dedicate this book to my dynamic staff, who are always willing and able to think out of the box and, over the years, have given me the support and encouragement to pursue a vision about what a public library can be. While I may have some ideas and a great willingness to experiment, their hard work and ongoing perseverance made the visions a reality and helped to create one of the most flexible, vibrant, and innovative community libraries in today's world. When I consider the buildings, the fun-filled spaces within, and the collaborative programs—Family Place Libraries, the Miller Business Resource Center, the Teen Resource Center, the Nature Explorium, and the Community Resource Database of Long Island—I realize that none of these accomplishments could have been the result of one person's efforts. It has taken a team of staff, board members, partners, and funders to fulfill our many dreams. For the chance to even tangentially change the look, feel, and role of the public library in our society, I will always be grateful to those who took this path with me and helped to make it all happen.

—*Sandy Feinberg*

dedicate this book to my parents, James M. and M. Jean Keller. They each fostered in me a deep appreciation for literacy and education, along with perseverance and determination in setting and achieving life goals. They also taught me, by example, to share my gifts for the benefit of others. My mother dedicated her adult professional life to her homebound students—all special needs children, most terminally ill with mental or physical disabilities. My father was extraordinary in his generosity of time and talent throughout his life, regularly driving Meals on Wheels to senior citizens into his mid-eighties. He dedicated the last twenty years of his life to Habitat for Humanity and other community organizations, full time, to make the lives of families in need worth living. Creating the Library Design Studio within a national architectural firm has allowed me to put my abilities, as well as the talents and gifts of my amazing colleagues, to use in continuing their mission: helping others by promoting literacy and lifelong learning, via the profession of architecture. My parents' kindness and care for others, regardless of status or circumstance or creed, has encouraged me to learn, grow, and share by creating space for children and families in diverse cultures throughout the world.

I also wish to make a special memorial note of my beloved yellow Labrador retriever, Lucy, who was at my side as I wrote this manuscript.

—*James R. Keller, AIA*

Contents

Color photographs can be found following page 116.

Acknowledgments

Designing Space for Children and Teens in Libraries and Public Places represents years of work, not only for the two of us but for the many contributors who have graciously given their time, knowledge, and expertise. Their willingness to share lessons learned and to envision the future of libraries and youth spaces helped to form the basic outline, significant concepts, and practical suggestions described throughout our book. The scope of their combined experience—from architecture to interior design to library administration to youth services—is evident in the manuscript's breadth and scope.

To begin our text, we conducted extensive interviews with architects, library administrators, and youth services specialists who represent a variety of building projects: Michael Madden, director (retired), Schaumburg District Township Library, Ill.; Hedra Packman, director of library services, Free Library of Philadelphia; Daria Pizzetta, AIA, Hardy Holzman Pfeiffer Associates (now of H3 Hardy Collaboration Architecture, LLC); Jeffrey Scherer, FAIA, Meyer, Scherer & Rockcastle, Ltd.; Ginger Shuler, chief of youth services, and David Warren, library consultant and director (retired), Richland County Public Library, S.C.; and Denelle Wrightson, AIA, PSA Dewberry. We acknowledge the architects, libraries, and photographers who have graciously shared their images and photographs for inclusion in the book. We thank our publisher, ALA Editions, for financial assistance in transcribing the interview/conversations that helped infuse colorful and thought-provoking commentary throughout the text.

In addition to our colleagues mentioned above, we acknowledge Sharon Breen, assistant director, Middle Country Public Library, N.Y.; Kathleen R. T. Imhoff, library consultant, Lexington, Ky.; Dr. Samira Moosa, board chair, Children's Public Library in Muscat, Oman; Gonzalo Oyarzun, director, Santiago Public Library, Chile; and Jirair Youssefian, director of design, VITETTA, for their contributions, not only to this book but to our professional development and the fulfillment of collaborative dreams and ideas for wonderful and dynamic spaces for children and teens. We look forward to continuing our work with them, as well as others, in striving for the best possible environments that can be created for youth by sharing ideas and working together.

We also thank Alan P. Hoffmann, president, and the partners of VITETTA, as well as the VITETTA library design team, marketing department, and especially Jesse Vaughn for support, encouragement, and assistance in preparing the graphic content for this book. In addition, we are grateful to the board and staff of the Middle Country Public Library for their trust and confidence in allowing us to create wonderful spaces for children and teens throughout the library's two facilities. A special acknowledgment goes to Owen Starr, graphic designer, TwoCreate, San Francisco, for the beautiful cover design.

Writing this book has been a labor of love. We acknowledge the challenges of writing a manuscript while working full time and creating the spaces about which we have written. We express our thanks to ALA Editions for being patient and cheering us into making this book a reality. The ongoing support of ALA Editions and encouragement from our friends and families—especially Richie Feinberg and Mark Mechowski—have made it possible to persevere and complete this work. We would also like to acknowledge our readers—fellow travelers in the journey to make the world a better place through the creation of better libraries and a literate society; we hope that you find beneficial information, confirmation, some consolation, and, most important, inspiration in these pages.

Introduction

Design is the creative mechanism employed to organize concepts into media and space. The range of discussion around design contained in this book is intended to include architecture, interior design, graphic design, themed design, and the continuum of these aspects as they inform space for children and teens. The use of design as a tool for defining and enhancing space is the focus of our investigation and discourse. It is our intent to present a balanced and objective presentation of ideas that will be helpful to library and design professionals in the quest to improve the quality of services for young people in libraries and other public places.

There is much to be learned in the area of design for children, and we hope that this book fosters inquiry, study, and exploration. Library administrators coping with the need for more space, differently used space, and renovated interiors are faced with a daunting task. In some instances, older buildings reach a condition in which they require major improvements and directors and boards are faced with refurbishing or adding to existing space. In other situations, new programs and services created by staff and then demanded by the community cannot be accommodated within an existing facility. Hedra Packman, in her article on the branch renovations of the Free Library of Philadelphia, summarizes the library of the future: "Public service must truly drive the design of every part of [a library] project. Special programs and library services of the future evolve from current successes, community needs, creative responses, and flexible interior environments that result from renovations" (Peterman 2001, 3).

The direction that a building project takes is reflective of the mission of the library. Growth of the Internet has affected many of the library's traditional roles, particularly reference services and access to books and media. The need for creating a sense of community and places for social interaction and civic engagement is influencing how library space is being used. Firmly establishing the library as a community center or destination is uppermost in the minds of many library leaders. Sam Demas and Jeff Scherer reflect on the library as a community institution: "As noncommercial, altruistic educational institutions, libraries fill a vital human need for communal exploration of ideas. . . . When designed and maintained with 'place-making' in mind, the physical library serves as a vital agent in community-building—bringing people together to promote a community's civic and educational values" (2002, 65).

In their book *Civic Space/Cyberspace*, R. K. Molz and P. Dain emphasize the role of the library as civic institutions:

Libraries' unique characteristics take on special meaning today, when thoughtful people worry about the fragmentation of contemporary life and the apparent decline of local activities that bound people together in the past. . . . We see new attention given to the meaning of place, to social interaction, not in anonymous commercial suburban malls or in chatting at home with computer buddies in the new communities of cyberspace, but in neighborhood institutions in real space. People are looking for social moorings. Libraries—stable, welcoming, venerable, but also modern—make good candidates. They are associated with education and culture and understood as communal property but not too associated with government. (1999, 205–6)

Expanded, renovated, or newly constructed libraries are often designed to provide spaces that address the needs of specific audiences. For many public libraries in the United States and abroad, service and space for children, their families, and teens have been identified as a priority. Consideration must first be given to understanding the needs of youth—at varying ages and stages of development—their families, and caregivers. Defining how services, activities, and collections will satisfy those needs drives the various elements of design such as color, furniture, flooring, shelving, and lighting. As we design spaces for young people, characterizing the library's mission to serve the literacy, educational, recreational, and social needs of youth is paramount.

Historically, children's space was in the basement, behind glass walls, too small, and limited to school-age children. Preschool and kindergarten services began in the 1950s and primarily included storytimes. During the 1980s, libraries began to open their doors to infants, toddlers, parents, and child-care providers. Since then, the field has been influenced by information on brain development and the critical role that parents and caregivers play in helping children gain literacy skills beginning at birth. James Keller summarizes the development of children's rooms: "The children's room tucked away in the back corner of a Carnegie basement is part of the library of the past. There is a very real need for these resources and programs [for early childhood] and we have probably only seen the beginning of this evolution, if not revolution. The children's library of the future is one of spatial and architectural significance" (James Keller, in Ramos 2001, 12).

Architecture has an amazing power to shape our thoughts and focus our energy in a particular way. Through the building of libraries that are created as dynamic community institutions and the design of space for children and teens, architecture adds to the message societies want to send to their own and future generations. Integrating the educational, social, and developmental stages of childhood and adolescence with creative and well-thought-out designs can enhance learning, discovery, and exploration. The marriage of design professionals with youth services library staff sets the stage for endless possibilities on how libraries can and will serve children and teens.

For youth of all ages, learning is active and interactive. In an article titled "Project Play," Andrew Blum reflects on designing children's spaces: "Designing for kids means engaging them, not controlling them. . . . If buildings are to succeed as social spaces they must be armatures for discovery; not dictating specific responses but providing opportunities for the widest range of experiences" (2005, 83–84). As Peter Moss and Pat Petrie (2002) see it, public spaces for children are designed

■ for the childhoods children are living here and now, as well as creating relationships and solidarities between children, between adults and between adults and children.

- as a community place for both adults and children to work on special projects of social, cultural, political and economic significance.

- to provide a wide range of opportunities from educational and task oriented to lightly structured for unsupervised play—sometimes with an adult and sometimes without—and settings where young people meet each other as individuals and where they form a social group.

Modern library space supports learning through movement, play, art activities, media, technology, group study, homework assistance and tutoring, drama, writing, child-to-child and adult-to-child conversation, and peer networking. The need for appropriately designed space for youth—and enough of it—is substantially affecting the way public libraries are being conceptualized and built. Jeffrey Scherer points out:

One of the fundamental misconceptions about designing libraries, especially space for children, is that the children's area is thought of as equal to, and coexistent with, other departments. But, in fact, because the developmental abilities of children and their age differences are so wide ranging, it really puts a different kind of pressure on [the children's department] in terms of accommodating all the variety of age and developmental differences.

To address specific users' needs and cater to a wide age range—birth to young adult—a variety of issues need to be considered. The patrons' age group and their wants and needs affect how the library goes about the process of designing the various spaces. It is imperative to separate those areas so that adolescents do not see themselves being perceived as children and schoolchildren do not see themselves as toddlers. In "Designing Library Space for Children and Adolescents," Lesley Boon states:

If the space is for children, it should tap into the naturally inquisitive nature of the child and his or her need to explore. If it is for adolescents, how they will (or how would they like to) use the space is the critical factor. If it is for both, it needs to be organized so that all the groups (preschoolers, school aged children, teens) can function well and share it effectively. (2003, 151)

Two major movements have sprung up during the past several decades that have influenced the direction of youth services and the way library spaces and services are envisioned. According to Clara Bohrer,

public libraries are reaching out to families with young children to actively support early learning . . . [and] translating research findings about early literacy into exciting physical spaces where families can engage in early literacy experiences. [Librarians] need to do all that they can to create active and exciting learning environments where families or caregivers with young children can engage in meaningful early literacy experiences right in their neighborhood. (2005, 127)

With the emergence of research data on the importance of early childhood development, "the public library is the only fully (and universally) accessible public institution that can sponsor or host early childhood development programs. It is the transformation of this new role of the public library that is, and will remain, one of the most significant aspects of its mission as we enter a new century" (James Keller, in Ramos 2001, 11).

At the other end of the spectrum, the reestablishment of teen services and ensuring need for specially designed areas have received increasing attention by library administrators, youth services librarians, and architects. Providing a healthy, socially engaging learning environment suitable for adolescents within the library setting presents many challenges for designers and architects, not the least of which include noise control, flexible furniture, contemporary media, food, and music.

The proportion and positioning of early childhood, school-age, and teen spaces; the size and variety of collections, furnishings, and interactive activity stations; the integration of media and technology; and the general tone or ambiance that expresses what the staff, board, and community find comfortable are issues that need to be thoroughly explored in any project. Every library expansion and renovation is unique, and the range of philosophies varies in the conception of space needs, how the space will be used, what specific ages will be served, and the reasons for focusing on youth. How libraries decide to build for children and teens generally begins with a strong philosophy or vision of one or more staff members within the institution who are supported by the administration and board. Research, exploration, community outreach, education, and flexibility work in tandem with the architectural and design process to achieve the final goal—outstanding architecture and interior design that render creative community learning space for young children, youth, and families in the public library.

Chapter 1 | Facilitating the Design

I t takes a lot of time, energy, and people—library staff, trustees, elected officials, supporters, architects, designers, builders, vendors, and lenders—to make building projects happen. Planning and organizational skills, perseverance, and commitment are required for any successful venture. Designing for children and teens requires additional attention to details, information, and expertise that goes beyond traditional library facility planning. In these types of projects, youth services staff need to be thoroughly involved in the planning process and, if the area targets older youth, teen involvement is imperative.

Deciding what should be built, how large the space needs to be, and how the overall design will be presented is determined in the latter stages of the process. To get to these latter stages, some initial steps need to be taken, including selecting an architect or design firm, forming a project management team, and deciding on a communication process. Following these steps can help libraries through the critical beginning stages of a building project.

SELECTING AN ARCHITECT OR DESIGN PROFESSIONAL

Choosing an architect or design firm is one of the most important decisions to be made. An architect has tremendous influence on the future of the library in that the overall design will impact programs, staffing, and how the community uses the facility. The director, board, town representatives, or elected officials usually select the architect. If a major part of the expansion, renovation, or building project is focused on youth, it is important to discover through interviews or an RFP (request for proposal) process if potential architects have ever been involved in designing children's or teen spaces and the value they place on children and families as a major audience for public libraries. It may also be valuable to involve children's staff in the selection process.

An architect should be brought on board as early as possible. In addition to designing and preparing plans for the library, an architect can help evaluate the existing building and site, assess alternative pieces of property, and prepare a program for the new facility. Architects assist the director and board in working with patrons and staff to help define the vision for the library, and their input early on can be critical to the successful implementation of the project. In conjunction with a project manager, they educate the project team on the entire building process.

The chosen architect should have the experience and capability to handle the project and a good track record on similar projects. Most important, however, the selected architect or architectural firm should be one with whom the staff and board

1

can form a good working relationship—one with whom they feel comfortable, who understands the goals and complexity of the project. The library will be spending months if not years with this individual or firm.

It is equally important for the client to carefully select an architect or design professional who demonstrates the desired creative force, someone who can encourage the design team to realize the vision through their creative talents and skills. The architect should not dictate operational matters to the library or attempt to alter services, programs, or collections requirements to fit some architectural scheme. Likewise, the library professionals (and others) should be comfortable with the architect before starting the process and not try to design the space. There needs to be a comfortable balance and sharing of ideas.

Professional Fees

One of the key components of any project's success is developing, managing, and maintaining the budget. The first outlay in the expenditures for a project is the payment of professional services: legal, library consulting, and design professionals. It is important to understand the range of fees that are customary for the services required and to have realistic expectations. Professional services are, by their description, based upon professional time and experience. The cost of professional fees is directly related to the professional's years of experience and rate, expected amount of time to be expended, and expertise.

Experience in most, if not all, professions brings compounded value to the client. This is true in law, medicine, accounting, architecture, and interior design. Telling us of his experience as a township manager for over thirty years and the success of the Horsham Township (Pa.) library project, Michael McGee stated, "I have learned not to hire an architect solely on the basis of price any more than I would hire a neurosurgeon on the basis of price." It is important to analyze cost relative to the value the library will receive from the design professional, just as one would evaluate a surgeon's credentials or an attorney's experience. Design professionals usually calculate their fees on a lump-sum, percentage, or hourly basis. Regardless of the computation method, the cost is always directly related to the rate, time, and expertise of the professionals who work directly on the project.

Selection Process

Many libraries have suffered over the past forty years because of poorly qualified design professionals. A carefully structured and balanced selection process empowers the library to make the final decision on the most appropriate architect or interior designer for its particular project. It can also happen that architect selections are made by poorly qualified staffers or a disinterested other party, such as when a municipal body and the library enter into an "arranged marriage" that is not beneficial to achieving the vision and goals. In this instance, it may be better to postpone a project until various issues and concerns have been addressed and the library has an important voice in the selection process. Working with a professional library consultant with regard to some of these situations may be helpful. The consultant can advise and also help assist in securing the services of the best architect or design professional and also help manage the selection process. The following steps for selection and the criteria for making the final decision are a greatly expanded version of those first published in Harvey (2005, 5).

1. Develop a list of prospective architects who have the basic qualifications for the project. This list can be as small as three and as large as ten. Referrals, word-of-mouth, neighboring libraries, local AIA chapters, state library associations, library conferences, design awards, and magazine articles all supply good ways and resources to identify architects.

2. Contact the firm by phone or e-mail to solicit an initial interest. Follow up by sending a description of the library and the project, and ask these firms to send information on their background, their capabilities, experience on similar projects, resumes of the individuals who would be involved in the project, a description of their understanding of the project and their approach, a list of references, an outline of how they charge for their services, and any other information that would be helpful in making an evaluation.

3. Research the architect or firm. Does the architect have a strong philosophy or design from a basis of research and development, whose buildings become tourist destinations—improving the image of cities and towns? Does the firm specialize in designing libraries and youth spaces? Does the architect have a philosophy regarding space for children or teens? Where are the firm's headquarters, and how will travel affect the cost and management of the project? The library board and staff may want a firm from their community or city. Conversely, it may be beneficial for the library and community to bring in a nationally or internationally recognized architect. Bringing in a firm renowned for excellence in libraries and cultural projects helps to assure a solution that meets the functional and aesthetic vision for the project and often helps with private fund-raising. A notable architect teamed with a local architect provides another solution that can be blended to bring acclaim to the library and city.

4. On the basis of the candidates' initial responses, select a smaller group and invite them to the library for an interview with the administration, selected staff, and board members. An interview should last from 45 minutes to an hour to give the candidate enough time to make a presentation and the selection committee or board enough time to ask specific questions. Have the list of questions ready in advance, and ask each candidate the same questions. The most essential part of the selection process is asking questions. The architect also needs to articulate clear questions to the committee.

5. In some instances, particularly for larger libraries, the selection committee may prefer to base the choice of an architect on the presentation of a specific design. This may involve fee-based selection, design competitions, qualifications-based selection, or an RFP. A consultant or library administrator often serves as a coordinator for the selection process and helps to create a time line and administer the paperwork. This type of selection process may extend the time line of the project.

6. Visit some of the architect's completed projects, particularly those with significant children's or teen areas, and talk with staff. Take notes. Was it a successful project? Did the architect creatively solve their problems? Was the architect available in an ongoing and timely manner? Was the architect or designer flexible and engaging as a partner?

7. Call references. Keep a written summary of the information collected, including the packet of materials sent by the architect, notes on questions answered,

references, and photos of other projects. Discuss the strengths and weaknesses candidly among the selection committee members. Draw up a chart of strengths and drawbacks to assist in the decision-making process.

8. Request information on professional fees and how costs are figured. Keep in mind that costs should not be considered as an isolated factor. In other words, if one architect's price is less, it is not necessarily the better value. The costs, qualifications, and services provided need to be considered as a whole.

Consider these criteria in your final selection:

- Experience in similar projects, particularly in designing libraries and youth space.

- Experience working on similar types of construction projects (school district, municipal).

- Ability to provide the appropriate services and staff to complete the project, and current availability to begin work.

- Experience of individuals to be assigned to work on the library's project. (To ensure good chemistry and communication between architect and library, it is imperative that the library staff meet the actual working partners before making the final selection.)

- Ability to connect fully and successfully with the library's goals. Look for common philosophies and values, someone who will share the staff and board's vision for the future of the library. There needs to be a match between the library's values and goals and those of the architect.

- Track record of successfully completing similar projects within a budget and time frame.

- Creativity outside of the firms' usual architectural work, such as involvement in professional organizations, partnering in creating a special material or product, or publications.

- Good presentation skills and well-prepared accompanying materials. Remember that the design professional will need to describe the project to the community and other stakeholders.

- Costs that are relative to the overall scope and extent of the project. Consideration needs to be given to the costs relative to the qualifications and experience of the architect or designer.

FORMING A PROJECT TEAM

The project management team should be composed of decision-making representatives from all stakeholder departments and divisions. For a project encompassing space for children and teens, the team should include the library director, the project manager or youth services librarian, the architect, the project manager or

The [Schaumburg Township District Library] first put out an RFP and short-listed those who responded. Then, before we interviewed, we visited libraries and projects that the architects had built. We were familiar with their work during the interviews and, in the end, we think it produced a better fit. It was a little easier because we saw some things that we could talk about—things we liked and didn't like—and got a better understanding of how [the architects] worked.

The key things we were looking for were a company that could handle a project of this size and one that they [the board and staff] could have a rapport with; an architectural firm that wouldn't control the process but would have it be more of a team process. Some of the architects were rejected because they seemed too strong—strong in a sense that it wouldn't be quite a teamworking relationship. Some of the architects didn't give the board and the committee the feeling that they were really collaborative.

—Michael Madden (interview, June 2005)

coordinator, consultants, and vendors. These individuals need to work together to plan, manage, and implement the project.

It is critical for the team to designate a principal arbitrator or day-to-day decision maker. On small projects, the library director often serves in this role. On larger projects, architect Sam Miller points out, "A big challenge is working with clients that have many heads; one strategy is to find the key decision makers and stakeholders and . . . work with them to identify who can make decisions day-to-day. . . . A strong client making decisions and leading is a great asset to the project" (Wallace 2005, 51). Library project management teams will be ahead if they make an early, conscious choice as to whom this day-to-day decision maker will be and communicate that choice to all parties.

Library Director

The library director needs to be involved in the overall direction of the project and represents the library's interests during the visioning and planning stages. A board member may also be willing to participate. In any case, the primary responsibility for the library project rests with the library director or key library administrator.

Library directors in small and medium-size libraries often find that they are performing two jobs—directing the library and overseeing construction—during a building project. It may be best to assign the administration of the library to an assistant director or department head in order to maintain the day-to-day operations. The library director can then concentrate on construction demands, problems, and issues as they arise. In larger libraries, a project manager often handles the daily construction tasks, but the director still needs to maintain overall control and be aware of the issues and how they are resolved. During expansion and renovation projects, problem resolution that involves change orders or a significant change in the design must be fully understood by the library director.

Project Manager or Coordinator

Enlisting the help of a project manager or coordinator facilitates the design and building process. Some larger architectural firms offer this service, but often the project manager is an individual employed by the library or municipality and generally trained as an engineer or architect. Many libraries prefer to hire an independent project manager or coordinator, one who is familiar with local ordinances, building codes, rules, and regulations and has worked with other library or building projects. The project manager is responsible to the board and administration, represents the library on the project team, and confers with the architect and other consultants working on behalf of the library. Selecting a project manager often follows the same steps and uses some of the same criteria as selecting an architect.

The primary responsibilities of the project manager are to keep the project on focus, within the time line and on budget. Project managers conduct the meetings, keep (or track architect's or construction manager's) official minutes, and follow through with many of the details assigned to the various team members. They are generally knowledgeable about construction work and often assist with problems and issues that arise throughout the building project. In tandem with the architect, they assist with the identification and hiring of other consultants or vendors who may be needed for specific tasks or jobs.

Architect

The relationship between client and architect is similar in many aspects to other professional relationships—client/lawyer or client/physician. The architect is the advocate for the owner in all matters of design and project implementation. This includes advocacy for cost management during construction. Part of the architect/client relationship includes delineating the responsibilities of the client, which need to be understood and agreed upon beforehand. A key element in the architect/client relationship comes in the area of visioning:

> Librarians and architects envision and experience the process of planning a new public library very differently. The divergence is crucial because the degree of harmony between the two professionals influences the final success of the new building they are designing. In general, the librarian brings an intimate knowledge of the library's functions and requirements to the project, while an architect contributes creative artistic talent and building expertise. In a well-run project, both professionals participate in the creative effort. (Curry and Henriquez 1998, 80)

Architects help clients determine their true needs and prioritize their wants. They are responsible for the design of a building or creation of an interior space based on the integration of design concepts and practices, environmental and physical conditions, and the vision and goals expressed by the library. "Throughout the design process, architects think in terms of facts, values, goals, performance requirements and in conceptual terms of privacy, security, territoriality, image, maintenance, physical comfort, audibility, visibility, etc." (Wallace 2005, 49). Architects turn design problems into advantages, limitations into design parameters. They analyze the building site or location and its particular strengths and weaknesses and often review the proposed sites, infrastructure, environmental issues, local weather, climate patterns, zoning, and nearby commercial operations that may affect the placement, entrance, and sight lines of the building.

Another critical job for the architect is to involve the community in the design process. This can often become a difficult process and requires tremendous communication and facilitation skills. Jeff Scherer explained it to us this way:

> One of the things that architects don't realize, and/or they aren't as aware of as much as they should be, is that the creation of a building in a community is a big deal. And if an architect is not savvy about how they orchestrate the participation of key people, they can find that bad decisions will be made because [a certain] person needs to impose their decision on the process just to make it clear to the politicians that they were involved. [The architect] needs to orchestrate the decision-making process in a very delicate way that lets individuals be empowered to make decisions that they are good at, but don't force them into making bad decisions simply to show that they can make the decision. . . . you need to build trust so that [the team] can actually make a decision together, which is the better decision in the long run.

A major area of concern when designing youth spaces may involve the youth services staff's desire to create a specialized theme area or design features. Architects often have knowledge of and access to other professionals who can assist the library with specific design needs that arise. They often partner with manufacturers to create custom and specialized building materials, furniture, artwork, and carpets.

Youth Services Librarian

In a major building project, the youth space may be only a part of the overall design. For smaller projects or interior renovations, the entire project may focus on children's or teen spaces. Whether large or small, it is critical that the youth services staff be involved. At least one representative should be part of the team, preferably at the beginning of the project. They often serve as principal advocates of library service for children and teens, expressing their knowledge and impressing it upon all team members, particularly those not directly associated with libraries. They need to be involved in answering questions and assisting the team in understanding the vision and mission underlying service to youth in their library. Lesley Boon emphasizes that

the designing of library space for young people takes specialist knowledge and skills. Most important is knowledge of behavior and information needs, combined with a love for children and/or adolescents. . . . When designing a library or library space for children and adolescents, many questions need to be addressed. For each library facility, the questions may be the same, but the answers must come from local knowledge and expertise about what this particular user group needs. (2003, 151)

Engaging and getting input from the youth services staff in the design of children's and teen areas greatly enhance information pertinent to size, design, activity areas, collection and program space, and staff areas. Their expertise with children, teens and parents, and library services for these audiences is invaluable. At all points during the process, the youth services staff involved with the project must be informed and seen as active, valued members of the team. Reflecting on a Philadelphia project, the architect noted:

In retrospect, if there is anything about the Free Library process that we could change or re-do, it would be to add a separate design meeting or meetings just with the children's librarian. We did spend a considerable amount of attention on the design of the children's area, but time devoted specifically to the knowledge of the children's librarian would have improved our understanding and success in the design solutions. (James Keller, in Ramos 2001, 11)

The youth services staff need to communicate their vision to the building team and become liaisons with the architects. They also need to understand their role and potential influence in the building project. Do they have a lot of say in how things should be done? Are they allowed to choose the colors, furnishings, or signage? It is important from the outset to be explicit about how things will function and who is responsible for these types of decisions. By being informed professionals and able to convey appropriate information to the architects and designers, youth services staff will be valued members of the planning team.

In an article on a Sacramento (Calif.) Public Library building project, the authors wrote about the role of the youth services librarian:

Establishing a common perception of all planning decisions became imperative during our lengthy planning process, and we learned the importance of taking complete notes in every meeting with architects, interior designers and other library staff. We also learned the power of our role in the planning process; as principal advocates of children's library service we must express our knowledge, and impress it upon all players not directly associated with libraries. (Chekon and Miles 1993, 24)

Consultants and Vendors

Depending on the complexity of the facility, good design requires integrating the work of acoustical, mechanical, electrical, plumbing, structural, civil, geotechnical, energy, and environmental engineers along with interior designers, landscape architects, security integrators, technology consultants, furniture and shelving vendors, and other specialists. Library consultants who are skilled and experienced at the building process can be of great help, particularly when designing spaces for children and teens.

The process of selecting and working successfully with outside consultants or vendors can be difficult, and it is best to work with the architect and project manager for selection purposes. It is important to understand who is out there and what is available. Writing RFP guidelines helps clarify the library's relationship with any vendor. Follow the same selection guidelines outlined above, such as checking references and other work the vendor/consultant has been involved with, as part of the process. With any consultant, a strong, clear contract is the library's best insurance, no matter who is chosen.

In any major project—expansion or new building—a Program of Requirements is developed (on the Program of Requirements, see chapter 3). This document serves as the guiding plan for the entire project and is often prepared by a professional library consultant. Library consultants should be familiar with library planning and design, management, programming, staffing, and materials requirements. They may also assist the library in operational planning and budget preparation and provide a subjective viewpoint throughout the project. During the hiring process, the library consultant should provide credentials and references for this type of work prior to selection. It is advisable to request samples of a completed Program of Requirements as part of the selection process and before finalizing selection of the library consultant.

ESTABLISHING COMMUNICATION GUIDELINES

Deciding the role, size, function, and targeted ages of the youth space within a newly constructed or renovated facility is accomplished over time during meetings, conversations, visits, research, and one-on-one interactions among team members. Most important is the ability of the team to communicate effectively (and synergistically) throughout the process. Success depends on the library's ability to communicate with the project team and vice versa. Turning goals into vision and vision into concrete implementation is difficult for the library alone; it can get more complicated when the library brings in the various members of the project team.

Good communication leads to improved, often larger and more dynamic spaces and inventive solutions that better reflect the library's mission as a community place for families. It is not unusual for an involved project team to create a space that had not been imagined before, to place the children's space in a different position within the library building, or to designate a larger proportion (though not originally planned) of the facility for children and teens. Following these communication principles aids in the smooth running of the project:

- Maintain a clear line of communication and direction. The project manager acts as a pivotal person, considering all team members' concerns and relating decisions to the library director, architect, or other team members who may be affected. It is important that team members and staff know that all decisions and directions funnel through this one person. This ensures that all are marching to the same drummer.

- Respect the expertise of each team member. The design and building process is a series of compromises as the staff discovers what does and does not work from a structural standpoint and the architects, builders, and vendors learn what does and does not work in terms of library service. "If the library thinks they know more about designing a library than the architect, builder or consultant, then they have the wrong partner. On the other hand, library staff cannot give away their power—expertise on how libraries work, how people use the library, and what the community needs" (Peterman 2001, 6). The importance of respecting the expertise of each team member or partner cannot be emphasized enough.

- Establish a common perception of all planning decisions; this becomes more imperative as the planning process progresses. It is important to develop rapport among the team members and an informal way of giving input on many aspects of the building. Understanding the ultimate objectives and clarifying the vision of the building project help all team members reach their individual goals as the team moves the project along to its final destination.

- Get to know every person who works on the project. Team members become like staff and need to be treated as equal partners in the project. Recognize limitations; architects, consultants, and project managers cannot save the world and solve all of the library's problems. Remember to consider the strengths and position of different team members.

- Ongoing planning, communication, and trust are essential throughout the building project. The threads of communication and trust must weave together to create a strong relationship that can lead to a better design. It is important to reflect on lessons learned as the process unfolds.

In a series of interviews with librarians and architects who worked together on building projects, some fundamental differences between the perception of the architects and design professionals and those of the library staff surfaced:

Librarians spoke more extensively about the need for personal flexibility, compromise and diplomacy. They alluded frequently to the different agendas of people on the committee and emphasized that tradeoffs were necessary if the project was to move forward. . . . In contrast, the architects emphasized the need for a strong, singular vision, which could be diluted by "too many cooks." . . . They rarely spoke about team dynamics . . . and were more focused on creating fresh, innovative interpretations of public library facilities that would make a personal statement.

The final major point that emerged from the data was an overall difference in perception between the architects and librarians about the nature of the building itself. Throughout the interviews, the architects concentrated on building form, the librarians on building function. The architects emphasized the "look" of the building exterior and interior, while the librarians were most concerned with "use." . . . It appears that form/function viewpoint difference exists even in the initial planning stages, and leads to a communication gap that both architects and librarians must recognize.

—Ann Curry and Zena Henriquez (1998, 88)

- Although the project manager or architect is responsible for taking official notes, it is imperative that each staff member take his or her own notes in every meeting with architects, interior designers, and other library staff. During the project, one of the telling points is how often the same issue is on the agenda. After so many weeks, everyone gets tired of talking about it, so the team must jointly find a solution and then record who is responsible for implementation. In any project, no matter the size of the team or project, it is important to state clearly who is responsible for each item and who must be informed of decisions made and actions taken.

- Get prepared before meetings and conversations—time is money. List the objectives the library has for each meeting or conversation and follow up on whether or how the issue is resolved. The results of "sidebar conversations" and secondary meetings need to be properly reflected in follow-up meeting notes.

- Follow through on those responsibilities assigned to library staff in a timely fashion. No library wants to be responsible for a time delay or for holding up another team member from doing his or her task. Be as accommodating as possible within the framework of the projected time line.

- Be prepared for delays, which can happen for any number of reasons: materials in production not ready; labor strikes; inclement weather; selected materials no longer available and other selections needed. Whatever the reason, it is good to make note of the issue at the meetings and decide if the team has control and can resolve the problem quickly. If one of the team members is the problem, this needs to be handled promptly by the project manager, library director, or board member, and when required by the library's attorney.

- Knowledge transfer is key. Library staff must end up with knowledge, skills, and internal expertise to manage and maintain the building. Outside team members will leave eventually, and library staff need the skills to keep the library running. Ongoing maintenance and technology issues must be considered throughout the entire project.

According to Graeme Murphy of Hamlet Management Pty. Ltd., using good communication techniques during the design process helps the architect, designer, and library staff to adopt and use the same language: "This is powerful evidence that listening has taken place and that the effort has been effective. Ownership and trust between the two groups begins to develop as one. On occupation and handover to the client there must be no surprises. . . . The process of feed back and consultation for the entire project must foster the culture of 'team.' It must be sensitively handled. It must be respected" (Murphy 2002, 5).

THE CREATIVE PROCESS

The vision for the children's or teen space evolves throughout the design process. The early stage of design should be a season of celebrating ideas; the more ideas in this early stage, the richer the results may be. The evolution of the vision for the space should be shared by the staff, board, design professionals, and community.

Lesley Boon expresses how important it is to visualize how the space could fulfill one's dream:

> Don't think within the constraints of what is happening in your library now; don't be reactive. Think, dream, create. Brainstorm all the possible activities, spaces, and attitudes that would serve your client needs best and be identified as best practice within the field. The only limit is your imagination. Not all things may be possible, but this is definitely an excellent start. Prioritize, from what is most important down to what you would love but could live without. (2003, 152)

At the 2008 launching of fund-raising for the first Children's Public Library in Muscat, Oman, founder and board chair Dr. Samira Moosa introduced the inspiration for the library:

> The idea first came to mind when a child who had spent a year in the U.S. was returning home and was asked what he would miss most about America. The answer was definitely surprising and a light bulb went on in my head. Ever since then, I've been obsessed with the idea of a public library in Oman.
>
> What stuck in my mind most was that if a child who has a great deal of access to books, like him, misses a library most of all, how must the majority of children in Oman, who do not have access, feel about it? How much are they missing out on? As the obsession grew, I started asking people and I realized that many Omanis shared my hunger for such a project. It's been at the back of our minds, but action has never been taken to bring the vision to the front of our thoughts—where it belongs. We have to believe in this project, in this vision. H. H. Said Haitham [Minister of Heritage and Culture] believes in it, and that is why he gave us the land. A vision only becomes a reality when you take action and work toward it. It is the only way for our dreams to come true.

Image Credit: VITETTA

Rendering of library entrance, Children's Public Library in Muscat, Oman. Architect, COWI/VITETTA. Used by permission of VITETTA.

Many libraries and spaces for children have started with the vision of an individual or small group of dedicated individuals, committed to seeing their vision through. The journey comes with variables, some out of the control of the visionaries. Sometimes the process takes a very long time, and this may be the reality. Sometimes patience is a needed virtue in planning and building new spaces—especially libraries and spaces for children. Perseverance is the engine that drives many successful projects to realization. A capital project does not just happen on its own—it takes vision, dedication, perseverance, persistence, and commitment on the part of all involved. The result will be a special library space for children or teens with collections, services, and programs that foster and stimulate the quest for knowledge and initiate the process of lifelong learning.

The most successful architectural space derives from a strong conceptual vision. It is important for the library to know—at or near the beginning of the process—what the goals are and what the conceptual vision is. Predesign meetings may be instituted to conduct internal discussions with staff and, in some cases, with board members. These preliminary meetings provide the project team with background knowledge of library plans and expectations, help set the overall parameters for the project scope, and encourage board, staff, and community involvement.

Clarity of purpose on the part of the library fosters synergy with the design team and also serves as the compass for project delivery. This clarity of purpose serves to keep the project on track throughout its stages of development. Without clarity of purpose—or vision—the project will drift and the result will more than likely be a disappointment. It is not unusual for design professionals to excel in their art and craft—designing—but to struggle with client communication. "Design is a process. The most successful design solutions share several common elements. First of all there is a clear goal, an outline of how to achieve the goal or mission, and talent, energy, and discipline to carry the design through" (James Keller, in Ramos 2001, 10).

Designing right is a reflection of listening well. Architects need to learn about staff and how they do their work. It is crucial for architects to meet with the appropriate stakeholders—from board members and administration to library staff and patrons—in order to hear about the library's true needs and wants. They need to know what role the library plays in the culture and aspirations of the community.

"The architect's design is only as good as the information provided him or her. Architects want to understand, to gather information/concepts, and transform them into design ideas. The most abstract but important part of design is getting that information" (Geoffrey Freeman, in Wallace 2005, 52). What can the library be? What makes it effective? How does it interact with the community? Families? Children? Teens? This strategic information is what makes a library unique and a truly valuable asset.

It's a balancing act. Although the input from staff, friends, board members, and others is important, it can be fraught with contradictions. Project architects and managers need specific information to determine customer needs, but each group that participates in the process adds another layer of time and information that is frequently extraneous to decision making. The balancing act is to get staff and community input while moving decisively on designs to meet future needs.

Understand "no." It is critical that the project participants enjoy healthy communication and that the word "no" be understood to be a business term and never a personal affront. In our work and that of the contributors to this book, the ability to say no to ideas or solutions and move forward quickly has been essential to the success of every project. It may, however, be worthwhile to vet an idea fully before saying no.

Trial and error lead to solutions. The creative process is organic and flowing. Many creative ideas simply do not work in the built environment or are not appropriate, but one good idea and sometimes even a bad idea may lead to a brilliant solution. Most often in the creative process, it takes trial and error to reach the optimal design results.

Take risks. A willingness to take risks with design is another element of success. Design risk does not have to be unconsidered risk, but the message here is to be open-minded and willing to brainstorm. It is important to share ideas and think about one's own vision and goals before the design process begins. Likewise, it is important to be willing to let go of ideas that simply do not work in real space. These same ideas may give way to alternate solutions that are imaginative and successful.

Be ready to compromise. The many successful spaces for children and teens are the result of collaboration between the professionals with expertise in youth services and the design team. Chekon and Miles recall their experience in creating the Kids' Place at the Sacramento Public Library: "Over the six years, the building program underwent many changes. The process was a series of compromises as we discovered what would and what wouldn't work from a structural standpoint, and the architects learned what would and wouldn't work in terms of library service" (1993, 21).

Avoid micromanaging the creative process. There is an old adage that "it takes a great client for an architect to produce great architecture." This could not be truer than in designing space for young people. The more interested in the design process and results, the better the results will be. But part of being a great client is also knowing when and how to allow the design professionals the license to create, imagine, define, and realize the project. Although the client should check or review the specifics of the design, micromanaging the design is the sign of a poor client or a poorly selected design professional.

Involving Youth Services Staff and Others

The creative process is dynamic, and library stakeholders are an important part of this process. The following strategies can help staff gather information, formulate their vision, and come to some consensus as a department before approaching the design team.

- Institute predesign meetings to conduct internal discussions with staff and, in some cases, with board members and Friends groups. These preliminary meetings provide background knowledge of library plans and expectations, provide an opportunity to elicit general comments about the project, and serve as morale boosters and team-building exercises.

- Identify the key staff members who will represent youth services on the project team. It is important that contractors, partners, and staff know that all decisions and directions funnel through specific people.

- In addition to working with the architect and project manager, the key staff members should set up internal meetings that allow for the involvement of other staff members (from librarians to clerks to pages to custodians) in every step of the process. Though time consuming, it is well worth it.

- Keep a notebook for staff to jot down ideas as the project is being developed. It is easier and less costly to revise the building plans to correct oversights than to make changes during or after construction.

- Be there to check every point of progress. Check that the assumptions about what would be done are actually happening as envisioned. Be prepared to press for what is needed and to compromise on less important issues.

How well the library staff and architect resonate determines how successful the project will be. Architect Jeff Scherer told us that the architect/librarian team needs to "get to know each other really well; spend time with the people who are going to use the space; and make sure that the staff (is working together). The 'staff issue' is a little bit more complicated to talk about because the staff (may have) several agendas at one time."

Hedra Packman of the Free Library of Philadelphia told us about getting staff to express themselves:

People were really strongly directed and encouraged, coached into speaking their mind. If people were more shy or inclined not to say what they really thought in a public forum (which was the design meeting), they would either go ahead and get over that inhibition and communicate it in a design meeting or, immediately after the design meeting, communicate it on more of a one-to-one basis with somebody at the library who could represent that input. So we didn't go through a whole design process, get buy-in from everybody else, and then have one or two of the key people really unhappy at the end.

Preparing Idea Boards

One way to prepare for the design process is by writing ideas on paper and sharing them with the design team. The ideas can be verbal or graphic or they may be photographs of spaces, furniture, colors, and other design elements that are appealing or that appear successful.

Some design professionals begin the visioning process by creating design idea boards. Often used to communicate ideas and images and to reference the concept to be developed during the design stages, idea boards are usually done before the concept design begins. They may include a collage of photographs, fabric samples, material samples, words, or three-dimensional objects (e.g., a slinky might represent flexibility or energy). This is a fun method that often communicates the ideas better than a description.

Having children and young adults create their own idea boards and present them to the design team and library professionals can form the basis of the design concept and often helps with the choice of furniture, equipment, activity areas, colors, and other design elements (figure 1.1). Architects and designers are essential in pulling together the various ideas presented by the teens, for young adults are often quite inventive and articulate in their preferences. This process can be enlightening and edifying for the design team and provides a great learning experience for the teens as well.

When the VITETTA/Swartz Architectural Group team worked with the Middle Country Library on the enhancement of the Selden building teen space, the

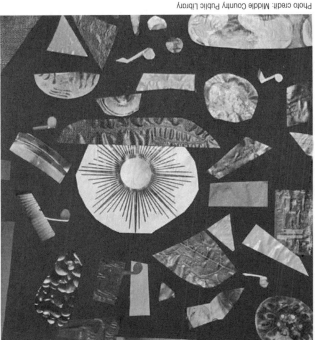

FIGURE 1.1 Teen idea boards, Middle Country Public Library, Selden Branch, Selden, N.Y. Teen space architect, Swartz Architectural Group; consultant, VITETTA. Used by permission of the teens and library.

design team conducted a series of design meetings involving representative teens and young adults. They asked each representative to create an idea board. The teenagers were enthusiastic about the assignment, and most of the participants prepared a board as requested. The design team subsequently had the participants present their idea boards—just as an architecture/design student presents a project to peers and jury—to key staff and the design team. The design team did not act as critics, however, but rather as information gatherers. The teens and design team immediately saw the wide range of ideas and contrasting opinions about how the space should look and feel.

In a subsequent meeting with the participants, the design team forged a common vision for the newly enhanced space, balancing the teens' ideas with the bold environment the library had already built. The palette of existing space included orange glazed wall tile, blue Marmoleum flooring, gold metal trim, purple painted metal deck, and blue painted structural beams. Some of the teens loved these colors and some detested them. The teams' challenge was to create a cohesive environment in this space that included the teens' ideas and reflected their taste but respected the interior design elements of this recently constructed and noteworthy building. The energy and commitment of the teen participants, and how they anticipated the use of the space, informed the design decisions at every turn.

Teen Focus Groups

The design process may include focus group meetings with children and teens, which can be a fantastic part of the experience. This age group has ever-changing tastes and ideas about what is "in" and "out." The tastes vary not only regionally but from neighborhood to neighborhood in urban areas and from town to town in rural areas. What is great for one community may be horrible for the next, according to teenagers.

When working with teens during the design process, it is important to recognize that this is a volatile period in their lives. Teens are influenced by many factors, including hormonal volatility to embarrassment. This is a biochemical reaction and a passing phase, but one that influences their reactions and participation.

In addition to getting teen ideas and perspective, an advantage of teen participation in the design process is that representative involvement teaches the teens a great deal about compromise. Every design project involves conflict resolution. Never does everyone on a design team agree on every point. Involvement allows the teens to learn how important they are as stakeholders in the use of public space. They also learn a great deal about how a building or its interior space is designed.

CONCLUSION

Designing and building library facilities and spaces for children and teens are the future for libraries that pride themselves on being community centers. As with the beginning of any building project, one of the most important activities involves selecting architects, design specialists, and library consultants, and one of the determining factors in those selections is personal chemistry. This factor should be considered as heavily as credentials, for without shared enthusiasm the design process will be unnecessarily onerous and possibly even unpleasant.

Designing a new space for children and teens should be one of the greatest experiences in one's professional life—even if it creates new and unusual experiences and stress at times. Forming a project team through sound selection processes and establishing communication guidelines will help the project go smoothly and efficiently. Integrating the youth services staff in the process is critical to making the vision a reality and the entire project a success.

A good building and good design depend upon the vision and clear articulation of that vision by the clients. How well the library and architect resonate determines the project's degree of success. It is imperative that staff inform the architect about how and what they need to do their work, since the architect relies upon the accuracy and completeness of the information the library shares. "In the final analysis, the threads of communication and trust must weave together to make a strong relationship that can lead to a better built design" (Wallace 2005, 54).

Chapter 2

Reflecting the Mission of the Library

Envisioning the new space is a joint effort on the part of the architects, design professionals, staff, board, and community. It requires an examination of the mission and roles of the library and how the library utilizes space to satisfy the needs of the community and, in particular, the needs of families and youth, birth through the young adult years. Ideally, children's and teen spaces need to reflect the library's philosophy of service and need to be designed as an integrated entity with a consideration of and an attraction for young patrons.

How parents and caregivers act within the library setting often influences how young children feel about and how often they come to the library. How children use the library affects their attitude and behavior not only when they are children but also as parents. The teen audience also needs attention from the library world. "Teenagers today long to be needed, to be respected, and to belong—and libraries are ideal places for these things to happen. By creating a space designed especially for teens, librarians present themselves with the perfect opportunity to embrace this age group full force" (Taney 2003, ix).

The future success of public libraries may well lie in our ability today to serve young children, their families, and teens in a healthy, appropriately designed environment—one that provides an introduction to the library for new users, serves as a laboratory of experimentation and discovery on what the "future" library may offer, and presents an exciting opportunity for garnering financial support and political backing.

The term *design* has many implications and meanings. The influence design bears on a single idea, mechanism, or space extends not only to the actuality of what is created but also to the organic nature of that which is created and how it will influence activity and thought. Design of space for children and teens includes the perceived physical space and the equally important intuitive space. That is to say, how the space is perceived and used, and what the dynamic of the interactions in the space will be, affects how the space, its contents, or its habitation influences users in their daily life.

At its foundation, a good design requires integrating ideas about how children and teens learn and perceive the world; understanding how architectural and design features can influence learning and usage patterns; listening to, interpreting, and incorporating ideas from the staff and community; and reflecting the current and future goals of the library. On the basis of their experience and knowledge, the design team provides additional outside views that not only add to the discussion but also bring critical skills of facilitation and organization to the process.

It is vital for the project team to gather as much information as possible about the core philosophy of patron service and how it is to be reflected in the design of children's and teen spaces. It is also important to uncover any serious disagreements between the children's or teen departments and administration regarding youth services. After reaching some central decisions such as the ages of the targeted audiences, the estimated size and scope of the space, and the basic activities and collections to be included within the space, the project team needs to gather information and validate its ideas through research, site visits, conversation, and exploration.

ALIGNING MISSION AND DESIGN

Public libraries today often think of themselves as community centers and take pride in their efforts to reflect the community they serve. When new facilities are built or old buildings are refurbished, the "why are we doing this?" part of the project needs to be understood by the entire design team. A critical consideration is how the new space will reflect the underlying mission and roles of the library. Each project is different, just as each building or space will be unique in its final design. The following vignettes offer specific examples of how the mission of the library is reflected in the design of a new or renovated building or space.

Creating a Model for Family Places and Teen Spaces

Three underlying themes consistently influence the development of the Middle Country Public Library: day-to-day communication with users; a focus on the library as a destination with a variety of interactive spaces, programs, collections, and services targeted to specific audiences; and partnering with local organizations to offer an array of on-site services. The children's department has traditionally been a leading service in the library. In 1979, staff created the Parent/Child Workshop, a program that targets toddlers, parents, library staff, and community resource professionals. Set up weekly as an early childhood learning center in the community room, this program offers a special space for toddlers and caregivers, focuses on parents and caregivers as teachers, and introduces families to community resource providers who can assist families with their various needs. The workshop, and subsequent services that resulted after its inception, influenced the development of children's services. Subsequently, the library became a living laboratory for the evolution of space, programs, and collections designed for parents, caregivers, family service providers, and young children beginning at birth.

Because of the library's customer service philosophy, the demand for the workshop and ensuing services pushed the library to think "out of the box." In the mid-1980s, Middle Country underwent a 25,000-square-foot expansion of its Centereach facility, adding 9,000 square feet to an existing 3,000-square-foot children's room. This new space included a designated early childhood drop-in space. During that same period, the library acquired an old school building, which housed a small branch collection, offered meeting rooms, and included an early childhood program room. Children's services continued to evolve and in the mid-'90s Middle Country became the national model for Family Place Libraries, an initiative developed in partnership with Libraries for the Future, a national nonprofit committed to the need for public libraries in a democracy.

Photo credit: Middle Country Public Library

Family Place Libraries, Middle Country Public Library, Centereach, N.Y. Architect, Hardy Holzman Pfeiffer Associates. Used by permission of the library.

Family Place Libraries (www.familyplacelibraries.org) elevates the position of children's services administratively and focuses on programs, collections, and space development for parents and young children, outreach to new and underserved audiences, and collaborative work with other family-serving organizations. Designing the space and activity centers in a Family Place library is a signature part of the program (see Feinberg et al. 2007). Family Place space includes

■ early childhood collections of board and picture books, toys, and AV materials

■ activity stations such as blocks, puzzles, train tables, a dollhouse or puppet stage, a kitchen corner

■ one or more early childhood computer stations

■ posters, murals, and other fanciful artworks

■ a parents collection with books, magazines, pamphlets, a computer, and displays

The demand created by Family Place activities, teen use and adult collections and programming encouraged another overhaul of both buildings in early 2000. The children's room in the Centereach facility had no windows, collections were overflowing, and the early learning activity stations could not accommodate the number of children and caregivers who wanted to use them. The Selden building presented other problems. It housed the Family Place Training Center (not wheelchair accessible) and a children's area that was very small and undefined. Because it was the national model, staff wanted to develop a "branch" version of Family Place space and add an elevator for access to the Training Center.

In addition to the demands for family space, there was no space for teens in either building. After fostering a dedicated cadre of family users with young children, parents often expressed the need for the library to do more for teens, both young teens and young adults. In early 2000, the library underwent a renovation and expansion project for both buildings to help fulfill its mission as a welcoming destination and anchor institution for families, young children, teens, and community organizations.

Creating a "Wow!" Factor

In late 1990, the Free Library of Philadelphia undertook the renovation of thirty-three branches, funded in part by a grant from the William Penn Foundation. Under the guidelines of the grant, the library agreed to redesign branch libraries to foster the mission of service to children and teens. Each branch was to include generous and flexible areas for storytelling, preschool programs, parent-child reading and learning, and various after-school and summer programs (figure 2.1). Another goal was to achieve the "Wow!" factor, which "meant that upon entering each branch library, an individual should feel a sense of uplift, enlightenment, or inspiration . . . and to reflect the special characteristics of each branch neighborhood" (James Keller, in Ramos 2001, 10).

FIGURE 2.1 Young children's area, before renovation (left) and after (right), Free Library of Philadelphia, Wyoming Branch, Philadelphia, Pa. Architect, VITETTA. Used by permission of the architect.

Photo credits: Joanne Bening/VITETTA

According to Hedra Packman, director of library services, children's services had always been a major priority for the Free Library of Philadelphia. That being said, the library did follow the old tradition of children's services. When the libraries were first built, there were no children's services at all. Then libraries were built with a children's department—a small children's department—placed on one side or in the back or hidden somewhere. Approaching the 1950s and '60s, children's departments became bigger, but not necessarily any more prominent.

One of the features of the 1990s renovations emphasized that children and teens were a major-priority audience, and that the design should reflect that physically. So suddenly, instead of the children being put in one area, children were everywhere in the library. The focus was on early childhood, homework help, seating, technology and computers, and the creation of a welcoming space. The library had already integrated nonfiction, and adults were put in a little quiet space off to the side or in a corner. The new arrangements reversed the way it had been done and reflected the philosophy that children are a major audience.

Designing Children's Space to Accommodate the Needs of Young Children

To address the growing functions of children's services, among other needs, the Schaumburg Township (Ill.) District Library embarked on an expansion project in the mid-1990s to provide space for early childhood activities, interactive media, computer training, the preschool library, a special collection of original children's illustrators' artwork, and integration of parents and caregivers. Schaumberg was one of the early libraries to promote the library as a community place with longer hours, a large and varied amount of collections and services, and a focus on the customer. Programming was an important part of library service. Ensuring that the space supported the programs became a primary goal of the building project.

For the children's area, creating a welcoming space that supported programming was the overriding principle throughout the design process. The noise and clutter, the disjointed space created by prior additions, and traffic flow reflective of the various ages of children and stages of child development greatly influenced the design of the building. Integrating noise in the younger areas and then moving onto quieter spaces for students and adults were important objectives that the library board and administration wanted to address in the new facility. This notion of noise and activity encouraged the library to place the children's department on the first floor bordered by the audiovisual collection and the adult popular reading room. A "park" entrance was created to entice children and families into the room and announce to all visitors the importance of children to the library's mission. The artwork and thematic spaces integrated books, book characters, illustrations, and activities into an active, lively children's room. The quieter functions (reference, adult literacy, administration) were placed on the second floor away from the bustle.

Following her work in Schaumburg, Architect Wrightson integrated the playful storybook theme into the children's area of the Southfield (Mich.) Public Library, including the design of an open book that functions as a canopy, denoting arrival and entry to this lively space (figure 2.2).

Using Space and Art to Foster Imagination

The image of the architecture influences children and families, and the accessibility and appeal of the library to this part of the customer base are essential. A prominent functional role demands a prominent location within a building. In the Richland County (S.C.) Public Library, youth services have always had a strong presence, reflecting the deep-seated conviction of their importance. Staff advocate proper attention to children's services in public libraries on a national level. When the library was to have a new building, director David Warren explained to us that "youth services would have a strong presence. Children were to have the very best—the best collections, multiple copies, well-trained staff, and programs. The children's room had to be a major focal point of the building. We wanted the space to integrate children with the whole library. It should be an exciting area. It should be something very, very special."

Photo credit: Gene Meadows

FIGURE 2.2 Young children's area with storybook theme, Southfield Public Library, Southfield, Mich. Architect, PSA Dewberry. Used by permission of the architect and photographer.

The building project emphasized the importance of connecting children to books. An underlying philosophy was to create a place of imagination that would entice children to come to the library and enjoy reading. Upon entering the building at street level, patrons have a view of the children's room on the lower level—the garden level—and can see the activities taking place there. Twenty-eight trees that are 40 feet tall grow in that space with parklike benches. Going down the escalator, patrons are greeted by "Wild Things" and then peer through a space of 20,000 square feet to a 48-foot Maurice Sendak mural. Ginger Shuler, head of children's services, told us that "everything about the room defines that it is for children. We wanted the children to walk in and know that the room is for them."

FORMULATING GOALS AND OBJECTIVES

The basic elements established in a building plan typically include an overview of required spaces and the functional relationships between those spaces. General characteristics such as ambiance, institutional character, and the library's vision and mission are considered in the overarching goals of the project. If the project involves the entire library, the plan considers the space needs of youth relative to the overall size, style, and ambiance of the building. It is during this part of the process that the overall importance and prominence of youth space becomes apparent to the architect.

Jeff Scherer, AIA, explained: "Instead of being this kind of a 'have to' thing, children's space is now driving a lot of the decisions. The percentage of space is going up. I would say from the mid-'70s to the late '80s [the children's room] was 10 to 13 percent of the overall space. Now it's pushing 20 to 25 percent." A simple and fair way to determine the size of the space to be devoted to children and teens is to calculate the percentage of floor space equal to the current or anticipated percentage of children's circulation and program use.

In addition to size, goals and objectives for the design of youth space often include the need for a welcoming environment for specific ages and families or a high-tech, dynamic look for teens. The integration of multimedia functions, active and quiet spaces, a separation of age groups, work and programming spaces, and other significant objectives that the library hopes to accomplish should also be considered. A significant step during space planning is whether the area will include special program rooms or thematic designs, both of which influence the amount of space required.

**Questions to Ask about the Scope
and Role of Youth Services**

How did this project come about? What are the primary goals? Secondary goals?

What is the guiding philosophy of the library pertaining to services to children and families?

What role does the library currently play in the lives of children, teens, and families?
What role will it play in the future?

How does the community served shape the philosophy/policy of service?

What attitudes will affect the services and design of the space? Is there an overarching vision of how best to serve youth? What population does the current youth space serve?

Has the library developed early childhood and parenting services? Is this a desired goal for the project?

Does the library feel that teen service is important? Is this an existing service? Will it be expanded in the new facility?

Does the library serve as a regional center, main library, or branch?

In addition to direct services for families, young children, and teens, does the library serve other professionals and providers from youth-oriented organizations, child-care centers, or schools?

How does the youth area function with other services and spaces in the building? Is it a prominent service of the library? Are there issues of primary concern such as noise, activity levels, or safety?

Are there adequate resources to support the current demands for programming and collections? What additional resources have been targeted to support new services and collections? What types of efficiencies can be gained in the project?

What is the current usage of children's and teen materials and programs? What demands are not being fulfilled?

What collections can be eliminated or downsized? Are books currently shelved too high for children to reach safely?

Is there enough space for seats to accommodate parents and caregivers?

Is meeting room space adequate?

LEARNING ABOUT THE DESIGN POPULATION

The success of any space reflects the staff's personal attention to and involvement with the entire process. Getting their input right from the start improves the architect's understanding of how the building should function and the audiences the library wants to reach. Staff must tell the architect what they need to do their work, for the architect relies upon the accuracy and completeness of the information the library shares. Staff have tremendous library expertise, street smarts, and skills in serving children. They need to bring this knowledge to the table and share their expertise with the architect.

The library must be specific: We need more space to serve our community. We like our old building but wonder if it is worth renovating. Should we demolish it or renovate it and add expanded space? Our community demographics are changing. We want the library to be a landmark building for our culturally diverse community. Our services are leaning heavily toward children and teens. We want to offer services to babies and toddlers as well as homework help after school.

Though board members or administrators may not be interested in the details of the children's space, they often set the tone for how much of the overall project is going to focus on children and teens, establish the role the library will play with regard to youth services in the future, and provide the funding support to accomplish

JAMES V. BROWN PUBLIC LIBRARY: AN EXAMPLE OF OBJECTIVES AND GOALS

In 2005, the James V. Brown Public Library in Williamsport, Pa., began exploring the possibility of expanding by adding a multifloor children's wing to the downtown building. The following summary report from the library consultant laid the groundwork for the architects.

Currently Children Services occupies approximately 4000 sq. ft. of disjointed space. Service suffers from crowded, inaccessible and "hidden" shelves of books and materials for children, parents and youth, and professional kits for teachers and staff who work in other libraries; inadequate and jam-packed office space for staff; two cramped programming rooms; an inadequate amount of seating for families and children; and no reference desk for librarians. In spite of these drawbacks, Children's Services does extraordinary work.

- Circulation for children's materials is over 150,000 on 40,000 items.
- Multiple programs, offered on a daily basis for infants, toddlers, preschoolers, and school-age children and their parents, are filled to capacity.
- A storymobile serves 40 child-care establishments in the county.
- The library has been selected to participate in two national initiatives: Family Place Libraries™ and Prime Time Library.
- Staff is recognized for their expertise and often speak to professional organizations and groups about family services.

The Library is undergoing a building project planning process to add a children's wing onto the existing structure that would house Children Services and the Lifelong Learning Center. Children Services space will house collections of books, audiovisual materials, and other resources for children, birth through age 12; computer stations; tables and a variety of seating for adults and children; specialized kits for caregivers, teachers and staff that work in other libraries; staff workspace, storage, and multiple and flexible programming space. The Lifelong Learning Center will house office space, storage for materials, a computer lab and tutoring/conference space for students and teachers.

A 9,000-square-foot area has been identified and cleared adjacent to the rear portion of the existing library building. A proposed 3- or 4-floor expansion including a basement has been discussed as a realistic goal. To reach this goal, the Library embarked on a fund-raising initiative.

Goals and Objectives

- Create an appropriately designed, welcoming and flexible environment for young children, youth and families.
- Gain space to satisfy demand for services that are currently provided and for the future growth of programs and collections.
- Further the Library's mission to serve as a regional center for librarians, teachers, caregivers and family support providers.
- Expand the Library's role as a vital institution that attracts visitors to the downtown area, instills a culture of reading and learning within the family unit, and employs an entrepreneurial staff.

the goals of the project. Gonzalo Oyarzun, director of the Santiago (Chile) Public Library, explained his view of the library experience for children and young adults and the underlying principles that influenced the building of the new library:

A children's and young adult library serves as a public square, where children and young adults can go and have fun; where they can feel free to choose, explore, and know; where parents and children can talk and know each other. It's an intimate place where children and young adults can meet and interact with others, assuming and respecting their differences and ages; an environment in which teachers and students can experience, together, reading far from the school's curricular pressure; a multimedia and interactive zone in which children have free access to books, new technologies, activities, highly trained professionals, comfortable furnishings, state-of-the-art infrastructure, and to their own scale. (Oyarzun 2009)

Most of the successful children's and teen space projects have been initiated because one or more board members or an enthusiastic library director saw the value of investing in youth services. In smaller libraries, a board member or director often acts in tandem with or in lieu of children's staff because of his or her background with (they may have been a children's librarian or teacher), interest in, or understanding of children. In most instances, designing and building spaces for youth have the support of one or more board members, the library director, and those who control the finances. Without this type of support, it is difficult to move forward.

Michael Madden, director of the Schaumburg Township District Library, described to us how he involved his staff and board during their building project:

From early on in the programming process, we brought in maintenance people, division heads, and pages. Every staff member had a say in their area—how it functioned and later on, when we were adding the finishes, we had this group decide on the finishes (our of a range that had been preselected). They could pick what they wanted their area to look like. Because of that, some of the rooms had high partitions, some lower.

The board was also very involved. They wanted to know how each area would look. They wanted to see the finishes, colors, and artwork, but they left the details of how areas would function up to the staff. They trusted the staff to make sure the building would work, but they did care about what it was going to look like. They also wanted to see what some things felt like, for example, seating and furniture.

Though some staff have strong opinions about whom the library serves and can envision how the new space will function, it is imperative that they add to their knowledge base and gather additional information. Children's staff should consider participating in ongoing meetings with each other and the architects/designers; reviewing literature on library services and space design for children and teens; conducting on-site and online visits to a variety of venues; looking at demographic trends in the student population and the types (size, ages, ethnic background) of families that are moving into the community; and assessing the needs, behaviors, and learning styles of children and teens.

Review Literature on Youth Spaces

It is important that the staff read books and articles not only about designing special spaces for children and teens but about the needs of children, parents, and teens and how they learn, the newest ideas in education, what resources parents need to help their children, and other topics. Do not limit the research to libraries. Consider information that covers other venues such as museums, parks, child-care centers, schools, and youth centers. Relate these ideas to the design and features of the new space.

Ask the Audience

Seek ideas from current and potential users including children, teens, and parents. They may come up with ideas not thought of by staff or the design professional. Having users participate in the planning and development of services and new space generates interest in and enthusiasm for the project. "This is your opportunity to involve others. Let patrons know what is happening. Explain what you are trying to achieve, listen to their suggestions and grievances, and get them on your side. Encourage ownership of the project. There is nothing like participation to encourage positive outcomes" (Boon 2003, 153).

Depending on the clientele and the situation, patrons can be asked about their preferences in several ways, including surveys, focus groups, design or idea boards (see chapter 1), and suggestion boxes. It is often best to target specific groups—elementary or middle school students, older teens, or parents of very young children. If a library decides to pursue these activities, it is recommended that staff work with a consultant to assist with the design of the surveys or to conduct the focus groups, or with a design professional to work on design boards.

Conduct On-Site and Online Visits

Going on-site and seeing various facilities for children and teens provides perspective on how space is presented, the variety of accommodations for different age groups, marketing messages and what different children and teens might perceive when interacting with the space, the range of materials available, and how different libraries and other venues address the needs of youth.

It is beneficial to visit other libraries and various children's facilities, especially in other regions, to benefit from lessons learned, and to see other solutions for serving youth. "People working in libraries are not aware of how differently space can affect their function because they are so caught up in what they are doing. In order for them to create and articulate a vision, they need to be taken out of what they do every day and allowed to think outside the box" (Geoffrey Freeman, in Wallace 2005, 52). Many of the best ideas for creating space are inspired by a completed project. Sometimes a poor attempt at solving a good idea in one location leads to resolution and success in the next.

Denelle Wrighson reflected on some of the places that influenced her design work:

After the [library] tours and the research we did for the [Schaumburg Public Library], we started going to children's museums. We went to Boston, Indianapolis, Ann

Arbor, and Chicago to see what they were doing, what kind of materials they were using that would hold up, and what kind of things [to use], like bubble walls. The Indianapolis Children's Museum—it's a wonderful museum—has a bubble wall, and a poetry wall [that the Southfield, Michigan, Library expanded] in words and shapes. In Oak Park [Ill.], they also use the words, I think, very effectively. I think learning to use the librarians as resources, in brainstorming ideas and having them bring in the students that are using [the library], also helps integrate the [staff and children] into the whole process, which is important.

- Visit other libraries, preferably during high-use hours, and talk to the library staff about what works and what doesn't work. When an architect has been chosen, arrange for the architect to observe excellent library services for children, parents, and adolescents in well-designed library spaces.

- Visit museums, recreation centers, parks, youth centers, sports facilities, and child-care settings. Many of the materials on display or used in various settings can be replicated or adapted for the public library environment.

- Peruse library furniture catalogs and attend conferences and trade shows that display children's furniture and equipment. Talk to library suppliers about what you would like; they can be very helpful.

- Have a look at other floor plans. In the beginning, it is often hard to visualize size. Comparing a library's floor plans with actual space helps staff prepare for proportion and size, what the new space will feel like, how patrons will use it, and whether the space is big enough to accommodate the many activities envisioned.

- Search appropriate websites. Look at photos, print out text descriptions, examine the types of programming and activities offered, and review public policies and procedures relative to youth. Understand that the design and functionality of the area tell a lot to those who enter the space.

- Do not forget to bring a measuring tape and camera to all visits. Keep a collection of photos, illustrations, websites, and other visual elements in one spot (booklet, notebook, box).

Research Community Demographics

Basic research on the demographics of a community provides the design team with estimates of the number of children and families who currently live in the area as well as the estimated growth (or decline) of the youth population. Other important information includes the ethnic diversity and education level of families, the performance of the school district, and the availability of other youth resources such as Boys and Girls Clubs, YMCAs, youth centers, sports facilities, parks, and children's museums. Gathering this information and preparing a chart of resources, ages served, programs offered, and other pertinent information help staff determine what the library can do to satisfy unmet or partially met needs.

For the Sacramento Public Library's expansion project, Terry Chekon and Margaret Miles learned about their population through a marketing study conducted on children's services in the central library's service area (see Chekon and Miles

1993, 21). Through this study, staff determined what specific services and materials were of interest to potential users. It confirmed their belief that there were a limited number of children living in the service area, and that many of them were from non-English-speaking families. The study also confirmed their conviction that the children's space in the new library would need to be accessible at times when families from beyond the surrounding area could visit.

- Find out what other resources for youth exist in your community. Visit these places and speak with the professionals managing them. Ask what services are being offered and what needs are unmet (at least from their perspective). Elicit their ideas and gain their support for the new library space for children and teens.

- Locate community reports created as the result of a community visioning process or the development of a long-range plan by the town or city council, school district, local business, or civic organizations. These reports often outline the need for community space (recreational and educational) for children and teens.

- The latest census report (even a dated one) provides a demographic breakdown by age, gender, ethnic background, languages other than English spoken in the home, household income, and the like. Extract information related to the number of children (preschool and school age) and teens in the community.

- Contact the school district and the PTA/PTO for recent reports or studies on the school district population.

- Search for information on local history and a general description of the library's service area. Your library may have this information readily accessible. If not, a web search often produces some historical as well as recent information on the local community. Search this material for information on youth services and the growth of the young population.

- After looking at the statistics and outlining the needs of young children and teens, it is important to consider not only the current needs of the design population but also the future needs. Function and flexibility are key.

Questions to Ask about the Design Population

Is the library in a working-class community? Low-income community? Wealthy community? How do family lifestyles affect usage?

What demographic information is pertinent to the design and expansion of the new space?

What outlying population areas make use of the current space? Projected space? Does the library serve a migrant population or summer population that severely increases use during various seasons?

What ethnic backgrounds are predominant in the population? Is this a changing statistic? What is the projected growth?

What is the size of the children's and teen population relative to the older population?

What other youth resources exist in the community? What other resources exist for after-school care and homework assistance? Do many children attend summer camp? Go on lengthy summer vacations? Do children need a place to hang out after school or during the summer months?

What gaps in service can the new space satisfy?

How is child care provided? Are parents the primary caretakers? Is there a need to serve grandparents? Nannies? Child-care centers?

CONTEMPLATE THE CHILD, THE TEEN

For the most part, children have not received special attention, in terms of space created solely for their use. Until Frederich Froebel developed the kindergarten concept in Germany in 1837, there was no formal approach for young children to grow and learn through social interaction with other children. Froebel's theories and practices were revolutionary, remain in use to the present day, and are among the earliest influences on the need of interior space designed primarily for active young children.

Kindergarten, where children from age three to seven learn through instruction, play, and independence from parents, required such an interior space. The typical classroom setting did not encourage play and interaction, and thus the creation of kindergarten was the beginning of the demand to create unique public spaces for young children. The kindergarten space must accommodate young children in the quest to learn social skills and develop self-esteem and cognitive skills. The early kindergarten was essentially classroom space that had a particular assignment and appropriate play space for young children (Richie-Sharp 2003, 1).

The implementation of kindergarten and the resulting demand for special space exemplify the synergistic relationship between architectural space and programmatic intention. The creation of space for youth has advocates for many different aesthetics, expressions of design, and programmatic priorities. The ideas and attitudes about space, programs, and design vocabulary may be broad in range, but the intent to encourage children—birth through adolescence—in academic and social development is a consistent element in planning regardless of the specific approach.

The primary responsibility of the designer in creating space for youth is to contemplate the child and the teenager. Scale, light, color, and texture are some of the components that inform the interpreter of interior space. The functional aspects—the security of the child or teen within the space, and their reaction to and interaction within the space—are equally important considerations of the design. Much of what informs design decisions concerning space for children and teens is the reactions and tastes of adults involved in the design process. The results of this process are varied in their appropriateness and success. Therefore the role of design in creating environments for youth is to maximize the benefit of the space for its inhabitants—children and teens.

"Children's space planning is influenced by cognitive development, learning styles and a shift in philosophy about realistic behavior expectations in libraries. Children's libraries should be designed for the user, who is a unique individual very different from adults" (Sandlian 1999, 5). To accomplish this goal, it is essential that the design team—which includes design professionals and library professionals—develop a clear understanding of the variety of uses to be encouraged within the space. The design must reinforce the function of the space and create the appropriate mood for a range of activities from social interaction to play, reading, computer use, and quiet study.

Parents and caregivers are important participants in the young child's environment, especially in the public library. Although the primary consideration must be to the child and the teen, the caregivers and professional staff must also be considered. The programs, collection, and technology and their synergistic relationship with the space will continue to influence the development of library space, just as in the development of the kindergarten. Two fundamental differences between designing space for children in the library and in the kindergarten are the need to allow for the ongoing change in the role of the library in the community and the need to accommodate a range of ages from birth to young adult.

In the preparatory stages of library design it is important to look at the needs of youth at varying ages and stages of development. Children are innately inquisitive and trusting and require a loving environment—a place where the love they give also is returned and where they can exercise understanding, gain knowledge through learning, and organize what they learn effectively. Pam Sandlian comments on the Denver Public Library's children's space: "The real difference in this library [is] the sense that children are unique human beings and their information needs are central to their development and growth. . . . Childhood is a time of discovery and every encounter is a learning adventure" (1999, 6).

Space in public libraries needs to reflect the latest thinking in brain development and early literacy. A major element in the Family Place Libraries initiative is the reconfiguration of space in the children's room. Focusing the library on its role as an early childhood and parenting center, Family Place emphasizes play, social interaction, and their relationship to learning to read. Space needs to include toys and learning stations (trains, puzzles, dollhouses, building blocks), early childhood collections and computers, and a designated area of the children's room. The Family Place drop-in space is extremely popular with young children and their parents/caregivers and needs to be well thought out in terms of noise and safety.

The notion that teenagers need special space in contemporary culture derives from behavioral patterns that include distinguishing themselves from young children, high noise levels, and the transition to adulthood and independence. The precursor to the library teen space in U.S. libraries is undoubtedly the family room or basement of the 1950s and '60s, commonplace in suburban homes. The notion that teenagers should be free—to be noisy, private, and independent—stems from cultural shifts.

In public libraries, children—particularly adolescents—may be viewed as a nuisance. Children and teens do not need silence to learn. They have a remarkable ability to focus on individual tasks while they filter out noise. Librarians must remember when designing youth spaces to allow for peer interaction, music, and movement

> Younger children like to sprawl on the floor or on soft furniture to read and share. They like places they can talk, and quiet reflective places where they can curl up with books and sink into that world. Adolescents need a variety of places. They need individual study spaces for research and homework. They need places to share information and ideas. They need a space that is obviously their own. It is best to arrange material for children according to the ways in which they think and act. Maybe using the Dewey Decimal Classification System and alphabetizing fiction in shelving areas is not the best way to go; ask them.
>
> —Lesley Boon (2003, 154)

while offering adults a quiet space to satisfy their own needs. "There appears to be a predilection for the chaotic. There are visual statements to indicate a different domain of existence, encouraging adults to keep away. The furniture is not always used in the ways imagined by the designer or manufacturer, and floor space is an important component of work and relaxation" (Boon 2003, 152).

According to Cranz and Cha in their research on adolescents in libraries,

Movement is the basis for early learning and continues to be the basis of health throughout life. Adolescents are not yet fully socialized to learning only abstractly, so they may need to retain movement in order to learn. Moreover, different styles of learning differentiate individuals—visual, auditory, and kinesthetic—so having all learning environments, not just those for teens, with options for different postural attitudes would be ideal. (2006, 49).

Gender is another important issue. Boys and girls use space differently. Boys tend to be independent and want to study or work alone. Girls tend to prefer working in groups and relying on each other for information and support. Boys take up more room than girls; they are louder and more active. During our interview, Jeffrey Scherer commented on the differences of behavior of different aged youth:

The thing that I find really fascinating is the "children helping children" issue. One presumes that [the interaction involves] either a librarian and a child or a parent and a child, but, in fact, there's a lot of very creative coteaching if you get a kid who knows something and another kid who doesn't know it. And at a certain age they are very helpful. . . . At other ages because of the peer relationship they won't help. So you get that break point in the teen years where [kids] don't ask for questions.

Space and many of the interior elements of teen areas are successful if designed to be multipurpose. Teens come to the library often for contradictory purposes and alternate between different sets of activities. They occupy a variety of postures including sitting, standing, perching, reclining, lying, leaning, as well as the range of social activities—chatting, studying, reading, taking notes, browsing the Internet, browsing the bookshelves, listening to music. These various behaviors require special design elements (Cranz and Cha 2006, 51).

Youth spaces in libraries should be designed to reflect and complement young people's wide-ranging educational and recreational needs, aesthetic sensibilities, and body movements. It is vital to understand the developmental milestones of the various age groups and to apply this knowledge to new library spaces. Through reading, visiting, and interacting with other librarians and youth professionals in other fields, librarians can gain insight into what spaces can and should be designed for optimal learning. This type of creative process will lead librarians, architects, and communities to a better understanding of the library of the future.

Questions to Ask about Separate Areas for Children and Teens

What ages are to be served? Will there be a separate area for early childhood, including babies, toddlers, and preschoolers? Will collections and space for parents and caregivers be provided?

What level of school-age youth will be served? Will there be a division of space between preschool and school-age children?

How close will the children's area be to the teen or adult sections? How close will the teen area be to the adult section? What about noise? Food? Music? Gaming computers?

How are young teen and young adult audiences to be served—as part of the children's room or in their own areas?

Will the area serve young teens and young adults? This is a large age range. Are there any thoughts about spaces and services for the different teenage years?

Will the youth department change organizationally as a result of the building project? How will the change affect management?

What about accompanying adults: parents, adult caregivers, and teachers? Should special collections for teachers be located in the children's room, or can they be located in a workroom area?

What other practical considerations have already been identified as important in the design of the children's space?

CONCLUSION

It is critical that the mission of the library be taken into consideration when designing new space, particularly the influence and position of youth services. In today's society, the public library's role as a community institution embraces services for children, families, and teens. During the initial planning stages, the project team should gather as much information as possible about the attitudes and commitment to youth on the part of the staff, board, and community. More important, the team should become educated and immersed in the behavior patterns, learning needs, and tastes of children and teens. Devoting time and energy to examine this commitment and to understand the various ages and behaviors fully will lead the team throughout the process and culminate in a successful expansion or renovation project, one that satisfies the end users.

At this point in the process, all of the research, on-site and online visits to spaces and places for children and teens, staff expertise, community input, and architect's and design professionals' experience converge to envision a new design. It is critical that the library and design professionals' processes of gathering input and synthesizing it into a cohesive design solution be managed effectively and without interference.

Chapter 3

Planning the Space
Furniture, Shelving, and Equipment

Once the design population and major goals of the project have been decided, the library professionals work with the architect and library consultants to determine the space allocation and requirements for each new area. Space planning offers a good opportunity for administration and staff to think in realistic terms, allows the design team to get all of their ideas on the table, and provides the architect with a road map for the overall scope and design of the project.

At the end of the space study, the architect and project team draw up the Program of Requirements, which brings all of the library's stakeholders together on the size and scope of the building or renovation and reflects the needs of the library and the community.

PROGRAM OF REQUIREMENTS

The Program of Requirements is a written representation of the proposed building project with each area detailed and described, so that the architect can prepare drawings that transform the words into graphic representations. The Program document typically includes an executive summary, background, and objectives of the project; what other studies have occurred; information on the library, the community, and the proposed library site; and details on each item of furniture and equipment, the quantity and extent of collections, and other facility needs such as special program rooms and workspaces. Figure 3.1 is a sample page.

The Program of Requirements, in which all of this important data is organized and recorded, serves as the basis of planning for the new or renovated building and provides all of the critical ingredients the architect will use to create space that functions well and is architecturally and artistically pleasing. The Program will be used as the document against which the design solution can be monitored and measured and serves as a checklist for library staff during the building stages of design, development, and construction, to make sure no element disappears. The Program of Requirements is generally approved by the board and administration before the project proceeds to conceptual design.

The space study begins with a detailed assessment of current resources. The next steps are to estimate future collections, furniture and equipment needs, workspaces (public and office areas), and storage and program preparation space and to decide whether there will be special activity areas, spaces, or meeting rooms dedicated to youth programs. Throughout this phase, major obstacles and issues are often identified, the overall size and scope of the project are explored, and the general adjacencies

Department: Early Childhood and Parent Center (Birth - 5 years)
Building Level: Two

Function	No. of Units	Unit Area (sq.ft.)	Unit Area (sq.met.)	No. of people	Extended Required Sq. Ftg.	Total Area (sq.ft.)	Total Area (sq.met.)
Giant Books	1	40	3.72		0	40.04	4
Baby Book Nests	10	8	0.744		0	80.08	7
Picture Book - Book Bins	48	18	1.674		0	864.91	80
45"H Shelving (Easy Readers)	20	18	1.674		0	360.38	33
60" H Shelving (Parenting)	10	18	1.674		0	180.19	17
Magazine Shelving	4	18	1.674		0	72.08	7
CD/DVD Shelving	4	18	1.674		0	72.08	7
Display Shelving	4	18	1.674		0	72.08	7
Display/Bulletin Board	1	100	9.3		0	100.11	9
Parent Information	1	50	4.65		0	50.05	5
Story Time/Activity Room (w/countertop & sink)	1	500	46.5		0	500.53	47
Story Time/Activity Room Storage	1	150	13.95		0	150.16	14
Puppet Theatre	1	0	0		0	0.00	0
Activity Area/Play Stations	1	500	46.5		0	500.53	47
Table and Chairs	20	35	3.255		0	700.74	65
Lounge Seating	20	40	3.72		0	800.84	74
Omani Seating Area	1	100	4.65		0	50.05	5
Educational/Gaming Computers	20	40	3.72		0	800.84	74
Parent Computers	2	30	2.79		0	60.06	6
OPAC Stations	2	30	2.79		0	60.06	6
Librarian Stations	2	70	6.51		0	140.15	13
Family Rest Room (w/Mother's Room)	1	120	11.16		0	120	11
Sub-total					0	5775.94	537
Internal walls and circulation @ 10%						578	54
Early Childhood and Parent Center (Birth - 5 years) Total Area						6,354	590

FIGURE 3.1   Program of Requirements sample page. Children's Public Library, Muscat, Oman. Design Architect, VITETTA. Used by permission of the architect.

and traffic flow are established. With a good start, the Program of Requirements clearly articulates the proposed functions of the new building or renovated space and gives the architect sufficient information to begin the design. The more comprehensive and accurate the Program, the better informed the architect.

ASSESSING RESOURCES

Administration and staff expertise and knowledge provide the most critical information during this phase of the project. The architect, design professional, or library consultant, if already on board, can be of great assistance. They have access to software that formulates the square footage requirements for shelving, seating, program space,

The [Schaumburg Township District Library expansion] was one of the first projects that I was involved with where the director really embraced getting everyone involved. From early-on programming, we brought everyone (maintenance staff, pages, librarians) in on the design. Then there was this core group—the division heads—that were providing oversight. Every staff member had a say in their area and how it functioned. Later on, when we were adding finishes, they could also choose from a selected set [of materials and colors]. The size of the children's room really came out of interviews with staff and the building committee when we programmed the space. These are the spaces we need. These are the [plans for] collections [and] seating. During planning, we discussed the needs of the department.

—Denelle Wrightson (interview, June 2005)

desks, work areas, and technology. If they were chosen for a specialty in designing youth spaces, they can provide invaluable ideas for creative spaces or areas, new collections, or diverse services that the library staff may not think of initially. They often have been involved with or have knowledge about exciting youth spaces that exist or are being built. It is the staff, however, that must determine what services will ultimately be provided within the new space.

Collections Assessment

Assessment begins by counting the number of volumes in each of the current collections, generally estimating how large the collection may grow (or diminish) to accommodate future needs, and determining the new collections that will be added to satisfy the needs of those populations identified through the planning process. It is helpful to estimate the size and scope of the collections the new space will have on opening day as well as future growth.

If a library is small and the collection inadequate, staff may need to identify and use standard guidelines to project collection size. These guidelines are often provided at the state level but may need to be modified or enhanced to suit the design population. Growth calculations are based on the library's current rate of addition (if the library is currently "maxed out," this current rate would need to be a best estimate) extended over approximately two decades. Decreases in collection size also need to be considered. The following list serves as a starting point for assessing children's, teens, and parent collections.

Preschool and School-Age Children

Books of various types (board, cloth, oversized)	Magazines
	Computer software
Picture books	Audiovisual collections
Easy Readers	Multimedia kits
Fiction	Toys and puzzles
Nonfiction	

Teens

Fiction and paperbacks	Magazines
Nonfiction (often housed as part of the adult collection)	Computer software
	Audiovisual collections
Graphic novels	

Parents and Professional Collections

Books	Magazines
Audiovisual collections	Pamphlets
Kits	

Other factors may influence collection size and scope. A regional library may need to house more substantial collections than a branch or small library. A special service focus may necessitate resizing the collection. For instance, a Family Place library, which emphasizes early childhood and parenting services, may need to increase the amount of board books, picture books, toys, and parenting materials. Another factor that may influence collection size is the increase in availability of electronic resources and downloadable materials, which would decrease the growth rate in reference, non-fiction, and audiovisual collections.

Shelving and Furniture Plan

The organization of the furniture and shelving—or furniture and shelving plan—must be concurrent with architectural space planning and design. Many modern office buildings are designed as what is referred to as "core and shell": The building is constructed with the elevator and plumbing core at the center, and the empty office space is later developed by tenants. Many library board members and architects are familiar with this concept of architectural development and planning. Designing a library building or space is absolutely the reverse of this approach.

It is essential that the library furniture and shelving layout be developed in conjunction with the building site orientation and architectural design. Detailed consideration is needed for the general location of collections and the height of the shelving and other obstructions that may interfere with views or sight lines critical to the visual management of the space. The Program of Requirements must be reviewed carefully to ensure that appropriate allocation of linear shelving is coordinated with the expected shelving heights. The accuracy of the projection affects the overall space required as well as the design team's success in meeting the sight line goals.

SHELVING

The size and types of shelving influence the amount of space collections occupy within the new space. Deciding on the age groups and the formats, sizes, and variety of materials helps the architect provide the appropriate space and layout for each type of shelving unit and the number of shelves needed. Books, magazines, audiovisual materials, toys, and games are best housed on specially designed shelving or storage units. Most of the library shelving and furniture vendors offer a variety of solutions.

From a planning point of view, a book stack is going to be one of the guiding forces of how you set the building up because it has dimension and it has to be accommodated and it has to have an aisle width of a certain dimension so that you can circulate. When you think about the whole structural system of the building, it is actually set up around the book stack and then everything else has to fall in place. (interview with Daria Pizzetta, October 2004).

Graeme Murphy illustrates collection planning supporting space planning: "East Melbourne staff analysed the current collections size and added expansion rates for each sub-collection and then the shelving system was developed and the spread [aisle width between shelving units] agreed. It was only then that the space allocation was made" (2002, 3).

One thing to keep in mind is that movable shelving is becoming a flexible alternative to fixed units. Shelving on wheels or castors allows for room management for programming and the delivery of special services. The Middle Country Public Library often conducts resource fairs (child-care providers, pet information fair, International Museum Day, working families, catastrophe readiness, Women's EXPO) and other large events using public floor space. Wheeled shelving enables the staff to make space available for this type of community programming. In the design of the new Village Branch Library in Lexington (Ky.), space limitation was turned into space flexibility through innovative planning and flexible furnishings (figure 3.2). Kathleen Imhoff, Lexington's executive director, summarized the goals of the design as four A's: adaptability, accessibility, aesthetics, and accommodation.

Many of the shelves are on wheels for easy moving and adaptability. When a program is planned that anticipates a crowd that is too big for the meeting room (over 75), the front shelves are moved into the meeting room and the front area is used for the program. Sometimes the shelves are pushed against the wall so that there can be two programs going on—one in the meeting room and one in the front open area.

Another "A" of good building design is accessibility. The high impact entrance has a remote controlled handicapped accessible front double door. The entire building is on the same level and the bathrooms are accessible. The library shelving is all low and the bottom shelves are not used. Much of the shelving is face out shelving for convenient selection. (Imhoff 2005)

Picture books are often housed on lower shelving units with tops for display or additional face-out shelving for marketing purposes. Children's nonfiction and fiction collections are typically shelved on 42-inch (106 cm) or 60-inch (152 cm) high shelving, not the standard 84-inch (214 cm) or 90-inch (228 cm) shelving in the adult room (note that these are nominal dimensions that may vary with manufacturers). Young children's collections often include items that need to be housed on special storage shelves, hung on racks (book/CD combinations), or displayed in specially designed bins or cases (board and cloth books, oversized picture books, toys).

Providing collections for parents or teachers often requires the use of standard-size adult shelving that can overwhelm a children's area. Placement of these materials should be kept in mind, particularly in reference to sight lines and openness. Many children's room designs opt for 42- or 60-inch shelving for parenting collections, taking this fact into consideration. Another shelving height that may be preferable is 48-inch (122 cm)—a dimension more common in metric systems than with U.S. manufacturers.

Teen collections generally work best with the standard 60-inch shelving and in some cases can accommodate 84-inch shelving to gain more shelving space. This height may work well against walls or the outer perimeters but, as in the other youth areas, sight lines need to be kept in mind.

Both wood and metal shelving for parent and young adult magazines is available from standard shelving manufacturers. Important considerations include the height of the shelving, the quantity of back issues to be made available, and the location of the magazines near comfortable seating.

Audiovisual and merchandising shelving may utilize more space than stack shelving and should be arranged carefully. Considering the ongoing extinction of current

FIGURE 3.2 Movable shelving on casters provides space for large programs in a small branch library (top), and special activity with movable shelving out of the way (bottom). Lexington Public Library, Village Branch, Lexington, Ky. Architect, Sherman Carter Barnhart; consultant, VITETTA. Used by permission of the photographer.

Photo Credits: Kathleen R.T. Imhoff

38

media formats and possibility of future uses of the shelving for other materials, it is advisable to invest in a merchandising or shelving system for audiovisual materials that is adaptable to new formats. Audiovisual shelving/furniture should be placed with the popular collections of the children's and teen areas and may be on castors for mobility or display.

Updated listings of vendors and manufacturers of standard shelving and retail fixtures are available at http://goldbook.libraryjournal.com. Design professionals should be familiar with products that accommodate the specific requirements of the library.

FURNITURE

The single most critical component of the library interior is the furniture; it must be inviting, comfortable, secure, durable, and attractive. The type, size, quality, safety, and aesthetic of the furniture either reinforce the design mission or destroy it. Too often in public sector projects, the first item to be reduced or eliminated from a design solution (budget) is the furniture. Too many times existing furniture is reused in a new or renovated library—furniture that is not functional, is unattractive, and does not bolster the aesthetic improvement sought. The decision to use existing furniture must be considered carefully.

According to Carol Brown, the basic design elements of form, size, and scale should inform furniture selection:

"Form" refers to the basic shape of an object (or a space) generated by lines, planes, volumes, and points. Individual furniture items are chosen with appropriate size and scale so that they are correctly proportioned to the overall size of the space and to other objects within it. Scale is an important consideration in regard to who will use the selected furnishings. For example, in order to provide furniture of the appropriate scale for children, the tables and chairs in a youth area are smaller than similar furniture in an adult area. (2002, 1)

Furniture for children must be at the appropriate heights for each designated age group. This information needs to be indicated in the Program of Requirements. It is essential that the data be accurate and applicable for each community and each audience. From one geographic area to another—or even one neighborhood to another—suitable heights of furniture may vary. It is important that this data be clear prior to the design professionals making selections and recommendations, for some furniture may not be available in appropriate heights, or there may be premiums for special orders.

Seating

The exact amount of space needed for reader seating varies with how the library is used, the types of collections it houses, and the size and variety of seats desired. Seating at tables requires less square footage than lounge seating. Tables and chairs in an early childhood area require less space than in a homework area for school-age children or teens. Easily movable seating may be desirable, particularly if the library is located near a school and children regularly use the space as an after-school study hall.

Computer stations require different seats than lounge areas. For casual seating in a children's area, cushions do not require as much room as a typical lounge chair. Adult lounge seats are also needed to accommodate parents and caregivers (figure 3.3). The most important thing to keep in mind with seating is who will be using it and for what purpose.

Children need a wide range of choices in seating because they come in different sizes and forms and use libraries in different ways. A sedentary 60-pound child coming to the library for several days of research has different needs than a restless 100-pound teenager coming to listen to the latest CD.

Chairs are the most important pieces of equipment in the library. They should be the first priority in equipment budgets and there should be no compromise for comfort and durability. Many library patrons will sit for hours of intensive study, and their comfort will determine their level of satisfaction with the library study experience. If libraries want to distinguish themselves from bookstores, chair comfort can be an important factor in that distinction. (Lushington 2008, 111)

The notion that all seating must be comfortable is true only if the desire of the library is for the customer to spend a great amount of time seated. In selecting the chairs for an urban branch library, the VITETTA team selected a chair that was comfortable to the majority of testers for about thirty minutes. This is the amount of time the library estimated that customers usually spend reading the newspaper or a magazine. The only other users of the library for these seats were individuals who wanted to sleep all day in the previous comfy seats. The library was contemplating abandon-

FIGURE 3.3   Child/parent area, Horsham Township Library, Horsham, Pa. Architect, VITETTA. Used by permission of the photographer.

Photo credit: Andrea Brizzi

ing the lounge seats but knew that the local residents—many of whom were elderly or parents with young children—would truly miss the opportunity to sit for a few minutes and peruse a newspaper. Therefore a moderately comfortable or "gradually uncomfortable" chair proved just the right solution for this setting.

Ergonomically appropriate seating is desirable regardless of the age of user, and for staff workstations this characteristic is paramount. Seating manufacturers, particularly office seating manufacturers, are constantly improving and developing flexible, ergonomically appropriate seating. The interior designer will be helpful in directing the library to a variety of solutions in this regard.

Youth services librarians often have strong opinions about types of seating and how seating needs to be integrated in different user areas. Chekon and Miles reflect on their experience at the Sacramento Public Library: "The designers had a tendency to choose furniture for its artistic statement rather than its functionality, and during discussion with them we had to be careful to emphasize user needs. The designers suggested stools for picture book area seating, but we pointed out that two- and three-year-olds require a seatback for support" (1993, 23).

Children's seating is often an afterthought of seating manufacturers. It is important that the sizes and proportions of the seating be carefully detailed, with the weight of the seating neither too heavy to move nor light enough to be tossed. Ordinarily it is possible to obtain samples of chairs prior to selection or specification. If this is not possible, it may be worthwhile to ask the manufacturer for references and to call other libraries that have used the chair to ensure that the selection is appropriate—durable and with the correct level of comfort. According to Carol Brown:

Chairs designed specifically for children come and go on the market frequently, because of the small quantities purchased relative to other furniture items. All of the major library furniture manufacturers offer chairs for children. Some of the chairs are of similar design to a line of chairs for adults offered by the same manufacturer. A good children's chair is not an adult chair with the legs cut off; the entire chair should be proportioned, with shorter legs and smaller members. The height of the chair needed will depend on the age of the children expected to use it and the height of the table with which it will be used. (2002, 76)

Seating Mix

Appropriate seating in youth spaces is required for parents, caregivers, children of all ages, and staff. Each of these constituents requires a unique seating solution. The children's room must have seating that accommodates the range in height and girth of the public. The right mix and placement of seating serve to reinforce the mission of the library in general as well as of particular user areas (see figure 3.4 and plates 12 and 15).

Referring to the "four A's," Imhoff notes that aesthetics is key:

The goal of the entire building design was to create a warm, inviting space where everyone would feel welcome and comfortable. Nontraditional furniture helped to create spaces where people could sit low on a stool, cuddle with their child on a sofa, hang-out with teens at a high ice-cream style table with tall stools or relax in a comfy seat to read a magazine. Part of the marketing plan was to create a positive perception of the library which would then translate into a positive image. (2005)

Seating mixed into the stack areas, clusters of seating, orientation of seating to natural light, and the aesthetically pleasing appearance of the seating all contribute to the successful use of the library. In addition to seating at tables, the children's area may include lounge chairs, rocking chairs, or oversized chairs for parents and children to read together. Sometimes a special waiting area with lounge chairs can be provided for parents or other caregivers waiting for children attending programs. Inviting, comfortable-looking seating encourages caregivers to sit and read to their small children. It is important to consider the shape and appearance of lounge seating in particular.

Librarians at the Sacramento Public Library commented: "The one chair that is perfectly adapted to library users throughout the building is the comfortable oversized lounge chair. . . . finished in a tough leather-look, its extra-wide arms are designed to be sat upon. The two in the picture book area easily hold a parent and child or two small children" (Chekon and Miles 1993, 23). Libraries may also consider a special type of seating that is particularly attractive to children, such as a treehouse, boat, carousel bench, or picnic table.

Galen Cranz and Eunah Cha provide a good example of seating choice relative to teen preferences:

A long, deep bench with a back that tapers from high to low marks one edge of the space and offers several types of seating—conventional right-angle seating as well as cross-legged seating—for more than one person. Because the bench is not subdivided, several people can sit together—half a dozen if the group can tolerate body contact, or one or two people lying down. Several leather-upholstered ottomans can be moved freely throughout the space. (2006, 50)

The mix of tables and chairs, lounge seats, sofas, one-and-a-half seats (great for parents and small children) should be included in the Program of Requirements. It may be beneficial to make minor adjustments in the development of the design, but quantities should be determined by library staff, not the design professionals alone. The quantity and size of seating should be determined before the building design begins. This is the ideal time to consider these important factors and to derive the quantitative listing of the requirements. This maximizes the efficiency of the design team in making selections and recommendations for the seating, focusing on qualitative characteristics rather than the quantities.

Upholstery

Whether to use upholstery or not and how much of the seating to upholster are questions to be resolved. For the Free Library of Philadelphia branch renovations,

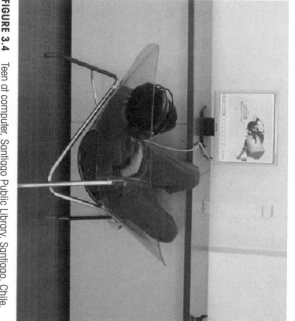

FIGURE 3.4   Teen at computer, Santiago Public Library, Santiago, Chile. Architect, Cox and Ugarte; Design Consultant, VITETTA; Industrial Designer, NAVE. Used by permission of the library.

Photo credit: Santiago Public Library

these issues were paramount for both health and maintenance, and decisions varied from branch to branch. One concern involved the presence of lice, whose transmission can be aided by upholstery. The need for easily cleanable furniture, not only for reasons of health but to manage the results of activity (magic markers, Play-Doh, snacks), was also a consideration. Vinyl seemed to be one alternative that was easier to keep clean, but even this was not a perfect solution since in some branches staff were concerned about the ease with which vinyl can be slashed.

On the positive side, there are many reasons why a library may choose upholstery. Colorful patterns, interesting designs, comfort, and attractiveness of upholstery material add to the warmth and ambiance of the children's room, and "funky" pattern enhances any teen area. Parents, young children, and teens alike are attracted to comfortable lounge seats and, even where it is not advisable to select a large number of upholstered seats, a few well-built and properly upholstered chairs can make an enormous difference in youth spaces.

Tables and Workstations

Fun, cozy, inviting seating attracts teens and young adults to use their space for reading, listening, and conversation. For teens, it may be better to design a less traditional workstation, offering a choice of standing or sitting. Curved work surfaces at two different heights can be accompanied by adjustable-height stools to accommodate varying heights of teenagers, either for standing or perching on stools halfway between sitting and standing. In "Body Conscious Design in a Teen Space," Cranz and Cha (2006, 50) describe workstations that are not designed for traditional right-angle seating but rather offer a choice of standing or sitting (as in figure 3.5). Curved workstations at two different heights are accompanied by adjustable-height stools. The space accommodates various heights, either for standing or perching on stools halfway between sitting and standing. The sit-stand position (also called perching) is particularly beneficial physiologically, since it allows the legs to rest while the spine's curves are retained.

Tables and workstations can be of various heights and, in the case of early childhood computer counters or tables, often call for an accommodation of adult seating space as well. At the Middle Country Public Library, the early childhood computer stations were designed to be 4 feet (1.3 m) wide and chair heights are adjustable, which allows for a parent and child—or two children—to work together easily (figure 3.6). Parents do not need to stand over or crouch down near the child. For other tables in the children's room, several heights were used in order to accommodate children preschool through the young teen years.

Tables can be square, rectangular, or round. Children and teens often prefer round tables for group work and conversation, and they have the advantage of lacking

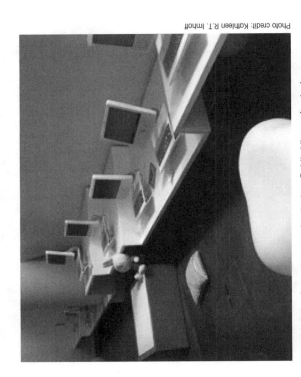

Photo credit: Kathleen R.T. Imhoff

FIGURE 3.5 Computer area, Amsterdam Public Library, Amsterdam, Netherlands. Architect, Jo Coenen and Co. Architecten. Used by permission of the photographer.

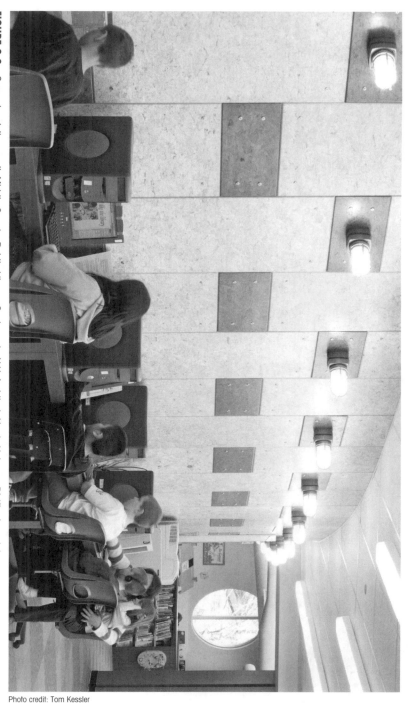

FIGURE 3.6   Computer stations wall, Middle Country Public Library, Centereach, N.Y. Architect, Hardy Holzman Pfeiffer Associates. Used by permission of the photographer, courtesy of the architect.

Photo credit: Tom Kessler

potentially sharp corners. On the other hand, square tables can be grouped together easily and may be more popular with teens. The type of base and the frame of the table are important considerations for the design team. Pedestal base tables are not appropriate for use in an area for young children because of their tendency to tip over. It is important to consider the appropriateness of pedestal base tables for older children for the same reason.

Many tables are constructed with cross-framing, which can present obstacles to chairs and people. It is important to check the structure of the tables being considered and ascertain that the chairs selected not only complement the tables but actually fit underneath. One of the most important factors to consider is scale; allow 9–10 inches of clearance between the seat and the table. Counters, particularly for computers and docking stations, are a popular alternative to the traditional reader table or carrel, but be cautious about the support details for counters, which are ordinarily custom millwork. Many systems furniture manufacturers and some library furniture manufacturers offer counter-type workstations that may be more flexible and therefore preferable.

Existing Furniture

Libraries are filled with existing furniture. It is noteworthy that in the hospitality industry the average life cycle for furniture and nonpermanent finishes (paint/carpet/

wallpaper) is approximately five to seven years. The library is the public equivalent of the hospitality industry, yet the furniture and finishes life cycle of public libraries ranges from ten years to sixty years or longer.

The success of the library's mission is reinforced or inhibited significantly by the selection and design of the furniture. Many renovation projects incorporate existing furniture into the mix of new design elements. It is important to consider the value of the furniture, before proceeding with design, in terms of both replacement cost and the environmental impact of discarding items to a landfill. In all situations, be wary of accepting donations of furniture for a new project.

Evaluating the existing furniture prior to a renovation project is a first step. Furniture that is still functional can sometimes be refurbished and used in storage or back room areas. In some cases, it can be donated to other public institutions or nonprofits. It is critical to balance the value of retaining, refurbishing, or replacing the existing furniture by performing a furniture inventory. Generally the interior designer is best skilled to perform the inventory. The interior designer measures each piece of furniture, determines its function and capacity, ranks the condition, evaluates it for code compliance and structural defect/soundness, and outlines the aesthetic characteristics such as wood/metal color, fabric pattern/color/style, manufacturer, and materials (figure 3.7). The inventory usually includes a digital photo record of each item or sample items. This information is instrumental in integrating some or all of the existing furniture into a new design.

It is important to recognize the desire to retain or replace existing furniture in the scope of the design plan. A design professional may have sources for refurbishing old tables and reupholstering chairs that can help save money and the environment. In the Free Library of Philadelphia renovations, the VITETTA team salvaged hundreds of chairs nicknamed the "Jetson chairs" because of their futuristic molding of an entirely stainless steel frame. The team relocated these chairs from Carnegie branches to modern branches built in the 1960s. These are wonderful seats—appropriately sized and extraordinarily strong—and were made attractive with new upholstery and an appropriate setting. Chairs are no longer constructed with solid stainless steel frames and replacing the Jetson chairs in kind was impossible; replacements would have been costly and inferior.

The decision to reuse or replace existing furniture must be made early in the process, prior to space planning. If existing furniture is to be integrated, the furniture plan must reflect the exact dimensions of these items; there are no "generic" or "default" dimensions to be used in floor plans when integrating existing furniture. Many items have unusual dimensions and must be measured and drawn accurately on the plans in order to ensure proper aisle widths, functionality, and comfort zones. Design professionals not familiar with libraries sometimes integrate standard symbols from a computer library into the floor plan. This method is likely to result in difficult or impossible furniture installations when the construction is complete.

Complete replacement of existing furniture is warranted in many libraries. Much existing library furniture is past its useful life, and other furniture is inappropriate or inefficient in space consumption. It is important to communicate to community stakeholders and governing agencies the value of appropriately furnishing a library as it relates to achieving the mission.

Quantity	Existing Room No and Name		Exist. Tag	Type	Manufacturer	Material	Color	W x D x H	Note	Condition	Disposition
1	100A	Quiet Reading Room		shelving unit, SF	Built-in	wood	maple	40 x 10 x 82	5"h base, 6 shelf		
1	100A	Quiet Reading Room		stand, atlas	Remington Ral	wood	oak	29 x 27 x 44	6 shelf, tapered legs, worn	fair	reuse if nec
1	100A	Quiet Reading Room		stand, book		wood	cherry	31 x 17 x 44	solid end, front and back	good	reuse
6	100A	Quiet Reading Room		table, study	Brodart	wood/p.lam/metal	oak/green copper/green	72 x 36 x 29	Libris series, wood bullnose edge - 4 tubular leg, slight wear	fair	reuse if nec
1	100B	Business Center		carrel, DF	Brodart	p.lam/wood	green granite/maple	61 x 42 x 29	16" H arched screen, 4 leg, grommet, powered	good	recondition
1	100B	Business Center		carrel, SF	Brodart	p.lam/wood	green granite/maple	36 x 33 x 29	16" H arched screen, 4 leg, grommet, powered	fair	reuse
4	100B	Business Center		chair, armless	Brodart	fabric/wood	green diamond/maple	18 x 18 x 36	wood ladder back, w/circle detail	good	reuse
4	100B	Business Center		chair, armless	Brodart	fabric/wood	blue-green stripe/maple	18 x 18 x 36	wood ladder back, w/circle detail	good	reuse
1	100B	Business Center		chair, task w/ arms	Now Seating	fabric/metal	green-blue stripe/black	27 x 21 x 38		good	reuse
4	100B	Business Center		computer					CPU, keybd, flat screen		
1	100B	Business Center		copy machine	Ricoh				Aticio 3228C w/coin machine Jamex 6557		
1	100B	Business Center		table, study	Brodart	p.lam/wood	green granite/maple	60 x 30 x 29	grommets, powered	good	reuse
1	100C	AV		book truck		metal	tan	28 x 16 x 40	double faced, 3 shelf - worn	poor	do not reuse
1	100C	AV		chair, arm		metal	brown	24 x 17 x 35	Windsor style, chipped paint (novelty)	fair	reuse
1	100C	AV		globe		wood	medium oak	37" dia x 50	wood frame, state of Pennsylvania worn off	fair	reuse
2	100C	AV		rack, display	Totalibre	wood/metal	oak/chrome	22 x 23 x 53	3 shelf w/handle and caster	fair	reuse
1	100C	AV		shelving unit, DF	Brodart	wood/metal	oak/blue	145 x 20 x 42	2 1/2" H canopy, 4" H base, 4 section, 3 shelf	fair	reuse
2	100C	AV		shelving unit, DF	Brodart	wood/metal	oak/blue	181 x 20 x 42	2 1/2" H canopy, 4" H base, 5 section, 3 shelf	fair	reuse
7	100C	AV		shelving unit, DF		p.lam/wood	black/oak	51 x 25 x 54	pyramid, 5 shelf, some missing trim, worn	poor	do not reuse
1	100C	AV		shelving unit, DF		wood/metal	oak/blue	97 x 29 x 54	slat wall back, 9" D slanted shelves, white base, oak trim, 4 shelf, 2 section	fair	reuse
3	100C	AV		shelving unit, SF	Built-in	wood	maple	24 x 10 x 82	5"h base, 6 shelf		
23	100C	AV		shelving unit, SF	Built-in	wood	maple	36 x 10 x 82	5"h base, 6 shelf		
1	100C	AV		shelving unit, SF		wood	maple	37 x 12 x 82	no back, 7 shelf	poor	do not reuse
1	100C	AV		shelving unit, SF		wood	oak	37 1/2 x 9 x 82	white p.lam back, 7 shelf starter (unfinished side)	poor	do not reuse
1	101	Storage/Mech		file, index	Cole	metal	tan	14 x 27 x 40		fair	reuse
1	101	Storage/Mech		file, index		metal	red (painted)	15 x 27 x 52		fair	reuse
1	101	Storage/Mech		file, index	Cole	metal	tan	24 x 25 x 38	side by side drawers	fair	reuse
1	101	Storage/Mech		file, vertical		metal	army green	18 x 28 x 50		fair	reuse
4	101	Storage/Mech		file, vertical	HON	metal	tan	18 x 28 x 52		fair	reuse
1	102	Storage/Elec		shelving unit		metal	gray	36 x 14 x 80	6 racks, hanging spools	fair	reuse
1	103	Fiction		display		plastic	blue	19 x 17 x 70	Danielle Steel - 2 sided		
2	103	Fiction		rack, spinner		wood/plastic	medium oak/black	27 x 27 x 62	4 column, 4 sided	fair	reuse if nec
5	103	Fiction		shelving unit, DF		wood/metal	oak/putty	218 x 21 (24) x 90	Type 9: cantilever shelf, individual supports, slotted together, 10"D base, (1) 9" D shelf, (5) 7" D shelf, total 7 shelf, 6 sections, 24" W wood end panel, 1 side	fair	reuse if nec
5	103	Fiction		shelving unit, DF		wood/metal	oak/putty	184 x 21 (24) x 90	Type 9: cantilever shelf, individual supports, slotted together, 10"D base, 7" D shelf, 7 shelf, 5 sections, 24" W wood end panel, 2 ends	fair	reuse if nec
1	103	Fiction		shelving unit, DF		wood/metal	oak/putty	182 x 21 (24) x 90	Type 9: cantilever shelf, individual supports, slotted together, 10"D base, 7" D shelf, 7 shelf, 5 sections, 24" W wood end panel, 1 end	fair	reuse if nec

FIGURE 3.7 Furniture inventory sample page, children's department. Architect, VITETTA. Used by permission of the architect.

Activity Tables/Special Furniture

Many examples of young children's activity areas, including furniture and developmental play tables, are available from library and child-care industry suppliers. The design team should make use of these manufactured items where appropriate and need not reinvent every wheel. Many of these products are the result of research and have been tested for quality, performance, and durability. The design team should, however, be given the opportunity for invention; some wonderful, appropriate, and unique elements of the activity space may be realized through the creative force of the library staff and design team.

Millwork and Casework

Millwork is cabinetry and woodwork (e.g., door casings, chair rails, crown and base molds) that is custom designed for a building interior. Casework is cabinetry that is manufactured in components and modified or organized to fit into an interior space. Most library circulation desks and reference desks are either millwork or modular library furniture. Most library kitchen cabinetry is either millwork or casework. Millwork is specially manufactured in a millwork/carpentry shop. Usually these are local shops that produce a range of millwork for commercial and residential installations.

Millwork can be extraordinarily beautiful and add exquisite effects to a library. Alternately, it can be poorly designed or executed and detract from both the functionality and aesthetics of the space. Libraries are generally better served with furniture components than with millwork for quality assurance. Modular or freestanding furniture offers flexibility and high-quality, pre-engineered hardware such as drawer glides, hinges, and keyboard trays. It is imperative that the architect who wishes to implement millwork solutions in libraries invest careful study and detailing to accommodate the functional requirements for the library and monitor the fabrication quality.

Casework or millwork is an appropriate solution for the cabinetry in a program or meeting room, workroom, or staff lounge. It is important to review counter and upper cabinet heights and clearances with the team. These requirements vary from library to library and from library to office space. Be careful to verify the specific dimensional requirements, including placement of appliances such as icemakers, taking note of 90 degree corners and hardware finish and function. The *Checklist of Library Building Design Considerations* (Sannwald 2008) is an excellent resource for design and library professionals during the planning phases and provides a comprehensive list of considerations for each project.

Questions to Ask about Cabinetry

Is millwork the optimal solution or would manufactured furniture be best?

What are the special requirements for data transmission, electrical, and plumbing?

How many cabinets, how many shelves, how many drawers, and what type/size of drawers are required?

Will the drawers/doors be lockable? Will they have a master key or be keyed separately?

What are the heights of the counter? Is the sink accessible?

What is the height of the upper cabinets (bottom and top—check the structure)?

What appliances will be integrated? Disposal? Icemaker? Refrigerator? Microwave? Plasma screen or monitor?

What will the finish materials be? Plastic laminate? Resinous hard surface such as Corian? Wood? Marmoleum?

Will the counter edges be self-edged (plastic laminate or wood) or PVC?

Displays

Display areas, exhibit cases, and bulletin boards must be integrated in the children's and teen areas and not designed as an afterthought. Some ideas to consider include a flat screen programmable display for events and programs, picture rails for art, and a place for seasonal decorations and collections. Tackable display walls can easily be provided in a few locations throughout the space; this helps organize (and limit) the number of displays and often serves the dual function of a sound attenuator.

An important part of the children's experience is the ability to display art or crafts created at the library. It is important to consider the placement of tackable surfaces for these displays in select areas of the children's space. A story/craft room often provides plentiful blank wall space, which can be covered with a tackable surface or fabric-wrapped acoustic panels to achieve several goals with one investment. Fabric-wrapped panels or upholstered walls generally provide a feeling of warmth in the story space as well.

Special display cabinets can be integrated into the youth space and the general public spaces of the library alike. Display cases need to be lockable and should be easy to access and maintain. The architect should consider integrating standard retail display cases into the design or creating millwork cases. Retail display cases often include appropriate lighting to highlight the items within the case.

Special shelving units can be created to accommodate fliers and pamphlets in an organized display, facilitating clarity for parents, children, and teens and helping to eliminate clutter. These units can be on castors to allow the library to store them out of sight during special library events or to vary their placement within the room (figure 3.8).

FIGURE 3.8 Display shelving, Middle Country Public Library, Centereach, N.Y. Architect, Hardy Holzman Pfeiffer Associates. Used by permission of A. R. Kropp Co. and Sons.

Photo and display unit design credit: A. R. Kropp Co. and Sons and MJ Industries

Questions to Ask about Displays

How will displays and exhibits be accommodated?

Will bulletin boards and exhibit cases be built in as millwork or purchased from a standard library manufacturer and installed or placed within the area?

Does the library have any permanent artwork for display? Is there a permanent art collection that needs to be considered?

PUBLIC COMPUTER TERMINALS AND OTHER EQUIPMENT

The number of computers available for public use varies widely from library to library. With each year, the amount of electronic resources being released and the daily demand for computer use influence the arrangement and use of space. In the young children's area, most libraries provide computer terminals with seating to accommodate two patrons—either a parent and child or two children. Teens often work in teams or compete in online gaming environments, which necessitates having enough computers to satisfy a peer-to-peer network. Teens also require individual workstations for Internet research or word processing. Today's computer world is a very interactive environment.

Many libraries aim to separate computer areas by age group—young children, parents, school-age children, teens—as well as by function—gaming, reading readiness, literature and learning, reference and Internet searching, online catalog, e-mail and social networking. Early in the planning process, the library needs to determine age groups and functions in order to help the architects and designers better plan for table heights, seating, number and size of computer stations, and adjacencies regarding which age group accesses what resources. How and where children and teens register for Internet use needs to be considered along with casual staff oversight of the area for security purposes. For young children, wires and plugs present particular hazards.

During the branch renovations of the Free Library of Philadelphia, the project team and architect decided that standardizing the computer furniture for all of the branches would save on costs and be the best solution for staff management and security. They considered the installation of computers and the accompanying furniture as part of the design of the building rather than as a typical furniture purchase. They needed twenty-four carrels with CPUs located at each computer station, easily accessible to staff and locked for security purposes. The architect standardized the design as part of the construction drawings process, which resulted in a contract with a manufacturer to build a product that later became part of the company's standard catalog offerings.

Other equipment desired for youth spaces may require extra counter space, cabinet storage, or specially designed workstations. Copiers, Ellison die-cut machines, whiteboards, poster machines, and photography equipment are just some of the special equipment provided in children's and teen rooms. At the Schaumburg Township District Library, the children's department has a special room that allows children to create materials for homework assignments, special reports, or personal creative ventures. The drop-in Teen Resource Center in the Selden building at the Middle

Country Public Library was created to be a wireless hub, providing laptops as needed, a TV and gaming setup, and café tables for board games. How to store equipment and materials was an essential part of the space design.

Questions to Ask about Computers

How many computers will be housed in the children's area? The teen area? For parents and other adults who work with families?

What kind of work will the children or teens be doing on the computers? Catalog access only? Reference and Internet searching? E-mail and social networking? Desktop applications? Reading, learning, and other educational applications? Gaming?

Are the computer stations stand-up? For individual or multiuser use? What dimensions will be used for each type of workstation? What type of seating will be used at the computers?

What equipment will be used at each workstation—monitor and keyboard, CPU, printer, speakers, scanners? Will printing be networked? Where will the printers sit? How much space will this equipment occupy on opening day? Will computer services be provided via a LAN or wireless access?

Will there be a separate computer training lab or computer services room? How will it be arranged?

Computer Labs

Although most libraries provide one-on-one computer-use tutorials, some libraries want to provide computer labs for youth. Labs require a different set of standards. The factors involved with establishing a lab must be analyzed thoroughly since setting aside space for a specific function can be inflexible in the library's overall plan of service. In many newer environments, libraries have opted to use wireless laptops for computer instruction, which provides for much more flexible programming.

At the Middle Country Public Library, space was developed for both individualized use and group functions. In the Computer Place (a classroom that was originally part of a school building and reconfigured to provide seventeen networked computers) librarians and teachers work with children as young as three years, their caregivers, teens, and seniors for specific periods of the day when staffed; computers are also programmed for instruction on specific software or online resources. In the recently expanded buildings, computers were placed throughout the Family Place, school-age, and teen areas to accommodate all ages of children, their caregivers, and teens.

At the Schaumburg Township District Library, the staff was technology conscious and wanted to create an actual lab within the children's department for instructional purposes. This was a big effort because there was usually only one computer lab in each building. With the expansion, they wanted to build a dedicated lab for children and decided that it had to be designed differently than the one for adults. Whereas the adult labs were set up in rows (one computer per person), the children's was designed in a U-shaped layout, placing the instructor at the head of the U. With this type of layout, the instructor goes behind the students to help them with their work. It makes assistance easier than if the computers and counters are in rows. The size of the desks was also considered; the children's lab included wider desks that could accommodate two children with one computer.

ADDITIONAL ROOMS AND ACTIVITY SPACES

Not only are children's and teen spaces in today's libraries furnished and designed to target special audiences, they often come with additional spaces or areas for multiple purposes. Many new or expanded libraries provide a separate children's storytime or activity room or, in the case of teens, food area. When designing such special spaces, including story/craft rooms and computer rooms, it is beneficial to place the rooms carefully within the plan of the library to accommodate multifunctioning. *Public Library Space Needs*, a handbook published by the Wisconsin Department of Public Instruction, points out that these specially built rooms "can alleviate the scheduling demands on the library's larger meeting room. Depending on the frequency of programming activities, a separate room can be advantageous. A separate room also creates a chance to locate the room within the children's library (or teen area), close to the material that the programming activity is meant to promote" (Dahlgren 1998, 20).

Architect Denelle Wrightson described the incorporation of programming space in the design of the Schaumburg Township District Library—one of the early projects to create the library as a community center: "Programming was always an important part of this library, so making sure that the space supported the programs that were offered was critical. This is the first library that I've worked on that had a classroom and craft room, a tech lab, and two story rooms. These created opportunities for more program interactions."

Pam Sandlian reflected on the Denver Public Library's "Kids' Place": "The craft room was designed with an abundance of cupboards for storage, washable surfaces, tile floors and of course a handy sink for continuous cleanups. Originally we intended on using the craft space for regular programs, classroom collaboration and science projects. Popular craft programs soon turned into an ongoing open craft project which was designed, displayed and well-stocked for use by families, classes, and individuals" (1999, 11).

To achieve full multifunctioning for these spaces, sliding doors can be used. Sliding glass doors and a theatrical blackout curtain were used in the Horsham Township (Pa.) Library Story Tale Place (see plate 1). This allowed the room to be used as a story or craft room with little or no distractions (curtain closed), for an expanded story area (curtains and sliding doors open to adjacent area), or for activity space for young children during regular hours when no programming is scheduled (glass doors open or closed).

The same design device can be applied to computer labs and small meeting rooms. In the case of computer and meeting rooms, the sliding doors can be transparent or opaque. It is important that the architect solve the means of egress, since a sliding door does not qualify as an emergency exit. This can usually be accomplished by inserting one fixed door that has regular hardware to achieve the proper door swing and means of egress. At the Lexington Village Branch Library, when its doors are open, the public computer area operates as a computer area for adults and teens (figure 3.9). When the doors are closed, the space operates as a computer classroom. The small meeting room doors can be open or closed, depending on the need for privacy (Imhoff 2005).

Many libraries provide spaces for play and learning stations such as a writing station, puppet stage, dollhouse, Lego table, train table, or block area. Teen areas often include a lounge area possibly with music piped in, a refreshment station, and game area with computers for online gaming as well as traditional board games. Some have small conference rooms or group study spaces as part of the design (see plates 2 and 3).

FIGURE 3.9   Sliding wood doors open (top) and partially closed (bottom) at computer room in converted Auto Zone Store, Lexington Public Library, Village Branch, Lexington, Ky. Architect, Sherman Carter Barnhart; consultant, VITETTA. Used by permission of the photographer.

Photo credits: Kathleen R. T. Imhoff

FIGURE 3.10   Shaker peg coat hooks at meeting room entrance, Lexington Public Library, Northside Branch, Lexington, Ky. Architect, Omni Architects; consultant, VITETTA. Used by permission of the photographer.

Photo credit: Frank Doring

During the planning process, librarians may not know just what types of special areas or stations the library will provide, but it is important to begin to think about whether such spaces will be part of the overall design. In addition to special rooms, other items to be considered include coat racks for libraries in colder climates, bike racks, stroller space, drinking fountains, and family restrooms with a diaper changer and step stool. In the Lexington Northside Branch Library the design team installed chrome coat hooks that are reminiscent of Shaker pegs—creating a contemporary twist on a local and historic theme (figure 3.10). The first person to recognize and use a peg for his coat (on opening day) was a child about five years of age.

Questions to Ask about Special Activity Rooms

Will the children's department have a separate storytime or activity room? How many children should the rooms accommodate? Will the children sit on the floor or on small stacking chairs? Should some adult-height chairs be supplied for the room? How many children should be accommodated at tables for craft activities? What is the height of the tables?

Will audiovisual equipment be built in? Will there be storage?

Will there be a children's or family restroom? With a changing table?

Will the youth services department serve children birth through young adult? If so, how will the space be delineated? Can a program room be shared?

What special activities or equipment will be allowed in the teen area? Group study? Game tables? Poetry board? Computers? Lounge? Refreshment station?

Should there be a separate program room dedicated to teen activities?

Will the special spaces have sliding doors, sinks, cabinets, storage closets, plasma or pull-down screen? Will there be a need for a performance stage (portable or permanent) or puppet stage?

Will the room have windows with shades or curtains? Will the shades be electrically or manually operated? Will shade/curtain cords be engineered to be safely out of reach of children?

STAFF WORK AREAS, DESKS, AND STORAGE

Planning workspace for children's services staff requires decisions about public service stations, office areas, program preparation space, and storage. Part of this process includes assessing current and future assignments and workloads, examining trends in service patterns, comparing local staffing patterns with those of neighboring libraries and other libraries of comparable size, assessing current office space available for children's and teen service staff, estimating the growth in staff that may occur after the expansion or renovation, and determining whether the staff needs special program preparation space.

When designing workspace, it is best to focus on proximity and tasks performed in a given area and how those tasks relate to other library operations. For example, several different individuals can occupy a single public workstation or program preparation area at different times during the workweek, whereas office workstations need to be provided for each staff member. The typical workstation requires 80–120 square feet (8–12 square meters); final space allocations are based on further evaluation of the specific routines to be accomplished at each station or within the preparation area and the amount of furniture, shelves, and equipment necessary to support those routines.

Public Service Area

Desks can be created from many different types of materials and products depending on the composition of materials used throughout the room. Eye-level service, particularly in the children's area, should be maintained as often as possible. Chekon and Miles describe the reference desk at the Sacramento Public Library: "The desk is low, only 29 inches high, making it extremely accessible to children, while still comfortable for the reference staff. It is large enough for two librarians and two terminals, with extra desk space for storytime sign-ups, etc." (1993, 23).

Keep in mind that desks can create a barrier to service and establish a negative power balance between staff and children or teens. Any desk configuration needs to remove this type of "feeling" or ambiance and promote an openness and willingness to engage. In the teen area, a simple kiosk may be preferred to a more formal desk configuration.

The service desk should be located close to the entrance to provide good supervision of the entire area. If the room is large, the desk may be closer to the center of the room. It needs sections for public assistance, including answering reference questions, with workstations for each scheduled staff member that include a telephone and computer with easy access to a printer. A large display calendar may list children's or teen events for the month, and a conveniently placed file of fliers and program materials may be adjacent. Several book carts probably need to be located near the desk, with shelves behind for reserves. Underneath the desk, all sections should be on mobile carts independent of the desk structure so they can be reconfigured easily. A copier in or very near the area is a must. If the desk doubles as a circulation desk, it needs the proper counter height for checkout activities and space for sorting and repair of recently returned materials. It is imperative that the staff inform the architect or design professional thoroughly about all of the functions that take place at the desk as well as those functions managed in other areas of the library. Each function/activity needs to be accounted for.

Questions to Ask about Public Service Areas

What functions will take place at the children's services desk? Circulation? Reference? Program registration? Weeding or reviewing of materials? How many service desks will be in the children's room?

Should kiosks be considered in lieu of desks? These can be located centrally or throughout the room.

How many staff members need to be accommodated at each desk? Will the staff sit or stand? How many computers will be at the desks?

How will staff print? Do you need a printing station? Fax machine? Copier?

Do you need ready reference shelves or files at the desk? Storage units? Room for book carts?

Office Workspace and Storage

In addition to public service desks or kiosks, there may be other workspace needs for youth services staff, including professional office space or a workroom for processing materials. Each office desk needs a computer with access to the Internet and a printer, a phone, and file space. Windows provide natural lighting and support a good work environment. If the office is adjacent to the public floor, any window that faces the floor area must have curtains or blinds for privacy when needed. Cork bulletin boards or tackable surfaces are popular, and coat racks and lockers are essential for personal possessions. If space is available, a meeting table with chairs can help promote good staff communication and teamwork and also be used for larger projects. Many staff members request a sink and counter for craft preparation.

Regarding the location of staff work areas, Nolan Lushington states:

It is essential that all staff members have a dedicated space where they can work. The staff work area is often located close to the service desk to allow observation of active areas, especially in small libraries where staff have to perform a variety of functions. In small libraries the work area will include partitioned space for the children's librarian. In larger libraries, the staff work area may be located away from the service desk in order to monitor another part of the children's area. Larger libraries may also have a separate office for the children's librarian. (2008, 104)

Storage is important to youth services librarians. Posters, prints, mobiles, flannel boards, puppets and puppet stages, arts and crafts materials, audiovisual equipment, and storytime books require a lot of space and special shelving and containers. At the James V. Brown Public Library in Williamsport, Pa., many factors influenced the building plans for the children's wing expansion. In addition to providing sufficient space for preschoolers, parents, and school-age children (families from the entire region often visit and participate in programs), the library has extensive outreach services that require the housing of collections for regional circulation. Storage space was needed for program supplies, teacher and caregiver resources, audiovisual equipment, outreach materials, and regional collections/materials. Though some of these materials could be stored in the new basement, a certain percentage had to be stored upstairs with staff workspace or on open shelves in the teacher collection area. Worktables or areas for processing and packaging of resource materials had to be considered and placed as close as possible to the storage areas.

At the Middle Country Public Library, the office space for full-time staff is on the second floor, away from the public areas. This provides "off desk" space for those staff who need to supervise, plan programs, write grants, prepare schedules, and so forth. In addition to office space for full-time staff, the library provides a small office area as part of each public service space where part-time staff house their work, make telephone calls, keep their personal belongings, and store their work on special projects.

Questions to Ask about Office Workspace

Will the children's staff office area be adjacent to the children's room or integrated within a larger professional office area? How many workstations are needed?

Where will employees lock up their belongings and hang up their coats? Where is the nearest staff restroom? Staff lounge?

What are the special storage requirements? Is storage needed for large pieces of paper and other programming supplies? For theme boxes? What size are the theme boxes? How many boxes will require storage? Is storage needed for puppets, dolls, toys, puzzles, or games? How many items?

How is audiovisual equipment to be stored? Vertical storage for large props? Costumes? Portable puppet stage?

Is a program preparation area needed? What type of furnishings? Cabinets and shelves? Counters? Computers and other equipment?

PROCUREMENT

There are many sources of furniture appropriate for children's and teen spaces in libraries, including traditional library furniture companies as well as established commercial furniture companies in the United States, Canada, and Europe. For large projects, additional sources to consider may be industrial design companies in both the United States and abroad. The library may be limited to domestic sources, depending on its location and the sources of funding (local/state/federal) and associated requirements. It is important to research the options for procurement and understand the restrictions before selecting furniture or shelving.

Many design professionals who are unaccustomed to working in the public sector may propose and attempt to procure furniture that presents legal obstacles and complications for the library. It is preferable to work with an architect or interior designer familiar with the requirements of public sector work. A design professional unfamiliar with these requirements must research the appropriate methods of procurement in a particular location, minding state and local statutes as well as federal law. It is advisable to consult either the governing agency purchasing agent or the library attorney before the furniture design phase in order to have an accurate interpretation of the local governance regarding procurement policies.

In many states an option for procurement may be the state contract system or the U.S. Communities Program (www.gogreencommunities.org). In some cases the only option may be to bid the furniture. Sometimes a foundation or other private entity may be able to procure the furniture with fewer restrictions than the public entity.

CONCLUSION

Space planning is a practical tool for helping the administration, staff, and architect become energized and engaged in the building project. The style and amount of shelving, seating, and tables; the amount of workspace and storage; and rooms designated for special purposes or audiences are determined during the space study process.

The space study often sheds light on the importance of youth services from the perspective of management and results in a common agreement about how youth will be served during the next several decades. "The programming effort is the cornerstone of the design process. The importance of this first step in the evolution of any design cannot be emphasized too strongly. . . . The next part of the process is the design, which can be organized into conceptual, schematic, and design development" (James Keller, in Ramos 2001, 10). After the space study and the Program of Requirements are completed, the design meetings move from "wish list" to realities of budget.

Chapter 4 | Relationships and Adjacencies

The allocation of space for each area of service, program, or collection is an essential part of the planning process. It seems rational that, in a public environment designed and intended for use by children and teens such as the library, a design philosophy be invoked that promotes service to youth and families. The role of design in creating youth environments in libraries extends to identifying and defining the importance of children and teens in the greater context of the services. Through this "defining" process, the project team gets a clearer picture about the size of and where to place the children's room, whether teen resources will get their own space, and how the spaces will be situated in the library.

The first and most critical step in this part of the process is developing the concept for the space organization. The second step is to develop a conceptual diagram of the adjacencies and relationships—often referred to as the "bubble" diagram or blocking phase of the design. During this phase, it is important that ideas about space relationships be organized conceptually, including placement and size of space, the adjacencies, entry to the space, exiting the space, noise and activity areas, quiet study areas, collections, program rooms, deliveries, returns, security, views, solar considerations, and site restrictions and opportunities.

Many questions arise regarding the size, organization, and zoning of space when the actual blocking (creating blocks of space to illustrate the basic building plan organization) or space planning begins. The blocking, or bubble, plan provides a global view to the project team about where the youth areas will be placed and their relative size in proportion to the whole library (figure 4.1). Each bubble represents an area that reflects the information gathered through the space study and recorded in the Program of Requirements. Bubbles can also reflect specialized segments of each area, such as the program room, early childhood and school-age areas, collections, media area, teen areas, or study rooms.

Graeme Murphy describes the positive aspects of creating a bubble plan:

> Developing bubble diagrams with staff provides an opportunity for them to review how functions interrelate in terms of people movement, line of site, trolley movement and their marketing. . . . Bubble diagrams and paste-ups are very engaging and fun for staff to develop. They also tap what is often not included in space planning—the emotional. Tapping this dimension gives the designer insight into how staff and customers relate to different collection formats and types, and the designer is given a better chance to get the look and feel of the collection in terms of how it is to the customer. They also enable staff to visualize and take control over how services are managed by experimentation and trying things out. (2002, 5)

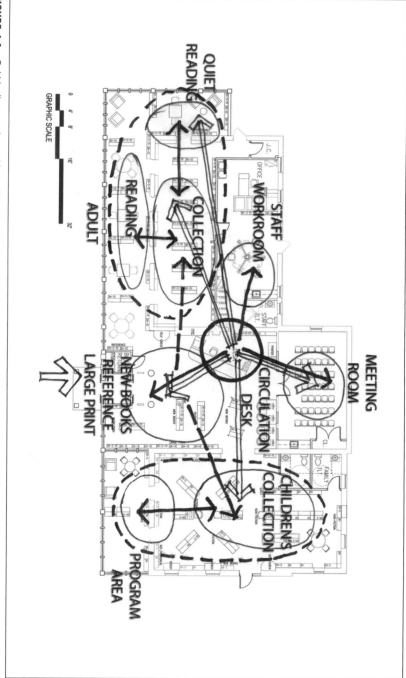

FIGURE 4.1   Bubble diagram, Lower Merion Township Library System, Penn Wynne Library, Wynnwood, Pa. Architect, VITETTA. Used by permission of the architect.

Image credit: VITETTA

PERCENTAGE OF SPACE

Decisions about the placement and percentage of space allocated for the children's and teen areas are critical to the external message to the community and to the programmatic success of youth services. Emphasis on the size of the children's and teen areas in proportion to the entire facility is a significant indication of the importance a library and community place on service to youth. During the past two decades, new libraries have had the foresight to increase their visibility in the community by dedicating larger and more dramatic spaces to youth services. And not only new buildings; many libraries and branch systems are redesigning existing facilities and reapportioning space for children and teens.

Beginning in the early 1980s, public libraries across the United States saw a growing emphasis on children's services, particularly in services for very young children. This movement gave way to the development of early childhood spaces (expansions, renovations, decorations, activity stations, toys) that were specially designed to appeal to toddlers and their parents. The popularity of the services influenced libraries to design and build for this audience. Rather than diminish space for school-age children, it was an opportunity to enlarge the children's room by expanding a building or reapportioning space originally designed for other purposes. The Denver Public Library, Sacramento Public Library, Schaumburg Township District Library, and Middle Country Public Library, four libraries mentioned throughout this book, were

> During the planning process (of the Kids' Place at the Sacramento Public Library), the location of the children's area moved several times in an effort to provide the square footage and separate identity it required. The original site shared the main floor with the business collection, but two less compatible spaces are hard to imagine. The next plan showed the children's area on the second floor, with more natural neighbors: adult fiction and nonprint. . . . However, both staff and architects felt that the second floor location was not easily accessible to children as they entered the building. So, in the next plan it returned to the first floor, sharing space with the popular library. While this combination was more workable than the earlier one, neither space was large enough to carry out the goals of the building program. . . . The architects came up with the new idea of expanding the lower level and creating a children's area on two levels. We explained that the children's area be located on the lower level only, with half of the room open to the first floor. This plan allowed the children's area to be integrated with the main floor and provided for natural light from street-level windows on the north and west walls. The change resulted in a 5600 sq. ft. space, 433 sq. ft. more than the building program proposed.
>
> —Terry Chekon and Margaret Miles (1993, 21–22)

committed to the vision of expanding their scope and range of ages served to include infants, toddlers, and parents. Michael Esmay, AIA, noted in an article on construction: "In my experience, the children's room is the largest specific area used in a public library, aside from the stacks" (2006, 122).

Designing space for teens also began to rise during the mid to late '90s. Although special collections for young adults—especially in large urban libraries—have existed for years, the notion of featuring and focusing on teen space is quite new. Among the pioneers in this area is the Enoch Pratt Free Library in Baltimore, which designated a mezzanine in the main library as "off limits" to all but teenagers and the staff assigned to manage the area. This area was created in 1996—very early in the movement to create special spaces for teens—and provides an interesting example because of the "off limits" rule for adults. The Phoenix Public Library was one of the first libraries to create an entirely separate room designed with and exclusively for teenagers.

Some libraries lack the wherewithal to build a new facility, expand an existing one, or develop separate rooms but have found ways to zone special collections, seating, computers, and design features to define a distinct area for young children or teenagers (see plate 16). This is particularly the case in small libraries or branches that cannot afford the luxury of square footage totally designated to specific age groups but need to be more flexible throughout the day or evening. Other branch systems that have no capacity to expand have determined that the children's and teen services will be given more space and that adults will get less.

Regarding the "carving out" of teen spaces in small places, Kim Bolan Taney comments: "The foremost thing to remember when discussing layout is that it's not the amount of floor space a library has, it's what you do with the space that matters. The smallest of library spaces can be the most creative, well-designed places for teens as long as they are arranged with careful consideration to its users and functions" (2003, 11).

That youth are one of the public library's single largest user groups is a strong argument for ensuring them a prominent location and sufficient amount of space. In the years following the completion of the thirty-three branch renovations of the Free Library of Philadelphia, the statistics indicated a jump of approximately 35 percent in use by children and teens. After the Teen Resource Center was completed at the Middle Country Public Library in 2003, teen program attendance along with the variety of programs (drop-in café, Battle of the Band, Anime Club, Science and Technology Club) increased noticeably, including the development of a very active teen advisory committee. When the Lexington Public Library's new Northside branch opened in 2008 with designated space for children and teens, the circulation more than doubled.

PLACEMENT AND ADJACENCIES

During the planning process, general layout issues are often discussed. Carol Brown elaborates:

> Because libraries are service organizations, the successful design of a library of any type is based on careful consideration of several factors that enhance the use of the library by its clientele and support the work of the staff. Two of the most important factors are those of relationships, or adjacencies, and the movement of the people and materials through the library. "Relationships" or "adjacencies" refer to the space-planning process in interior design, are determined by studying the library's philosophy of service, its use of materials and services, and its policies and procedures, and involve deciding what spaces and functions will be adjacent to other spaces and functions. (2002, 2)

The foremost matter is where to place the youth areas within the larger context of the building. For some libraries, the children's and teen rooms are of prime importance, and the administration and board make it clear that services for youth are number one. For others, the library clearly sees itself as an adult-oriented institution and wants to address the needs of youth only nominally. To determine the overall prominence, the project team needs to consider the library's mission and goals and not rely on anyone's personal viewpoint. It is important to keep in mind that the determination of placement and adjacencies properly reflects the results of the space study and input from the staff and community.

Physical and Visual Accessibility

Families, children, and teens bring energy and vitality to the library environment. Noise, security, visual control, and access are all essential factors in locating youth spaces. It is important that the children's area be easy to access from the building entrance and that every opportunity to showcase the children's area be maximized. This does not mean that the children's area must be immediately at the front door but rather that it be visually accessible—if not also physically accessible—in a direct line from the entrance. In all but the largest libraries, it is preferable that children be able to see their area when they walk into the building. The location of their space needs to be made obvious through a welcoming entrance, colorful signage, or the overall design of the entire facility.

Entry-level placement of the children's area provides the most accessible and safest location in terms of movement for young children. Eliminating the need for children (especially young children) and parents to use stairs, escalators, or elevators to reach the children's area is a positive aspect of entry-level placement. This placement also serves to add color and life to the library. Lesley Boon emphasizes that "students may

---

A new subset of library users is tweens. They are not young children, but not adult readers either. Some libraries are finding that this group benefits from an area set aside specifically for them, either within the children's room or in a room of their own.

Teen readers are another growing population of library users who are obviously different from adult readers. Including a young adult room is becoming more common in library expansions. I have seen many young adult rooms that are barely used or that are used by older patrons. A fishbowl atmosphere and a sterile environment seem to be the cause.

Successful young adult rooms I have visited have included comfortable seating, computer stations, and teen-related books and periodicals in a welcoming environment. [When I addressed teens regarding their space] their articulated needs called for a fairly large space, to be located within the library in a way that addresses noise and security issues.

—Michael Esmay (2006, 122–23)

FIGURE 4.2   Before renovation (left) and after (right), children's area, Free Library of Philadelphia, Charles Durham Branch, Philadelphia, Pa. Architect, VITETTA. Used by permission of the architect.

be reluctant to use places that are in the back corner or are accessed by many stairs. Spaces need to be user-friendly and have visual supervision. Spaces need to accommodate strollers and wheelchairs" (2003, 156).

For many of the branch renovations of the Free Library of Philadelphia, Hedra Packman explained, "we had to have a preschool center that had some kind of mural or some kind of artwork that defined the area, whether it be the rug and something else that people could see when they walked in—not just a carpet area, but something that would be visible so you would know where the preschoolers were located." Figure 4.2 shows some of the results.

In cases where it is architecturally infeasible (as in some renovations) to locate the children's area on the entry level and where it is determined that for security reasons the children's area needs to be placed differently, it is imperative that some visual connection or cue be given regarding its location. To create a vibrant children's area and tuck it away in a basement or third floor without clear visual identification is counter to the goal of creating dynamic, child-friendly spaces.

Although it is a level below the street entrance in a "garden level," the children's area in the Richland County (S.C.) Public Library is immediately visible from both the street and the entrance. Upon entering the building and before ever going to the children's room, visitors are greeted at an information desk. This is a thoughtful solution for placing the children's area in a focal place yet giving over the prime real estate to the popular adult collections at street level. It also provides an extra measure of security for children in this downtown location. Director David Warren told us of the importance of the children's room placement:

First of all, it had to be a major focal point of the building. While we didn't want it right inside the front door—we knew that wasn't going to be appropriate with all the other things we were designing—we didn't want it to be a hidden space. While the children's area is on the lower level, the garden level, it is immediately visible to all who enter. It has a huge opening of glass doors that can be closed, but I don't think we have ever had them closed but once, and that was on the night we had the grand opening for our benefactors' black-tie dinner.

In the Northside branch of the Lexington Public Library, the children's area is located at the right back portion of the open plan library, with the children's program room visually accessible at the back corner (see figure 4.3). This configuration places the children's area in the most focal location when entering the building; research indicates that most people who enter a building look or move to the right. Adult patrons, who have no need to access the children's space, turn a sharp right and enter the general collections, periodicals, and café. The teen/young adult area is to the left of

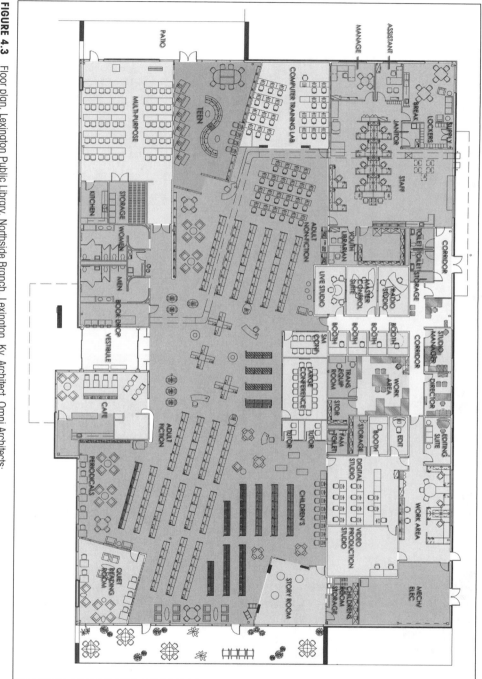

FIGURE 4.3   Floor plan, Lexington Public Library, Northside Branch, Lexington, Ky. Architect, Omni Architects; consultant, VITETTA. Used by permission of VITETTA.

Image credit: VITETTA

the entry—the opposite direction from the young children's collection and an intuitive redirection for teens and young adults.

Daria Pizzetta, interior architect for the expansion of the Middle Country Public Library, described some of the basic concerns about the placement of teen services:

We were concerned with where to place the [young] teens and let them feel like they had their own place without feeling like they walked into where the babies are. Although they are still a part of the juvenile department, they don't want to be with their five-year-old brothers and sisters. They want their separate space. We also had conversations about how to draw teens and young adults into the different sides [children's and adult] and how to delineate what is what. It is very visual when you walk into this library. It is very easy to see and read what is going on in each side of the building: split down the middle into two major components of the library [with teen areas in both sections].

Safety and Security

Safety and security issues come to light when designing public spaces for children and have particular significance for libraries that serve all ages but may not have the staff or resources to monitor all areas. A basic consideration is the distance from the entrance and circulation areas. Although it is important for children to see their room (or experience visual cues to the room) upon entering the building, it should be zoned far enough away from the entrance to provide a safe environment for rambunctious (and often running) toddlers. Nolan Lushington explains:

Child safety is a major concern in our security-conscious society. Children need to be closely monitored by staff for safety and security reasons. Staff as well as parents and caregivers need to know where children are at all times. Therefore, security and safety concerns often dictate design.

Keeping children in their own part of the library where caregivers and staff can see them is a major design objective. It is especially important to keep children from running out of the first floor of a building and into automobile traffic or from escaping down a staircase or elevator. (2008, 60)

The converse of the concern for security of children posed by "running away" or by predatory behavior by non-caregiver adults is that of egress. It is beneficial for the architect to meet with the local code officials and fire marshal early in the planning process—preferably during concept design. These officials are tireless advocates for the health and safety of the public. They are allies when included in the solution and may have an adverse reaction when a plan is inappropriate or unsafe.

Safely moving large groups of children *out* of a building in the case of fire or other emergency is of utmost concern. It is important to contemplate how the "lost child" or large groups of children will move out of the building and to identify the location outside for safety and recovery by caregivers if separated. Many library professionals overlook this important consideration in deciding where to locate the children's area. The ground level is obviously the safest place for the children's area in regard to means of egress, but it is important to balance the varying and often competing safety concerns to find the best solution.

If the new building site or existing building constraints do not allow for placement of the children's area on the main entrance level of the building, then it is critical to consider the traffic flow into and out of the children's space as it relates to the building entrance, public access stairways, and emergency exits. For visual security it may be a worthwhile investment to construct glass-enclosed elevators in multistory buildings, especially where the elevator opens directly into the children's space. Glass doors or a glass cab and enclosure permit staff, parents, and others to see if a child moves into the elevator without a caregiver.

The additional cost of a custom elevator cab or glass doors varies with the details of the elevator, but they cost significantly more than a standard elevator. Therefore it is important to include an accurate amount in the budget for special elevators where they will augment the safety and security of children using the space. This will be money well spent if the building configuration requires it, but if avoidable the money could likely be used elsewhere in the library.

Transparent railings on balconies and stairways may also be preferable to opaque railings. Balcony rails in children's spaces should be seriously considered for height requirements regarding safety. Any railings that are higher than the height of children must be closely monitored for safety reasons. Changes in the level of the floor create negative situations for children who are frequently corrected by parents, caregivers and librarians" (Brown 2002, 110). Two other basic safety concerns are furniture and bathrooms; no furniture should have sharp corners, and bathrooms should be close to staff areas for observation.

Once inside the space, it is preferable to design the area with a flat floor. "Any construction in a children's area that encourages climbing, jumping, and running is important to include an accurate amount in the budget for special elevators where and cannot be mounted or climbed on are preferable to low rails, which are obvious hazards. Vertical glass (or other) enclosures provide an even more secure solution and can be designed as attractive features in the space.

Another safety factor within the children's room involves accommodations for adult caregivers. According to Kathleen Imhoff, executive director of the Lexington Public Library, "The fourth 'A' of excellent building design is Accommodation. The building is designed to be a safe and secure place for children, teens, adults and seniors. It is a place for coming together for all of the people in the . . . community; a place for enjoyment and celebration" (2005).

Providing chairs for adults to sit close by or adjacent to the young children's area is a must if the library does not want parents or caregivers leaving the area. At the Middle Country Library, there are only a few signs, but one states that children are not to be left unattended. The entire children's space invites parents and caregivers with collections, computers, and a place for them to sit. They can interact with other parents. It is a natural setting, like sitting in a park, and it is rare that they leave their children alone.

In new buildings, optimal space planning eliminates visual barriers that would present management and security concerns in the public areas. In renovations, optimal space planning eliminates most of the visual barriers. Many libraries have been designed with shelving 90 degrees from windows but obstructing the sight lines. Shelving organizations that are 90 degrees from the windows and provide clear sight lines are ideal, but many architects prefer a gridlike floor plan that obstructs most or all sight lines, providing only the day lighting benefit. This preference must be subverted to the more important concern for visual management and security in public library spaces—especially for children and teens.

In some instances, safety and security measures are not obvious until the building or renovation is complete and staff begins to work in the space. In the Selden branch of Middle Country Public Library, the children's department experienced two problems. The Family Place area was separate from the elementary-age children's space (through a vestibule and around a corner), and there was no way for one person to monitor both areas. Eventually a security camera was added to the Family Place with a CCTV on the librarian's desk. In this same building, the children's section was located on the mezzanine floor with a steep staircase to the lower-level adult services floor. These stairs were readily accessible to the Family Place area. The library staff, working with the architects, came up with the idea of a latched gate at the stairway entrance, one that could not be opened by toddlers or preschoolers.

CCTV and mirrors are generally mandated because of poor space organization and planning. If the architect or design professional presents a plan that obstructs sight lines, it is the obligation of the library to direct replanning to alleviate this problem before preparing construction documents, bidding, and construction. If the library is contemplating CCTV or other video monitoring, it should consult the local government for protocol and liabilities. It may be advisable to consult legal counsel as well, for installation of such monitoring devices implies responsibilities that must be understood and carefully maintained.

Traffic Flow

How families with young children enter the library and move to the children's space is a consideration not only for the families themselves but for other users of the library. Babies and toddlers are generally ensconced with strollers, and parents often have their hands full with diaper bags, return materials, toys, and food. Barrier-free travel patterns help transition families into and out of the space. Parking areas for strollers are advisable. In her article on early learning and libraries, Barbara Huntington discusses various issues related to the location of the children's area:

Once in the building, the location of the family area can make the visit easy or challenging. The distance it takes to walk or carry a toddler to the appropriate area as well as the route that must be taken to get there can either encourage or discourage repeat visits. Routes that require stairs or walking through adult or quiet areas to get to an elevator or their final destination can be physically and emotionally challenging for those accompanying young children. Adults who encounter angry stares and concerned looks as they escort an exuberant toddler to the appropriate space or try to calm a fussy baby as they make their way to the exit will sense they are not welcome and perhaps the library really isn't a place for babies and toddlers after all. Reconfiguring space and traffic patterns to eliminate or minimize such experiences creates a more welcoming and accepting environment increasing the likelihood of return visits. (2005, 51)

How children and teens "travel" to their respective spaces is a key ingredient in placement and design of the youth areas. "Young children should not have to walk through adult spaces to enter the children's area, to walk to the circulation desk, or to use a rest room. . . . Within a children's space, school-age young people and teens should not have to walk through the preschool area to get to their own materials and services" (Brown 2002, 3).

Another issue concerns meeting rooms. If a separate programming room is not available for the children, it is best to place the library's main community room adjacent to the children's room, since the children's department will need ongoing access. This may necessitate two entrances—one from the adult area and another from the children's room. For traffic flow and safety, adults should never need to walk through the children's area to access the meeting room—or any other space, for that matter.

Separation of Ages

A major decision concerns the various age levels of the youth to be served and the need for the separation of ages. Will there be one children's room that accommodates children, birth through twelve or eighteen years, or two distinct areas (children and teens), or even four distinct areas (early childhood, school age, young teen, and young adult) such as at the Children's Public Library in Muscat, Oman (see figure 4.4, plate 20)? If there is one area, how will the needs of each of the various age groups be addressed? One solution is to provide a space-defining element such as a fish tank or low shelving as a natural boundary between the early childhood area and collections for school-age children. Deciding how the various ages will enter and travel through their respective space needs to be considered thoroughly during the planning stages.

Lushington points out that moving through space is relative to the various age groupings:

> The children's room will have several distinct areas arranged to invite children and their caregivers to move through the space and the service it supports in accordance with the child's conceptual development. Because of the wide range of ages and things done here, there will be a noticeably different ambience from those areas within the larger areas. Transitional areas between each of these spaces will house services used commonly by both age groups such as the computer area between pre-school and middle school. (2002, 133)

Another consideration regarding the separation of ages is the "spillover" of teens from the teen space. Teens take up a lot of room and, when things get too tight, like to sprawl throughout the space and beyond. Placing the teen area adjacent to a computer area, a meeting room, or an adult nonquiet area is preferred to an "invasion" of the younger children's area.

Creating space for children and teens with which adults do not become annoyed must also be considered during the space allocation and design stages. Avoid placing it near an adult area where many patrons want to read and have a little quiet. Having a children's area where adults can see it, or interactive where grandparents can take their grandkids, is good. But most adult users do not want to hear a toddler crying or parents and children engaging in conversation. They also do not necessarily want to listen to teens conversing and horsing around. Adults want their space too.

Staffing and Management

The importance and logistics of providing services to families, children, and teens must be considered not only when determining the location and size of the youth spaces but also in assessing the internal organization and management of youth services. A prominent functional role demands a prominent location within a building as well as adequate workspace and staff to support the role. This means that the location of staff desks, sight lines into and through the space and collections, and placement of learning activity areas are all important (see figure 4.5).

Jeffrey Scherer mentioned that desk location differs with purpose: "How the librarian's desk is positioned is different in the children's area perhaps than it is in the teen area. The teen area is more as a friend and roamer, and the children's area is more of a helper and a proactive relationship." In the Middle Country Library, the librarians are situated so that they can see the entire room— a 360-degree view of what is happening around them. The

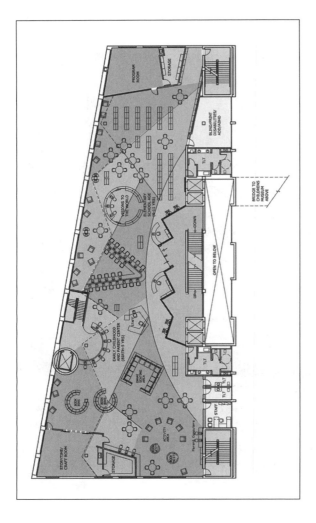

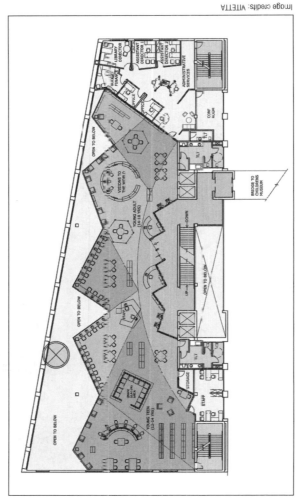

Image credits: VITETTA

FIGURE 4.4 Second-level floor plan, early childhood and elementary spaces (top), and third-level floor plan, young teen and young adult spaces (bottom), Children's Public Library, Muscat, Oman. Architect, COWI/VITETTA. Used by permission of VITETTA.

17,000-square-foot room builds up with the low stacks, beginning with picture books on one side, leading to the early childhood area and reference shelving on the other side, which leads to the collections and spaces for older children and young teens. There are two desks in the front center of the room where children and young teens can see that there is a person to help when they first walk in.

Improving sight lines reduces operational costs by both reducing needed staff numbers and augmenting staff visual management capabilities. The 25,000-square-foot Horsham Township (Pa.) Library was fully operational at times with only two staff members in its first year of operation. This was made possible by excellent sight lines throughout the building, shown in figure 4.6.

Libraries that elect to create special space for teenagers are often constrained by existing space and furniture. Many, if not most, new library building programs, however, do include special space for teenagers. In medium-size and small libraries these areas present management challenges. It is preferable that the young adult space be located where staff can visually manage it without being intrusive. Visual management is critical for the safety and security of the space, yet a feeling of seclusion, separation, or at least special identity is critical to its success. In a community library such as the Horsham Township Library it was acceptable to set the young adult space out of the way while still in view of the reference librarian (see figure 4.6). This is not a solution that works everywhere, but if it is planned for the staff assignments and job descriptions can be handled accordingly.

A key decision that the library must make in locating the teen space is how to separate the area from children's services yet manage and staff the space. As the popularity of focusing on teen and young adult audiences grows, even small libraries are designating staff resources to their space to maintain the desired separation yet provide the necessary support and oversight. Teens need to distinguish themselves from younger children and no longer want to be identified as children themselves. A decision to colocate the teen area—particularly the young adult area—within a children's department negates much of the desired effect. It is recommended that the method of staffing this area be resolved before the space is designed or created.

INTERACTIVE SPACES

Activity stations are among the most important considerations in the children's space. "The first impression one gets upon entering a new environment is influenced by the look and feel of the physical space. Size, location, design and content communicate messages for and about the target audience, as well as the purpose and type of behavior to expect within the space" (Feinberg et al. 2007, 97). Lushington summarizes the general goal of interactivity:

The overall result of the children's area design should be an intriguing combination of creativity, function, and flexibility. Children should be engaged by areas that stim-

FIGURE 4.5 Sight lines from staff point through collections to teen and computer areas. Lexington Public Library, Northside Branch, Lexington, Ky. Architect, Omni Architects; consultant, VITETTA. Used by permission of the photographer.

Photo credit: Frank Döring

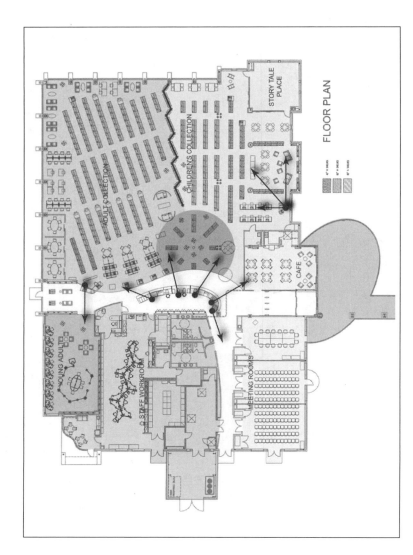

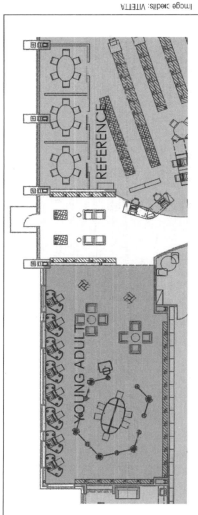

ulate their imagination while suggesting a variety of behaviors. Alternating busy and quiet environments should offer children a choice. The area should be easy to change both for short-term display and long-term changes in function as children change. Parents and other caregivers should have an opportunity to sit with children to read to them and enjoy their reading skills. There should be an opportunity for individual consultation with children for teaching and discussion. (2002, 137)

Activity areas can range from play tables and other cognitive activities for children from birth to five years to social activity areas for young adults such as tables for game boards and lounge seating for peer-to-peer interaction. The design of these areas starts with the development of the Program of Requirements, for it is at this stage that the conceptual thinking should begin.

FIGURE 4.6 Floor plan illustrating sight lines from staff points (top), and young adult and reference and study areas (bottom), Horsham Township Library, Horsham, Pa. Architect, VITETTA. Used by permission of the architect.

The location, security, and accommodation of space for activity areas vary with the activity. The designers may not be familiar with the learning skills of the various age groups or may have preconceived notions about what is appropriate, so library staff may need to mentor them regarding special needs and expectations for these activity areas. This is when the design team must pay close attention to the staff. When inappropriate or uninspired ideas or solutions are presented, they should be rejected.

Play and Social Interaction

Well-designed environments encourage verbal interaction between parent and child and lend themselves to casual interaction among children and other adults. Space in the children's room and in library programs needs to support early literacy, play, and social interaction. Keep in mind that the younger the child, the more interactive the program and space. Pam Sandlian provides a vivid description of an interactive children's room:

The [Denver Public Library] was designed to take advantage of the exploratory nature of children. Instead of a quiet, stern research center, the library became an information adventure. Every nook and cranny was filled with appropriate books, images, computers, interactive software, videos, stuffed animals, pillows, pop-ups, scissors, glue-sticks, copiers and printers. This cornucopia of materials organized by interest and age levels provided an atmosphere of discovery, invention and self-actualization. (1999, 7)

The library's environment models for parents and caregivers how to organize space for children and what to expect of children within that space. Integrating books with play and activity stations tells parents that play and social interaction are essential to emergent literacy.

Traditional library settings, with their rows of book stacks, banks of computers, tables, chairs and reference desks, communicate a message that libraries are quiet orderly places for reading and study. The family centered library is a purposefully designed public space that welcomes very young children and families, is filled with developmentally appropriate activities and materials, and encourages play, interactive learning and socialization. (Feinberg et al. 2007, 97)

Although these spaces are socially engaging areas and, in most cases, are very comfortable for toddlers and preschoolers, there are also children who seek shelter from the noise and interaction. A "cubby" or protective area with picture book shelves or a fish tank can often calm the overly anxious child or soothe the rambunctious toddler. These spaces can also provide a quiet area for infants or a nursing mother.

Noise is a factor in any interactive space and particularly affects where the children's and teen areas need to be placed within the library. "Children and adolescents

One of the fundamental misconceptions about designing libraries, especially space for children, that I have learned is that I think too often the children's area is thought of as equal to, and coexistent with, other departments. But, in fact, because the developmental abilities of children and their age differences are so wide ranging, it really puts a different kind of pressure on the youth services department in terms of accommodating all the variety of ages and differences. What is really interesting about children's areas is that you cannot define the task in advance like you can in all the other departments. The most successful children's areas are those that understand the structure of how children learn, don't try to box them in, and allow for space to evolve and change fairly rapidly over time. The space needs to be flexible.

—Jeffrey Scherer (interview, June 2005)

need to make noise and discuss things with each other and their parents/caregivers. They learn through social and educational conversations" (Boon 2003, 156). Adults often like to see young people, but they may not always want to hear them or be with them. "Many adult users prefer children's spaces that are separated from the rest of the library by glass walls or by the shape of the building" (Brown 2002, 109).

From the Schaumburg Township District Library's perspective, noise was a big issue. Director Mike Madden explained that the administration wanted to put the services that were functionally noisier—such as circulation activities, audiovisual and browsing collections, and the children's area—on the first floor:

We didn't want the children traveling through the quieter areas. That was one of the biggest complaints that we had from the public in our old building—the building was too noisy. We knew that we couldn't make the whole library real quiet, but we tried to make as much of it as [quiet] as we could. It was decided to place the children's room on the lower level with media and new books, near the circulation desk. Reference and other quieter services were located on the second floor.

Boundaries

Within the children's area, the arrangement of the collections, displays, and seating can help create zones. A skillful space planner, architect, or interior designer can create environments within the space without using walls. The collections can be attractive room elements that either divide or bring the space together. Seating may be in clusters or groups to create intimate settings that are comfortable for children and caregivers. A mix of lounge seating for parents to read to small children, lounge seats for children of different ages, and groupings of tables and chairs at appropriate heights (both tables and companion seating heights) helps to create a welcoming environment. Ceiling heights, colors, lighting, carpeting, and graphics can also be used to help create zones. Figure 4.7 shows one example.

Young children need unobstructed spaces that they can explore safely. Nooks, crannies, and partial enclosures provide safe boundaries for language enhancement, imagination, and play. Children appreciate small intimate spaces and, if designed properly, the layout and structure of the space help children define what behaviors are appropriate in the library setting. Creating areas in which adults and children can be together also helps libraries avoid the "lost mommy or daddy" syndrome.

A variety of design strategies can be used to create appropriate spaces. Picture book-height shelving can be arranged so that play and learning stations (e.g., block or puzzle table) are incorporated within the alcove. A large dollhouse can be situated to provide a partial barrier for a writing center. A small portable puppet stage and puppets in a crate can be easily moved from section to section. "A children's space should include furnishings and objects that they can use and touch freely without an adult saying 'don't do that.' Spaces should include items that do not have to be protected from use by children" (Brown 2002, 110). Open floor space needs to be integrated as part of a preschool area for toddlers and preschoolers, who often sit on the floor to look at books and play with manipulatives. Round tables, plastic corner protectors for shelving, and plastic inserts for wall plugs are added safety considerations.

In general, age-specific spaces include areas designed to enhance the development or age level of the targeted audience. "Allowing users to have control and ownership of the space, creating a balance between independence and guidance, and isolating the space, while simultaneously providing connection to the rest of the library, are some of the other essential concepts that enhance the area for families" (Demas and Scherer 2002, 68).

Integration of Adult Caregivers

When designing a new room or renovating an existing area, it is critical to provide space for young children in tandem with resources for their parents and caregivers. Parents and caregivers need comfortable seating in the children's area so that they have a positive library experience with their children and want to bring them back. To make space inviting for parents and caregivers, libraries should provide, in addition to comfortable furniture, access to parenting resources. Lounge chairs, benches, a coffee table (which serves as a great puzzle table for toddlers), and displays aimed at parents set a welcoming tone. Having a dedicated computer and collections for parents either in the children's room or adjacent to it creates a sense of place for parents. A quiet, semiprivate area, possibly a special room, is a plus for nursing mothers. Cultural sensitivity should also be accounted for in the planning and provision for nursing mothers.

Teen Zones

Design can reinforce the success of the teen space through the use of elements that create a place where teenagers feel comfortable and special. Working with teens during the 1990s, the Phoenix Public Library created a large space with varied zones includ-

FIGURE 4.7 Children's space with varied activities (top), and colored wall alcoves (bottom). Hjoerring Public Library, Hjoerring, Denmark. Architect, Bosch & Fjord; Interior Design, Lammhults Library Design. Used by permission of the photographer.

Photo credits: Laura Stamer

ing collections, conversation areas and small group meeting spaces, a food and music area, and seating. The style, colors, shelving, seating, lighting, and flexibility presented an overall mood of welcome and engagement for young adults.

In 2006, the design team at the Middle Country Public Library created the Teen Resource Center with several "zones," or activity areas. In the main area, the creation of a performance space was central to the planning process, which included the teens themselves. At one end of the space a performance floor was created with a stage curtain as backdrop and theater lighting and sound baffles above. This space is used for small concerts by the teens, poetry readings, and other special events. At the opposite end of the room, a juice bar features colored lighting controlled by an LED that glows through a resinous material. The juice bar was specially designed to reflect the ideas and notions of "cool objects" presented by the teens. This is a functional furnishing yet funky, fun, and a magnet within the space (see plates 2 and 3).

Among the anticipated uses—music, computer use, socializing, and homework projects—was a desire to have quiet space for study and reading. The result was an anteroom adjacent to the primary teen space where teens could socialize, see films, watch television, or read. It was not envisioned that the quiet space would always be quiet, but that this zoned space could be programmed to be quiet when desired.

In both the conscious direction given by the teen focus group at Middle Country and the practical observations of other teen space designs, there is another side to space usage by teens that is not to be overlooked. Teens frequent the library for a variety of reasons, and the more options provided the better the array of experience. But somewhere in each library a core of students who see the library as a resource for study and quiet learning can probably be observed. In his interview, Jeffrey Scherer reflected:

One of the most interesting phenomena that I have witnessed in the last couple of years is the presumption, especially in kids from pre-teen to teen, that they are really interested only in telephones and computers, which is, in fact, not true. I think a lot of teens that come to libraries are very interested in print as well. And so making sure that you take care of that is an important piece.

The placement of the teen space in proximity to adult collections and study areas enhances the experience and reinforces one of its most fundamental purposes to be an open door to intellectual freedom. The role of the library as this open door is for all ages, but the need is particularly acute for teenagers. Fostering access to information through access to adult collections, the Internet, and well-informed staff is essential in planning the teen space.

Acoustics

The acoustic quality of library space is often overlooked during the design process. It is important to set the criteria for acoustic design, just as it is for the quantity of bookshelves or computer tables. The success of the library will be impeded if the library is too noisy or possibly even too quiet. It is important to distinguish the sound levels desired or acceptable for meeting rooms, quiet spaces, performance spaces, and public areas, including a café, a Friends' bookstore, and children's and teen spaces.

Although it is not always necessary to involve an acoustic consultant in the design of a library, it is advisable in the case of special requirements or construction types. Generally, it is important to balance hard surfaces with soft, sound-absorptive surfaces in order to maintain acoustically comfortable space. This does not mean that carpet must be used on the floor or that all ceilings must be acoustic tile (the ubiquitous white tile originally developed for office buildings).

If hard-surface floors are preferred, for example, it becomes important to factor in the use of sound-attenuating materials on the walls, such as fabric-wrapped tackable panels or wall upholstery. The ceilings can be coated with spray-on sound-absorptive material such as SonaKrete. The ceilings can also be perforated metal or wood lay-in tile with sound-attenuation batting above (a particularly successful solution for meeting rooms). It is also important to take into account the sound-absorptive characteristics of books. Be aware that the weeding or reduction of collections in a renovation may cause the space to become more "live," and it may be necessary to add sound attenuation where it was not needed before the renovation.

It is particularly important that areas near high-conversation points (circulation, librarian's desk, lounge areas, activity stations) have sound-absorptive materials. These areas are often constructed with hard-surface materials, which can amplify the conversation instead of minimizing it.

The time to consider zoning spaces according to acoustic expectations is at this adjacency matrix and bubble diagram stage of the planning. If the library is to be a dynamic, people-friendly place, then it must accommodate the range of normal sounds—from conversation to the jubilant shriek of a small child—without creating chaos.

Materials used on walls, floors, and ceilings, the location of doors and windows, and the acoustic treatment of ductwork all affect sound control in a library. Plumbing fixtures, air dryers in restrooms, and mechanical systems can be causes of and considerations in the acoustic design of the library. Outdoor factors include vehicular and pedestrian traffic, sports fields, airplanes, and trains. The use of airport-style toilet rooms is increasingly popular for libraries, since they improve security and reduce vandalism. It is critical, however, that these "open" restrooms are engineered with negative air flow and appropriate sound attenuation. This means that the air flows from the public spaces into the toilet rooms and out through exhaust air vents/ducts (in the toilet rooms), and that the sound does not transmit into the public areas.

Intrusive noise can be controlled by the grouping of spaces and by the layout of rooms. Architects have traditionally grouped noisy elements of a building together. For example, main HVAC units are usually placed close to a receiving or mechanical area rather than near a quiet, public reading area. An engineering team (mechanical, electrical, plumbing, and structural engineers) with experience in designing libraries is most likely to understand the unseen engineering factors that affect the acoustic quality of the library, such as the depth of the structural roof deck required, sound isolation devices, and placement of ducts and penetrations into and through the building that are critical to sound and vibration control. If the engineering team does not have experience with libraries, it may be necessary for an acoustic consultant to participate. Such an expert provides recommendations not only for the envelope of space in the library but also for the wall construction, partitions, ceilings, and mechanical, structural design as it pertains to acoustic concerns. This includes handling apertures in the interior walls for electrical outlets, switches, and duct penetrations as well as decks and pads for air handling units, chillers, and other motorized devices on the roof—all culprits in contributing unwanted noise in the library.

CONCLUSION

The key to creating successful space for children and teens is prioritizing the relationships and other factors specific to the mission and needs of the community served with a focus on specific audiences and proper functioning of the library. It is important not to start with preconceived solutions but to develop the criteria and priorities in advance of the planning and design process. The space relationships and their correspondent needs and considerations govern the adjacencies of space throughout the library, ranging from specific concerns such as the placement of a space near the entry to general issues such as sound isolation from a nearby roadway. The most important step in determining the relationships and adjacencies is to develop an understanding of the interrelatedness of the design elements, including accessibility, safety and security, traffic flow, the separation of ages, sight lines, interactivity, zoning, and acoustics. Keeping an open mind in exploring options during the blocking phase (as well as subsequent phases of design) is the best strategy for accomplishing a well-thought-out and functional design.

Chapter 5 | Architectural and Environmental Elements

Architecture is created by material, form and void, light and shadow, scale and depth. These are some of the cerebral elements of architecture that are intrinsic to cognition of place. Through consideration of the cerebral, physical, and emotional aspects of design for children and teens, the next generation of space for youth in libraries will be elevated to a higher standard. Ginnie Cooper, executive director of the Washington D.C. Public Library, said that "library buildings are the way we say to the community—this is what you are worth" (2005). Creating great spaces for children and teens tells them that they are worthy of excellent design and architecture.

In a panel presentation on top building trends at the 2008 ALA conference, Joan Frye Williams talked about the importance of creating signature buildings that are unique to a community. No one model prevails; every building "has a 'conversation' with the people who use it, and the conversation should be about users." Inventive use of materials, shapes, and transitions that are the hallmarks of centuries of great architecture are no less effective or important in youth spaces than any other.

BASIC ARCHITECTURAL ELEMENTS

The most effective, dramatic, and timeless design features in a children's or teen space are the basic architectural elements of any great building design. The floor surfaces, the wall textures, the ceiling, the fenestration (windows, doors, skylights, and the like), and the volume of space itself—defined together as the *envelope of space*—are the building blocks for creating great space for young people. The cognitive skill and perception of children are vast, and adults often overlook this and design "down" to them. Children's space should be great space—fantastic space—and underscore *space*.

The space can be imaginative, inviting, and exciting without any props or themes. Framing views, capturing the enchantment of the context such as rural landscape or urban scale through fenestration, is as essential as it is free. It is the architecture that makes the space timeless and inspired. Architecture has the power to enchant, mystify, and inspire people of all ages. There is no magic age or moment at which the transformation to space perception occurs. As library consultant Susan Kent noted, "Libraries must be places of wonder and excitement" (2005). It is critical that the architecture of children's space be considered. Rather than creating a drywall box and inserting decoration into it, start by thinking about the space itself.

The Minneapolis Public Library children's area is a fine example of architectural space and elements. The children's envelope in this library is magical in its architecture (see plate 4). Architect Cesar Pelli and his design team celebrate the architecture of the entire library building through the children's space, with its expanse of windows and views to the streetscape, accessible level changes to create drama, built-in display units that feature book characters and books, and architectural columns that are at once pure to their purpose and evocative of trees or tree canopies. Juvenile themes or contrived elements that become tattered by time are not found in this marvelous and enchanting space.

Architectural volume and color are among the most defining elements of space for children. The use of architectural volume to create interest and define activity is ancient. Although many of the Carnegie-era libraries built in the United States may be flawed in terms of message and service delivery in the present time, these buildings exemplified the use of volume to define space and the activity that was expected within it. There are positive lessons to be learned from these buildings, and the elements they incorporated defined the basic components of the twentieth-century library building.

Architectural interplay of volume, scale, texture, fenestration, structure, and architectural decoration—when creatively and carefully considered—add little, if any, cost to the design of the children's space. These are the components that serve the function for the building's entire existence. These are the elements to celebrate, the creation of a truly timeless space—one that will be great and enduring for children of all ages. ImaginOn, a mixed-use (library and theater) facility in Charlotte, N.C., serves as a prime example of the interplay of volume, scale, proportion, and color (see plate 5).

Scale and Proportion

Children and adolescents perceive scale and proportion from their evolving perspective, and no two children perceive or understand a space in exactly the same way. Designing space for young people demands consideration and accommodation of many factors. It is essential for adults to consider their own childhood experience, not necessarily for application but for awareness.

Think of visiting a place as a child and then returning only years later as an adult. The place seems smaller, different. Buildings that seemed to loom and foreshadow us as children are often either quaint or modest. A theater that seemed to swallow us up in its vast arena is, in fact, humble and small. The school doorway that made us feel that we were entering a giant castle is now just ordinary. Design can forge the union

Architect Julie Eizenberg commented on her work with the Children's Museum of Pittsburgh:

Experiential stuff is missing from most institutional settings. . . . The value of being alive, and of enjoying the activity you're doing, is considered secondary to almost every other thing architects can come up with. I think minimalist architects have awakened to the abstract idea of what experience is, but there's also a social dimension to it. . . . We're doing it the soft way. Soft means easygoing or informal—as opposed to the hard pure forms and big gestures of most contemporary architecture. . . . It values the rambunctious and unexpected. . . . I like buildings that are happy to see you. . . . It doesn't matter if it is kids or adults, you've got to think like a child—you've got to think the world is wonderful.

Jane Warner, director of the museum, added:

We made a decision that we would be progressive, not reflective, and that we should honor the time that we live in as much as honor the time they [the old Pittsburgh barons] lived. Rigorous irreverence is a more appropriate approach to designing for kids than the typical tacked-on color that counts as playfulness. . . . A building for kids doesn't need childlike colors or cutesy animals to provoke joy and curiosity. . . . We don't do cute.

—Julie Eizenberg and Jane Warner in Blum (2005, 84–86)

of programmatic intention and its accommodation through architectural and interior space. Creating environments for young people, especially in the public library, presents wonderful opportunities to connect with the child or teen and to reinforce social and intellectual development.

For generations architects followed time-honored principles in the development of building designs related to scale. From the *Ten Books on Architecture* by Vitruvius to the rigors of the Ecole de Beaux Arts, scale and proportion have had their place in formal thinking about architecture. Only in recent generations has the execution of proportion and scale in design become democratized, eliminating formal expectations or guides as to the aesthetic harmony or discord created by scale. This is not to say that the current generation of architects universally fails at this task, but rather that there is no prescribed notion or method regarding scale. Nevertheless, there is a universal harmony and balance that when achieved contributes to the aesthetic success of a building. Altering the norms of scale is a device that can create interest. Frank Lloyd Wright changed the scale of the entrance to most of his buildings—lowering the entry, dramatizing or simulating grandeur in the succeeding formal spaces.

Scale is vertical, horizontal, and three dimensional. Perhaps no architecture demonstrates this more theatrically than that of architect Frank Gehry's Disney Center in Los Angeles or his Guggenheim Museum in Bilbao, Spain. Much of the perception of architecture comes from its vertical scale, since human beings walk upright. Likewise, much of the perception of scale for children is horizontal, since children crawl or walk on the floor and sit close to it. "Young children like small nooks or portals that are in scale with their own size. The interior design of children's space can include two or three small intimate spaces that children crawl into or through" (Brown 2002, 112). Accordingly, the horizontal scale is a component of the library's design that can make the space inviting to children or confusing. Patterns that define direction and identity of specialized spaces for children reinforce the mission of the library and can add depth and definition to the space (see plate 6).

The purveyors of children's amusements offer some lessons in the use of three-dimensional scale. Amusement rides and theme park venues often play with scale to create fun elements: teacups that you can sit in (rides), fun houses with floors that drop to create extra-tall walls, candy canes and lollypops that are larger than adults. An unusual juxtaposition of architectural elements in the children's area can create fun features that are timeless and enchanting. The three-dimensional elements of design can also be the basic form and shape of the architecture and interior, creating the most magnificent of children's spaces.

Form and Void

The creation of space using form and void is something that almost every small child experiments with through building blocks. Structure, balance, interest, form, and void are components and resultants of this early part of child play and development. What then, could be more appropriate or more intriguing to children than form and void in architectural space? Form and void may be rooms or shapes within a space for special features. These can be manifested in changes of walls, ceilings, or the insertion of a unique form into a space.

FIGURE 5.1   Bowl-shaped story room at children's area, Santiago Public Library, Santiago, Chile. Architect, Cox and Ugarte; Design Consultant, VITETTA; Industrial Designer, NAVE. Used by permission of the library.

Photo credit: Santiago Public Library

Architects Cox and Ugarte used form and void in the Santiago (Chile) Public Library by inserting a bowl-shaped story nook into the two-story children's space (figure 5.1). The element creates a void at the floor level, and the large wooden form dramatically informs children and caregivers that this is a special place to investigate. The necessary insertion into the same space of the child's toilet room creates another form—complete with colored-glass windows into the lavatory portion of the room. Cox and Ugarte also used voids throughout the library to connect people and bring light into this massive and previously dark building—formerly a government warehouse.

The most basic necessities and practical elements can be creatively woven into the space to generate interest and stimulate the imagination. The use of form and void to express the use or special nature of a space can even make it more intuitive. The ceiling may have level changes to accommodate ductwork, lighting fixtures, or the building structure. Simple variations in the ceiling level or voids/openings can also create drama and indicate place.

FIGURE 5.2 Museum Corner, interior view from children's area, Middle Country Public Library, Centereach, N.Y. Architect, Hardy Holzman Pfeiffer Associates. Used by permission of the photographer, courtesy of the architect.

In the expansion of the Middle Country Public Library, architect Robert Almodovar used the pentagon to emphasize the uniqueness and importance of the Museum Corner, in which rotating interactive museum displays encourage learning about a specific area of interest. Prior to the expansion, the Museum Corner had literally been created in a corner of the existing library using bookshelves. With the expansion, the new pentagon-shaped Museum Corner is not only at the outer corner of the children's area but also reads as a form from the interior and exterior of the building. Its distinct red-colored siding, location, and form denote the important function of this space in the library. The pentagon also serves as the backdrop for the entrance to the planned children's Nature Explorium (figure 5.2, plate 7).

Form and void can also be thought of as wall and fenestration. Children's spaces can capture views through geometric shapes in windows—large circles, triangles, parallelograms, trapezoids, and even the standard squares and rectangles. In the creation of space for youth, it is not necessary that all fenestration cleverly distinguish forms, as illustrated by the delightful and inviting children's area of the Indianapolis

Marion County Public Library system's central library, which is lined with continuous glass walls that visually invite visitors. The exterior north facade brings in wonderful reading light, and the south-facing atrium facade allows views into the expansive and dynamic public atrium. As illustrated in figure 5.3, in the Fayetteville (Ark.) Public Library, architects Meyer, Scherer and Rockcastle combined a convex form for the computer terminals, a concave form for the "Read Aloud" nook, and ceiling forms, special lighting, and a pattern of interior fenestration to create a space that both invites children in and provides acoustical separation.

The principles relevant to architectural form and void also apply to furniture and other interior design elements. The form of a chair can be sleek, with clean lines, or organic, with rounded edges and comfy-looking shapes and textures. The form of the furniture conveys the message of invitation or exploration from book bins to the rocking chair.

Rhythm

Although rhythm is most often thought of in music, repetitive patterns or "movements" are applicable to architecture and design as well. Architects throughout the ages have employed the rules of balance, proportion, and rhythm with formulaic methods. Even the masters of the Bauhaus—a style of Modernist design developed in Germany that has influenced many areas of architecture, graphic design, and interior design—used basic concepts of rhythm within their art and architecture. Although, in recent generations the importance of rhythm in library architecture has often been disregarded, the use of rhythm with the architectural elements can create interest, excitement, and even beauty in libraries and spaces for children.

The creation of balance—harmony and rhythm, form and void, structure and space, light and surfaces—is crucial to great design. Working with the architect or design professional, a good management team, including library staff, increases the

FIGURE 5.3   Reading nook and computer area, Fayetteville Public Library, Ark. Architect, Meyer, Scherer and Rockcastle. Used by permission of the architect and photographer.

Photo credit: Assassi Productions

When selecting furnishings, the basic design elements of form, size and scale enter into the decision-making process. "Form" refers to the basic shape of an object (or a space) generated by lines, planes, volumes, and points. Individual furniture items are chosen with appropriate size and scale so that they are correctly proportioned to the overall size of the space and to other objects within it. Scale is an important consideration in regard to who will use the selected furnishings. For example, in order to provide furniture of the appropriate scale for children, the tables and chairs in a youth area are smaller than similar furniture in an adult area.

—Carol Brown (2002, 1)

likelihood of creating a beautiful and well-loved building. The library building should be beautiful. It should be harmonious. It should be loved and visited by the public. That is not to say that any design, regardless of how thoughtful and successful—from the logically planned, handsome, neoclassical Nashville Public Library to the innovative, futuristic Seattle Public Library—will not have critics. Over time, acceptance and appreciation win the day.

It is important that every member of the design team have a sympathetic bent toward creating a building that has rhythm. The rhythm may be classical, baroque, jazz, or rock and roll, but many Western libraries of the latter part of the twentieth century read like a cut-and-paste of unrelated musical scores. These buildings have no continuity or rational expression of logic. Columns are in the wrong places. Windows do not capture views or bear any relationship to one another. The interior spaces are victims of form and void rather than beneficiaries. As we enter the second decade of the new millennium, it is important to achieve balanced, harmonious, efficient, and lasting architecture for our libraries, with a rhythm of joy in the spaces for young people. The Rancho Mirage (Calif.) Public Library illustrates the use of harmony and rhythm in the staggered lighting plan, simple rhythm of shelving height, and harmonious interior organization of seating and artwork, as shown in plate 8.

A unique example of a beautifully conceived and successfully executed building dedicated to children and teens is ImaginOn at the Public Library of Charlotte and Mecklenburg County. This joint-use facility, developed as a partnership of the library and a children's theater group, serves as a model for future facilities for young people. The building suggests through color, form, void, rhythm, and scale that this is no ordinary place. It is not mistaken for a branch bank or downtown hotel. The exterior is transparent, dynamic, and inviting, and the welcoming continues inside (figure 5.4, plate 5). ImaginOn engages one from first sight, continues to engage throughout the visit, and stays in the mind as a fond experience long after. It is a place where all who enter indeed do "come alive."

A WELCOMING EXTERIOR

Although designing space for children and teens is thought of mostly in terms of interior space, the exterior architecture and open space also influence children and present opportunities for creating youth-friendly environments. The designers of theme parks have understood the importance of fantasy and scale to delight, amuse, and attract children since the creation of amusement gardens in medieval Europe. Bakken

Photo credit: Tom Kessler.

FIGURE 5.4 Children's computers with whimsical seating and interior motifs, ImaginOn mixed-use facility for children, Charlotte, N.C. Architect, Gantt Huberman Architects with Holzman Moss Architecture. Used by permission of the architect and photographer.

Amusement Park, north of Copenhagen, Denmark, was created in 1583—thirty-five years before the Pilgrims arrived at Plymouth Rock. The civic role of the library may not necessarily afford the expression of whimsical architectural motifs from Bakken to Disneyland, but the exterior language and scale of a building can relate to and invite young people into the building.

An example of architectural expression that reads from outside in is the addition to the Franklin Institute in Philadelphia. When architects GBQC created the 1990 Futures Center addition, they elected to complement the 1932 neoclassical edifice, designed by architect John Windrim, with an equally dignified contemporary addition. The historic structure conceals a Pantheon-modeled hall, and the exterior form and void of the addition express a sense of expectation. Window frames are painted playful secondary colors against sand-colored brick, evoking the scientific exploration to be discovered inside (including an IMAX theater). The GBQC website once offered these words from its founder, architect Robert Geddes:

> Institutions are social forms and architecture embodies them in spatial, physical forms. And the form of a building, like the form of an institution, derives from necessity and association; that is from both the operational and symbolic aspects of human endeavor. Thus, the Futures Center building and site design responds to the facility's institutional mission, its unique urban context, its program of spaces and its social and public purpose.

The spatial form of a library building can also convey the spirit and function of the activities inside to create interest and be inviting. The design of the Horsham Township Library places the children's area on the most prominent face of the building. The street facade is mostly transparent—showcasing the children's department and a portion of the adult department reading and stack areas. To the left of the Horsham street facade (see plate 9) is the Story Tale Place, a special room for story hour and crafts. The mass of this room is different—solid stone with narrow, low windows, a clerestory banding, and a round clerestory window atop. The multicolored clerestory functions as a beacon, especially by night, to denote the importance of the children's programs that take place inside.

Since the image of the architecture influences users and potential users, the accessibility and appeal of the library architecture to children and teens are essential. The twentieth century saw the development of a vast network of public libraries in the United States through the Carnegie Endowment and similar local philanthropic gestures. These buildings offered something unique to many communities in North America, regardless of size or location. They offered a civic center where literature could be accessed freely, by both adults and children. "The ubiquitous Carnegie library . . . enriched modern life by making elite culture the common property of everybody" (Karal Ann Marling in Jones 1997: xi).

To the generation of library committees that sponsored them, these designs brought a sense of nobility to the citizenry. This notion was brought into a discussion about the role of the public library at a symposium sponsored by the New York City Department of Design and Construction and the AIA New York chapter, where architect Joshua Prince-Ramus stated that "there is a certain moralism of the Carnegie Libraries. . . . The library is the last vestige of free public interior space" (2005). Or, as Theodore Jones expressed it, "Library construction committees often chose the Classical Revival because it was beautiful and seemed to them philosophically appropriate for a public library building. Since the Columbian Exposition, the Classical Revival represented to Americans democracy, opportunity, education, and freedom—all important themes in public library development" (1997, 67).

Still, as wonderful a gift as these monumental edifices were, they need not be imitated in our postmodern world. Today it is essential that design foster the mission of inviting children and teens into the library. Public library systems such as those in Baltimore, Chicago, New York, Philadelphia, and Washington, D.C., are very cognizant of the need to counter the formal conveyance of their numerous historic branch libraries and have or are undergoing renovations to achieve their mission. These historic buildings are often handsome in scale, proportion, and use of materials, but they do not necessarily speak the language of invitation; rather, they are imposing and even intimidating. A formal staircase and often Beaux Arts lobby may imbue wonder, awe, and even inspiration, but these buildings require rethinking to foster the mission and the message of service to people. Yet some recent library building projects have still succumbed to the formalism of classical architecture, for the idea that "library" equals neoclassical ebbs slowly.

Director David Warren commented on creating a welcoming building:

I think one of the things that we wanted to do [at the Richland County Public Library] was to bring children in the front door so that they can get a feel for the library and [so that other] people can see children coming in. We think that if children come when they are young and have a feel for this building, they will be less intimidated, and hopefully not at all intimidated, to come into the library. And we really want people to see children coming in. We want the whole library to be welcoming to the children.

The library as museum or repository of books is a worthy icon but not an appropriate architectural model for modern libraries or spaces for children. Children are 35 percent of the population of the United States and represent higher percentages in other countries. Considering this large component of the public served is essential to the creation of new and expanded libraries. It would be counterintuitive to create a new children's learning center or children's museum for a community by designing a neoclassical structure to house it. Likewise it is counterintuitive to create new library buildings intended to serve a significant population of children and parents modeled after ancient Greek temples. If the place in the library for children is to be prominent, then it is worthy of denoting the prominence as an architectural expression through its visibility, unique architectural form, or other design means. Examples can be found in Charlotte's ImaginOn, in the Middle Country Public Library's expansion project, and in the Foster and Partners concept of an inverted conical Children's Library Place for the Free Library of Philadelphia expansion (figure 5.5).

Interior architect Daria Pizzetta described the particular relationship developed between the exterior wrapping of the building and the children's component of the library in the Middle Country expansion (see plate 18).

The design started out with an orthogonal plan for the existing space (the original building was a big rectangle shape). We then designed a "wrapper" on a tilted angle

FIGURE 5.5   Exterior rendering of Central Library expansion with children's tower, Free Library of Philadelphia, Pa., design competition. Architect, Foster and Partners. Used by permission of the architect.

Image credit: Foster and Partners

imposed on three sides of the rectangle. This produced a corner that "sticks out," which is where the early childhood area is located. This Family Place space occupies a prominent corner "sinking" into the landscape, which is significant because that's where the kids are.

The exterior of the library influences how a person enters the building not only physically but psychologically. The programming planned for youth spaces can actually drive the massing (size, shape, volume) of the building, the location of some of the expansion, some of the addition itself, and the exterior look of the materials or orchestration.

Glen Holt's description of ImaginOn expresses this well:

ImaginOn . . . is intuitive. From the vista at the entrance, there are sight, light, and color cues—of books here and computers there, of bright wall decorations here and theater box office and stages there. And, like the entrance to a spacious world's fair-style exhibit hall, the intuitive message is "Come on in and explore." Of course, there are brochures and some signs, but even little kids figure out pretty quickly where they want to go and what they want to do next. On the whole, the interior of this building is wonderfully self-evident. And, ImaginOn is adaptable both now and in the future. In the present, the building's spaces lend themselves to the immediate tasks at hand as library and theater professionals work to develop and organize their services to meet and exceed user expectations. In few other library buildings in America will one find such malleable spaces, including spaces still lightly used until good ideas come along to fill them (see p. 100, fig. 5.14).

(see p. 100, fig. 5.14).

ImaginOn is a building that carries out the message in its portmanteau name: It gives the people of Charlotte and Mecklenburg a great gift. It says, "your library and your civic officials care so much about you that they built you a library/theater where you will experience dozens of sights, sounds, and feelings that will fire your imagination—where you and your children are encouraged to Imagine On." (2008)

THE LOBBY

The lobby is among the most important spaces and often the most overlooked component of the contemporary library. Many building programs include only the minimal area required for an air lock—if that. This space deserves, however, to be considered carefully. The lobby—or a portion—is indeed where one enters the building and adjusts to the new climatic conditions. The vestibule—a part or adjunct to the lobby—is where the sand and water fall off the shoes, where coats are loosened, and umbrellas are withdrawn (see figure 5.6). The optimal hardware for this space is a double set of biparting, electrically operating doors with sensors—spaced far enough apart that wind, heat, or cold does not permeate the lobby or, more important, staff and customers inside the library. The vestibule should have the appropriate mechanical system to offset heat gain/loss, which may include an air curtain in particularly hot or cold climates.

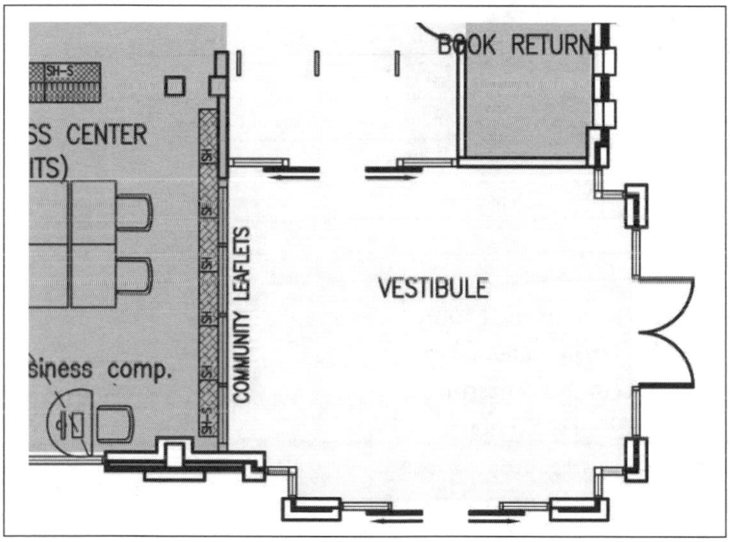

The lobby itself should be ample in space, providing an orientation to the library. The lobby does not need to be a room per se, but it should be an area designated in the Program of Requirements for the normal functions of a lobby. The lobby may contain special exhibits or information, including a staffed information kiosk. It could also include a coffee bar. The lobby optimally will have the public toilets nearby and integrated special displays to promote programs and popular collections. It should also provide a clear direction into the library through either a clear line of sight or an intuitive relationship to the interior spaces, especially those designed for children and teens.

An interesting feature at the Middle Country Public Library that has become a huge plus for children is the welcome desk in the lobby (figure 5.7). Patrons particularly love the staff member—a person sitting there just saying hello and helping

Image credit: VITETTA

FIGURE 5.6 Floor plan of entrance lobby/vestibule with double set of automatic sliding doors, Lower Merion Township Library, Ludington Library, Bryn Mawr, Pa. Architect, VITETTA. Used by permission of the architect.

FIGURE 5.7 Welcome desk and sign, Middle Country Public Library, Centereach, N.Y. Architect, Hardy Holzman Pfeiffer Associates. Used by permission of the architect and photographer.

Photo credit: Tom Kessler

them with directions. No confrontation. "Can you tell me where to go for the Mother Goose program? Do you have a notary? Do you have a fax?" And the greeter saying, "Just go right over there. They will handle your problem." It has become a centerpiece, overwhelmingly popular and very important to children and teenagers. When they come in, you hear, "This is neat. What do you do? Who are you?"—because it is just one friendly person sitting there, not an officious person saying "shush" or anything like that. Everybody says goodbye, and the little children might comment, "See what I made in the program," or show off their shoes.

The lobby is for *all* of the library's visitors. The important point here is that it is for children too. The feature heights, signage, and visual information, even floor patterns, should consider all of the customers, including the youngest.

The lobby is the place where patrons are first acquainted with the library. It must be inviting, light, and pleasant. Public notices, fliers, and free newspapers may be useful, but they tend to clutter the lobby and make the space appear messy and uninviting. It may be beneficial to assign an interior space for the usual community fliers and forms—perhaps near the meeting room or the toilets—and keep the lobby clutter-free.

Although space in a library is always at a premium, it is imperative to provide ample gathering space in the lobby for clustering. This may occur when people see others they know or arrive/depart in groups. It is important not to cheat this area in allocation of square footage during programming and design phases and not to clutter it up after the library opens.

The lobby at the Middle Country Public Library Centereach branch is the most dynamic feature of the building—and the one that was the most controversial in the community when the facility was being renovated. It has made a significant difference to how the users see the library. According to Daria Pizzetta, the interior architect, it presented special issues during the planning phase: "It is hard in a suburban area. We weren't going to build a fifteen-story building where the whole bottom floor could be a lobby. We had to do it within the confines of where we were—in the middle of a housing area. With the lobby, we wanted to tell people—and I think we absolutely accomplished this—you are in a very special place." According to the library's welcome desk log, many people say, "Is this a library?" And when they discover that it is, they say, "Oh, this is so wonderful." From the littlest person to the biggest person, somebody goes, "Oh, Wow." Or, like, "Whoa! Where am I?" When they enter the lobby, they know the library is different. They know they are in a special place.

RELATIONSHIP BETWEEN EXTERIOR AND INTERIOR

Relating the outside of the building to the inside presents some interesting opportunities for young children and teens. Various shapes and textures of materials introduced on the exterior and repeated in some form within the interior generate a feeling of completeness or wholeness as part of one's library experience. Children enjoy seeing the shapes, colors, and textures that stand out individually but together form the whole. Architect Daria Pizzetta explained the use of materials at the Middle Country Public Library:

I think that traditionally Hardy Holzman Pfeiffer [the architects] experimented with materials, and the Middle Country expansion became a laboratory of experimentation with the exterior material. While we had used the materials many other times and in other places, how the composition comes together is always an experiment and always a departure from the last project; we're always building on our knowledge of construction materials. A particular trademark is repeating exterior materials within the inside of the building.

We used several components of the children's room to enhance the exterior of the expansion, one of them being the Museum Corner. We wanted to emphasize that. So on the outside of the building you could read it as a shape or mask and then on the inside of the building it's the same thing—a five-sided shape, which is built out of a separate building material. It is constructed of hardy planks and painted red. So you can say, "I know that room. It's on the inside of the building too."

WINDOWS AND NATURAL LIGHTING

A critical aspect of relating the exterior and interior design of the building involves the adjacency between the outdoor and indoor environments. Lighting can affect how the library looks and feels. Good light is needed for study, and intimate lighting may be excellent for reflective areas. Spot lighting can be used for special effects. Thoughtfulness in integrating natural and artificial light in the space to illuminate tasks properly and, as important, to influence the environment and create mood is an essential component of the design plateau. Lighting designer Richard Renfro simplifies: "Light is the medium through which we interpret space."

As sustainable design permeates thinking about buildings in the public sector, concerns about energy efficiency and environmental responsibility rightly take center stage. Along with considering the effects of daylight as it pertains to the reduction of demand for artificial lighting (energy), it is equally important to consider the effects of daylight on library users as well as personnel and their work areas. Marilyne Andersen speaks about the advantages of natural light in buildings over using artificial lights, if appropriately controlled: "In a typical building, lighting accounts for 25–40 percent of energy consumption. By allowing more natural light to penetrate and controlling both its light and heat components, the financial savings could be considerable. In addition to its health and financial benefits, natural light also provides an almost 'perfect white light' that has a number of visual benefits. Best of all, natural light is of course, plentiful" (quoted in *Science Daily* 2006).

In the often challenging task of replanning within an existing building, it may be better to place a collection area or program room, rather than a reading area or workroom, in interior space. More ideal candidates for these interior portions of the building are mechanical rooms, toilets, storage rooms, and receiving rooms.

Just as the children's library tucked away in a basement corner is becoming a thing of the past, so too should workrooms tucked away where they never see the light of day. Workrooms should be located in direct proximity to natural light. If exterior wall exposure is limited, then an open plan workroom configuration will allow natural light to permeate a relatively large area that might otherwise be void of daylight. In the Horsham Township Library all of the building services are at the south edge of the building, including mechanical, deliveries, workroom, and staff lounge. A rectangular workroom furnished with flexible, open workstations allows daylight to permeate the entire workroom (figure 5.8). Daylight also fills the staff lounge.

The color may change and evolve throughout the day with the movement of the sun. No space, architecturally, is a space unless it has natural light . . . and artificial light is a static light . . . where natural light is a light of mood. And sometimes the room gets dark—why not?—and come another day, you see, to see it in another mood—a different time . . . to see the mood natural light gives, or the seasons of the year, which have other moods. Sunlight shining on different spots at different times of the day can generate an interest in time and space.

—Louis Kahn (1978, 17)

We humans, like all other animals, live in a world that is marked most basically and most invariably by cycles of day and night. This external fact of life has its counterpart in our bodies; somewhere in the dawn of time these fundamental rhythms were etched into our brains, so that we would be organized in synchrony with our environment.

How the brain does this is through an elaborate system of signals kicked off by light. Light strikes our eyes, certain nerve cells in our eyes detect the wavelengths of natural light, they signal the brain, and the brain sends messages to virtually every system of the body to rev up or ramp down. By virtue of this control center, among others, the performance of bodily systems is coordinated one with the other.

—Hara Estroff Marano (2004)

And the cloud that passes over gives the room a feeling of association with the person that is in it, knowing that there is life outside of the room. . . . so light, this great maker of presences, can never be . . . brought forth by the single moment in light which the electric bulb has. And natural light has all the moods of the time of the day, the seasons of the year, [which] year for year and day for day are different from the day preceding.

—Louis Kahn (1978, 18)

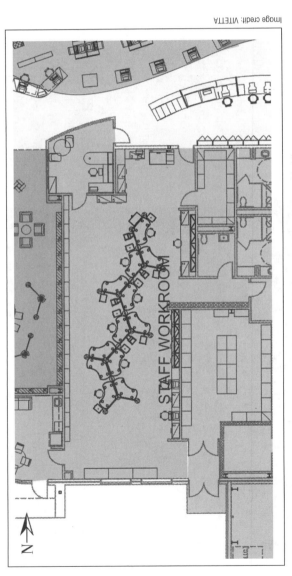

FIGURE 5.8 Floor plan of workroom with 120 degree workstation layout, Horsham Township Library, Horsham, Pa. Architect, VITETTA. Used by permission of the architect.

FIGURE 5.9 Children's story/activity room, Lexington Public Library, Northside Branch, Lexington, Ky. Architect, Omni Architects; consultant, VITETTA. Used by permission of the photographer.

In many libraries, collections of current newspapers and magazines adjacent to a comfortable reading area are located near windows. Windows also provide a view to the world outside the library. Windows allow patrons and staff access to the outdoors, whether it is for mood, weather conditions, or neighborhood ambiance.

Windows designed for children can be placed low enough so that even the youngest can see what is happening outdoors, as in figure 5.9. They can relate to the weather, see people walking and cars moving, appreciate the landscape, and understand the relationship of the neighborhood to the library building.

The windows of the Middle Country Public Library are prominent, and families see the gardens outside the windows when they enter the children's room. When kids walk in, they see a big round window at the far end of the room and feel like the garden is part of the library (figure 5.10). The windows extend the library out, connecting the reader with the local landscape. There are also two low round windows for toddlers in the Family Place through which even very young children can see the gardens outside and the cars going by. This places them; they actually know they are in a place and where that place is from the inside, and that they are still part of the surrounding environment—something that research on day-care centers has shown is important for learning.

Form and void interact with light in the Horsham Township Library story room through a circular clerestory of multicolored glass panels above. The colored panels refract prisms of color onto the floor and walls as the sun moves around the earth each day. The clerestory also serves as a lantern that glows at night for passersby to call attention to this prominent form—Story Tale Place—situated at the most important corner of the facades (see plates 1 and 9).

Window Coverings

It is equally important to consider the negative aspects of natural light in the workspace and make accommodation to manage these effects—primarily glare and heat gain—through the use of effective window treatments. Windows that face the north (or south in the Southern Hemisphere) do not necessarily need covering. Northern light is wonderful light for reading and does not present glare for computer screens. Windows on the other exposures likely require shading. This principle is particularly applicable when the building is built on a true north-south axis. Since few buildings actually face true north, the architect should reference true north in the early concept design drawings so that everyone on the team understands the relationship of spaces to the sun. The architect may also want to perform more advanced study models of the sun—in its ever-changing relationship with the building—to determine placement of overhangs and other screening devices during seasons of peak exposure.

Window shading can be handled architecturally with overhangs, louver devices, and garden walls. Many attractive products are available as part of curtain wall designs (metal framing and glass walls). Interior architectural shutters, some with louvers, have been popular in past times and can still be an attractive and lasting means to shade the interior during peak exposure.

Interior window treatments range from curtains to venetian blinds to roller shades. Each shading device has its application. Curtains tend to date and need constant

FIGURE 5.10   Child-height circular window, Middle Country Public Library, Centereach, N.Y. Building Architect: Hardy Holzman Pfeiffer Associates. Used by permission of the photographer.

Photo credit: Tom Kessler

upkeep, and venetian or italian miniblinds are easily damaged in public environments; they also harbor dust on their horizontal slats. Vertical blinds are another solution, but they also suffer in public environments. Simple, heavy-duty roller shades such as manufactured by Draper or Mechoshade have proven successful for controlling the sun in public spaces. These shades are durable and come with shade fabric available in gradations of density all the way to blackout. These shades can also be specified with dual rollers for sun screen backed up by blackout shades—perfect for meeting or program rooms where video or film may be shown. One important detail with shades is the cord. The architect should either specify a cord clip out of children's reach or have the shades electrically mechanized to operate from a keyed switch.

Many architects now prefer dot screens to shade western, eastern, and sometimes southern exposures. This application can dramatically reduce the solar gain in a building yet permit unobstructed views out of the building most of the time. This type of screening was used at the east porch elevation of the Northside branch of the Lexington Public Library (see plate 10). The dot screen at the exterior glazing is opaque during times of direct exposure to the sun (as shown) and transparent otherwise. The glazing type is also critical to solar and heat gain or loss in a building. The architect should clarify glass specifications as part of the presentation of the building palette and systems during design development.

Lighting

Lighting design is highly technical and is usually the job of a lighting engineer or consultant coordinated with and directed by the architect or interior designer. Libraries are difficult to light correctly because of the variety of lighting levels and types of fixtures needed for bookshelves, tabletops and desks, glare control, spatial definition, orientation, and the interaction between natural and artificial light. Maintenance issues, circuitry, and the lighting control system are also important parts of the lighting plan. As with signage, it is best to address this element in early stages of the design process rather than after the fact.

Using a variety of lights and lighting schemes can affect the mood and ambiance of different sections of the library. Indirect and diffuse ambient lighting can be used to impart a quiet, cozy atmosphere, and spotlighting provides a way to highlight materials or display. Direct light (natural and artificial) provides general lighting schemes for reading and book shelves. Kim Bolan comments that "lighting is crucial in a teen area primarily because teens will be spending a large amount of time studying there. [It] also creates atmosphere, which directly affects the mood, appearance and function of a space. For instance, lighting can play a key role in making a small room appear larger. . . . Mirrors are also quite effective in creating the illusion of a large space" (2003, 75–76).

In the Horsham Public Library, the VITETTA team used a variety of artificial lights to draw teens' attention to the type of activity that should occur in the teen space. Small spotlights accent the collections, specially painted walls surround the room, and floor and table lamps define where computer use and reading are appropriate. It is the interaction of the lights, paint, and floor patterns that sets the tone for the space and makes it come alive. An innovative design team may also employ specular lighting to cast light on objects to create both highlights and shadows for dramatic effect.

Daylight is an important part of any sustainable lighting program. Placing the children's area adjacent to northern or eastern light is optimal—with ample windows. If the orientation and design provide excellent day lighting, it may be beneficial to consider sensors to reduce the artificial lighting during the day. Mechanized shades can also be installed with daylight sensors. This is especially helpful if the space has a western or southern exposure, which does not provide optimal light for a library. All on/off switches for lights or shades need to be inaccessible to children.

The lower heights of children's area bookshelves do not restrict direct light from fluorescent fixtures and the sun as tall adult shelving does. Nevertheless, it is important to define the expectation for appropriate lighting levels in the children's area. Too much light is as counterproductive as too little. If there is too much light, the space is unpleasant and the light "hurts the eyes" of the children and adults. Lighting configurations that do not rely on the direction of the shelving are the most flexible and usually the most effective in distributing lighting evenly to the book spines—even at the low shelves. Shelving layouts that run perpendicular to the lighting or at 45 degrees or other angles achieve this effect.

If lighting is to run parallel to the shelving, the precision of spacing is critical. Many libraries find themselves in a bind with this configuration, for it restricts the rearrangement of shelving and other furniture. How many libraries do you see with linear fixtures directly above a shelving canopy? This is a significant waste of energy and does nothing for the library environment. Lighting arrangements that are parallel to the shelving pose another problem. The customer, while browsing, generally blocks up to a third of the light (or more) through his or her vertical positioning in relation to the stacks. Shadows result and often the customer must jockey to find a standing position that does not block the light. When the lighting is 90 degrees or some other reasonable angle from the shelving, light comes from both sides of the customer and is not restricted, providing a more even light.

It is advisable to verify any maintenance requirements pertaining to lighting in advance of fixture selection and specification. It may be possible to incorporate varied styles of lighting fixtures and yet have to stock only a few bulb types. Another important design consideration is the height of the lamps above the floor. It is critical that children cannot reach lamps to unscrew or dismantle the bulbs, yet it is important that the maintenance staff be able to access fixtures with a ladder rather than a lift device. Pendant-type fixtures should either have covers to keep debris and insects out of them or be completely open at the top and bottom in order not to trap insects, debris, or dust.

GARDENS AND OUTDOOR SPACES

In today's world, there is a growing awareness of children's need for access to public places and outdoor learning opportunities that enhance their health and well-being, provide a variety of educationally appropriate formal and informal play activities, promote direct experience with nature, and foster a sense of community and responsibility for the natural environment. A children's outdoor learning environment, contiguous with the library, can serve as a relevant learning space that takes advantage of the library's public accessibility, trained public service staff, and inclusive approach to serving all families. It also provides a wonderful opportunity for the library to connect with its community on environmental issues and helps to celebrate and sustain shared natural resources.

Exposure to natural environments through play leads to exploration and discovery, engaging both the physical and mental abilities of the child. Access to educationally appropriate outdoor environments during the early years is critical to developing nature-literate adults and, in the long run, a sustainable community. Through hands-on outdoor learning activities, children and their families become engaged in and knowledgeable about nature and their surroundings and are introduced to the importance of individual and community responsibility for the environment. This type of learning leads to an understanding of and appreciation for the natural world.

The public library, as a local community institution, can be part of the environmental solution. By integrating the concepts of early learning, family-centered practice, nature literacy, and sustainable communities through the sharing of local resources, library leadership ensures the appreciation and preservation of a common good. Well-developed outdoor learning environments for children work effectively and function comfortably with traditional library policies and practices. They provide a local community "place" for visitors to learn about and use plants, trees, and other natural materials for fun and play, storytelling, conversation, and social interaction.

Guidelines for developing outdoor environments are described in the *Learning with Nature Idea Book* (NADF 2007). Elements include an entry feature (both the interior and exterior of the building), climbing/crawling area, "messy materials" area, building area, art area, music and performance area, planting area, gathering/conversation place, reading area, and water feature. Naming and identification, visibility, variety, durability, visual appeal, and regional significance regarding materials use and regulatory standards are other essential ingredients for a successful space.

In 2007, staff from the Middle Country Public Library attended a presentation conducted by the Dimensions Educational Research Foundation on the concept of outdoor learning environments for children. During the presentation, featured models and demonstration sites were attached to churches, museums, schools, child-care centers, and youth centers. No library models were noted, nor were there any in development. Why?

With a 5,000-square-foot outdoor space adjacent to the children's room, the Middle Country library staff began to explore developing the first library-based outdoor learning environment based on the guiding principles promoted by Dimensions. Library staff, landscape architects and designers, and educators used workshops to create the initial design for the library's outdoor area (figure 5.11). In 2008 the library committed to the concept, hired a landscape architect firm, and the Nature Explorium was initiated. The completion date is targeted for the spring of 2010.

Although developing an entire area may not be feasible, many libraries integrate outdoor learning opportunities on their grounds. At Harborfields Public Library of Greenlawn, N.Y., a local sculptor created metal animals and placed them around the property for children to enjoy. The Port Washington (N.Y.) Public Library developed a small garden in full view and accessible from the children's room. The Reading Garden at the Middle Country Public Library, adjacent to the Adult Reading Room, regularly engages children and their parents. Created by a local sculptor, the fountain is ensconced with nymphs, a metal tree, metal books, and a pirate ship, providing a sense of wonder and place for pennies (see plate 17). The Princeton (N.J.) Library created an outdoor terrace with a handsome security "fence" for safety, as did the Lexington Public Library for its new Northside branch (figure 5.12). At the Santiago (Chile) Public Library the entire plaza is an outdoor space for children and families—a frequent place for concerts, films, and performances in the mild Santiago climate (figure 5.13).

Even with very little outdoor space, landscaping can enhance the child's experience at the library. Art objects, sculpture, and whimsical benches and seats serve to welcome visitors of all ages and provide a sense of adventure and imagination even before one enters the building. At the entrance of the Middle Country Public Library, a bench with a life-size little girl feeding a cat garners many comments. Children often pet the cat or leave a french fry in the milk cup—a sign of engagement and fantasy.

IMAGINON: A SPECIAL JOINT-USE FACILITY

Although this book is not intended to explore joint-use facilities in depth, one unusual and excellent joint-use facility dedicated to children and teens is worth mentioning: ImaginOn.

Lois Klikka, library manager at ImaginOn, gave us details. The Public Library of Charlotte and Mecklenburg County (N.C.) and the Children's Theatre of Charlotte, each with nationally renowned programs for young people, were both facing space constraints that led to the planning and development of a joint-use facility for children and teens. The resulting facility includes library spaces for children and teens, an animation/film/music production studio, interactive exhibits, computer labs with age-appropriate early literacy and creativity software, classrooms, rehearsal spaces, a

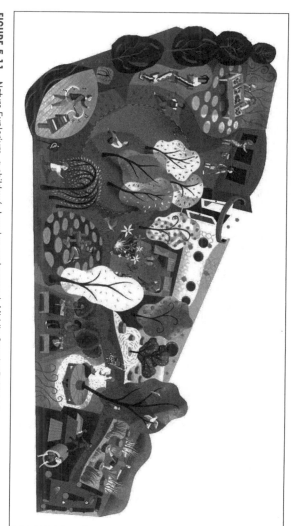

FIGURE 5.11 Nature Explorium, a children's learning environment, Middle Country Public Library, Centereach, N.Y. Used by permission of artist Heidi Younger.

Image credit: Middle Country Public Library

99

FIGURE 5.12 Outdoor terrace with security enclosure, Lexington Public Library, Northside Branch, Lexington, Ky. Architect, Omni Architects; consultant, VITETTA. Used by permission of the photographer.

FIGURE 5.13 Multiuse entrance plaza, Santiago Public Library, Santiago, Chile. Architect, Cox and Ugarte. Used by permission of the library.

Photo credit: Santiago Public Library

FIGURE 5.14 View of dynamic and inviting Park Family Story Lab, ImaginOn mixed-use facility for children, Charlotte, N.C. Architect, Gantt Huberman Architects with Holzman Moss Architecture. Used by permission of the architect and photographer.

Photo credit: Tom Kessler

gift shop, two state-of-the-art theater venues seating 570 and 250, and full production shops for scenery and costumes (figure 5.14).

We now find ourselves akin to a children's museum, utilizing traveling exhibitions, self-directed activities, and block programming rather than the traditional library story time model. We're all about the visitor experience. Block programming means we offer more frequent, shorter interactive programs and/or activities that are on the floor, scattered throughout the building, and do not require preregistration. Our goal is to have something fun for every age level, birth through 18, within an hour of when they walk in the door. We have so many large group visits that we needed to program differently. This year we're working hard to take technology out of the lab and onto the floor, to have bite-sized "morsels" of tech skills or games that can be enjoyed anywhere in the building. We're also working with preteen focus groups to come up with a more inviting environment and services for the 8–11 year old crowd. We're rearranging the Spangler Children's Library to create a larger space for babies up to 23 months (screen free). As far as partnership activities, we have also developed an ImaginOn Library–Children's Theatre team that plans and implements an annual calendar of what we call "shared initiatives"—the programs that we offer jointly or in support of the partner organization's programs.

SIGNAGE

Signage, or way-finding, is critical to the success of an overall design, whether for a large or small project. Plans for how people will find their way throughout a new building or space should be designed in close consultation with the library staff and other project team members. It is important, right from the start of the design process, to think about different ways to indicate to visitors where things are, using signs, color, symbols (use international symbols), floor layout and patterns, and pointers on the flooring. The arrangement of the library—architectural structures, furnishings, and flooring—should help users find their way and minimize the amount of signage in the building.

In *Interior Design for Libraries*, Carol Brown includes an entire chapter on signage. "A sign system should complement the architecture and the rest of the interior design of the library [or room]. The same elements of good design that apply to planning each feature of a building should be considered when designing the sign system. The dimensions of signs should be in proportion to the scale of the building and furnishings" (2002, 92).

The essential word here is "system." Consistency in types of signs for particular purposes helps patrons learn how to use the library quickly and easily. A signage system should be developed for the various types of signs needed in a library setting, including orientation and way-finding, identification, instructions, regulations, general information, and current awareness. Making signs simple, uncluttered, and standard is the main goal.

One decision that rises up during the design process for children's space and needs to be resolved is whether to give the room or space a special name. "Children's Room" or "Teen Room" are still acceptable, but often the staff want to create a special name. "Family Place" is one alternative for an early childhood area, but the name is trademarked and can be used only by libraries that are trained as part of the Family Place initiative. Some libraries now refer to departments as "family services" rather than "children's services."

In any case, the children's and teen areas provide an opportunity for creativity in naming and providing special signage. This can generate a lot of discussion and some controversy, since everyone thinks of the area somewhat differently or may want to focus on the particular age group they favor. In "The Kids' Place," Chekon and Miles recall that the selection of a name at the Sacramento Public Library led to lengthy discussions: "Some staff felt 'Children's Room' or 'Children's Department' were too stodgy, and would turn off young teens who were part of the group to be served. At the other extreme, a name like 'Discovery

In a program of the State Library of Victoria, Australia, Robert Sloan presented these suggestions:

Keep It Simple: Information overload has an inverse effect on people's willingness to seek out the detail. On viewing large blocks of text, viewers will either leave the facility or just ask an employee. Thus the text should be in concise messages and clear English. The use of internationally relevant pictograms equally caters to those whose first language is not English. The purpose of each sign should be minimized to a specific action, such as providing direction, promoting an event or giving instruction on the operation of a service. This will allow the viewer to progressively step through the facility. The number of signs should be reduced to a bare minimum, allowing for the use of other way-finding cues. A suite of standard signs should be established, based on a well developed master plan and adopted as the facility's standard to ensure that a consistent image is maintained for signage. Consistency will assist the user become more aware of the system and help them locate what their looking for.

—Robert Sloan (2002, 1)

Center' promised a wider range of materials and experiences than we could offer. 'The Kids' Place' was a compromise" (1993, 22).

For teen spaces, naming or not naming the area can also be an issue. Kim Bolan stresses that there is no "right" or "wrong" name for a teen area. In her research, "young adult" and "YA" were not recognizable to the audience, and the teens themselves didn't have a clue as to what "YA" stood for. She emphasizes that having teen involvement in the selection is critical and that the term needs to be clearly identifiable and universal. According to the teens, the name needs to be inconspicuous, short and to the point, catchy, and something that goes with the theme (if there is one). It should not contain the word "center," be corny, use "YA," or be a play on words (Bolan Taney 2003, 91–92).

Whatever the name, special graphics may help to convey that these areas are user friendly, age appropriate, fun places to be and to learn. The primary sign that identifies the space can be bold or dramatic in order to reinforce the importance of the space. This is an area of design where focus group participation and review can really assist the design team. It is important to consider the reactions of the age groups served. The signage should not overwhelm or compete with the building design, but it should complement the architecture and design, reinforcing the clarity of the space and the library mission.

CONCLUSION

The architectural style and elements of design reflect the aspirations and tastes of those who sponsor the project and the team that generates the design for the project. It is important to recognize the role of design in fostering the mission of library service to children and teens. Yet youth services can be fostered in an array of environments, and there is no right or wrong solution, although there are perhaps degrees of better solutions. The cost of creating a space does not necessarily impact the success of the space; simple solutions can often be the most effective.

It usually takes a confluence of support and participation from the uninformed as well as the informed to create learning places for young people. One person's vision can dramatically change the child's universe forever. "Each Carnegie Library reflects the efforts of the architecturally and bibliographically untrained community leaders who dictated their library's design and administration. These local endeavors resulted in [the construction of] 1,689 libraries over a short thirty-year period" (Jones 1997: vii). For the new century, it is important that libraries re-create the vision to reflect young audiences more succinctly and dynamically.

Perseverance and determination are essential to achieving the desired results in creating places for young people. To create these spaces, basic architectural elements need to be taken into consideration. Scale and proportion, form and void, rhythm, a welcoming exterior and lobby, natural and artificial light, outdoor environments, and signage are critical to the overall architecture as well as the function of well-designed spaces for children and teens.

Chapter 6 | A Welcoming Place

The public library is a place with unique energy. Individuals gather peacefully to gain access to information and to share in a community place. The architectural intervention, interior design, and technology can coalesce into a dynamic people place and have a transforming effect in shaping lives. The design, programs, services, and staff come together to create an inviting place. A welcoming public library with special spaces for children and teens has great potential to influence individuals and society in a positive way. For many young people the public library offers the first glimpse of independence, confirmed and symbolized by the issuance of the first library card.

The role of design in creating environments for youth can extend from decisions to create themed environments that suggest storybook qualities to more subtle, but nevertheless intentional, architectural expressions that spark the imagination. Both approaches have their advocates. There also remain professionals who believe there is no worthy rationale to warrant either approach and, instead, believe that the child's imagination is expected to be complete and not in need of any encouragement. This latter view, however steadfast, is contrary to the consumer industry that thrives on selling products to children and teens.

THE INFLUENCE OF MERCHANDISING

It seems no less important in designing spaces for children to consider the impact of the space on the child than to consider the appeal of a box of children's cereal on the supermarket shelves, including its placement at the height of the cart's child seat. Think of the toddler reaching out toward an attractive product on the shelf. One has to consider the elements of design—color, pattern, images—that capture the attention of the child. This is not to say that building space intended for use by children and adolescents should aspire solely to attention-catching devices and marketing gimmicks. It is essential, however, to consider the appeal to and reactions of young people to various design devices when planning space, especially in the public arena.

Architect Robert Miller described for us his perspective regarding the design of the recently completed Ballard branch of the Seattle Public Library (figure 6.1):

There is a . . . pronounced emphasis on the kids' area in Ballard, however, it is not adorned with the stereotypical bright colors and animated icons. These are icons adults have placed on children. Children themselves have limitless imaginations, as evidenced by the ability to find hours of amusement with something as simple as a

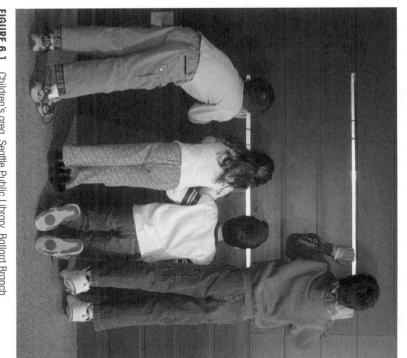

FIGURE 6.1 Children's area, Seattle Public Library, Ballard Branch, Seattle, Wash. Architect, Bohlin Cywinski Jackson. Used by permission of the architect and photographer.

Photo credit: Bohlin Cywinski Jackson

cardboard box. The space has a curved window wall system that refracts light and views into, over, and under flora and fauna. It has special bookshelves, special reading benches and accommodations for reading groups.

The children's area also has a few "surprises" such as a periscope that can be discovered in the cracks between the siding boards. The Ballard space has "vitrines" that display disassembled instruments but also look into the meeting room at a kid's eye level. These puncture through the reflective curved metal wall skin of the multi-purpose room that bounds the children's area. The entire building has a green emphasis and serves double duty as a learning tool for the relationship of the user and the environment. We have tended to treat the children's areas to more closely parallel the adult areas with added imaginative twists to make the space their own and also reward the inquisitive and curious. Hopefully they will leave the library with an awareness of their environment more cerebral than Teletubbies and teddy bears.

Merchandising, lighting, scale, and clarity reinforce the message—whether the message is for a sugar-coated breakfast cereal, Teletubbies, or children's literature. Design is integral in creating an environment that encourages a particular behavior or mood. Lack of good design can hinder the message or even obscure it. Much of the success of mass-merchandising retail giants lies in clarity. The reduced need for sales staff to assist the customer underscores the profitability of the venture and encourages self-reliance on the part of the customer.

It is important to consider this effect when designing youth spaces in a library. If finding reading materials can be likened to finding a needle in a haystack, then the mission of promoting literacy and self-reliance will be obscured or eliminated. Planning clear, logical sequences of space—open and uncluttered—serves to reinforce the self-reliance and development that is at the heart of service to children and teens. In the children's room at the Middle Country Public Library, "there is an accent wall that wriggles around, that brings the toddlers back into the Family Place area, and it's something that is very orange and bright and lively. They can follow this curve to where they are going to go and have their seats and have their programs take place too" (Daria Pizzetta, interview, October 2004).

THEMES

Architectural elements are the most timeless and cost-effective features to use in creating space for children, but several leading library and design professionals in the past decade have promoted themed environments as a way to engage young people and enhance the ambiance of the library's space. Borrowing cues from amusement parks, these libraries have implemented forest themes, castles, and other whimsical elements in an effort to make the library relevant and attractive to children and families. These themes range in complexity and cost from murals on the wall to complete themed environments, constructed of fiberglass and other strong materials similar to theme parks such as Disney and Universal. The proponents of themed designs offer a viable approach to making the library more attractive to youth and have been successful in reaching many people through these special environments. Still, themed environments need to be approached with caution. Nolan Lushington explains:

> Children's facilities are often designed to attract children with playful concepts. . . . Trying too hard to make it into an actual ocean liner [train station, castle, town] can look cute and corny and be boring in time. Murals, furnishings, and equipment should encourage children's imagination to make them what they will. The platform can be a deck, a balloon floating in the sky, or a space station depending on the child's imagination. . . . Classic and durable images should grace some of the walls of the children's areas and should flow naturally from the library's function to stimulate the imagination and offer children a variety of materials and ways to experience these materials. (2002, 131–32)

Achieving whimsy, imagination, and awe in library design is an outgrowth of the entertainment industry. Though the human imagination is unquestionably more vivid than graphic media, there exists an intrinsic relationship between brain development and visual stimulation. A child comprehends images in a picture book long before he or she can read text. It stands to reason that, likewise, the same child will relate to a color on the carpet or a storybook fantasy long before or even concurrent with developing their imaginations. The human response to visual stimuli is the engine behind travel magazines.

The imagination must be fed in order to grow. It is also true that creative visioning is not equal among children, teens, and adults. Some young people have vivid imaginations; others may be more limited to understanding what they actually have seen. The more a child or teen sees, the greater their kit of information from which to formulate other imaginative scenarios.

When asked about using any special kind of description or design language for the children's room at the Schaumburg (Ill.) Public Library, Denelle Wrightson, architect for the project, responded that the specially constructed indoor garden in the children's room was playful. It brought literature alive.

It's just very nice to experience the life-size characters [Tom Kitten from Beatrix Potter's Peter Rabbit series and Tomie dePaola's wonderful characters], because to a child they are bigger than life. Usually children are reading a "little" Beatrice Potter book and making those connections makes it really playful. It's like they are really in Peter Rabbit's house or pretending to be Peter Rabbit. . . . Going through the illustrations first, seeing the connection; this is a piece of art that then becomes put with words. "Entering the garden" and going into the illustrations that are out of scale and lifelike is a lot of fun. I like that progression and tie between literature and life-size characters. There's almost a traditional sense of connection to those murals that you would have found at the beginning of the last century, and a lot bigger; they are timeless too. We focused on characters from books that would have a life, not trendy.

The most important consideration in this approach is that the environments do not become awash in "little kiddie" design features that are akin to baby talk. Although themed environments can be a wonderful and appropriate mechanism to bring children into the library, it is important to consider that this is just one method of creating space that is inviting. Keep in mind that young people have vivid and active imaginations, and that the environments that are specially created for children may better serve the task by allowing for spontaneity and stimulation of the child's imagination. Strong, single-minded themes may be limiting. Many recent children's library spaces seem to be like the coloring book that has already been colored—there is little room for the imagination.

Like children's spaces, the design of teen areas is heavily influenced by a themed approach. Kim Bolan cautions us to "try to stay away from trendy themes that involve permanent or costly items" (2003, 57). These areas may attract teens initially, but they often become stale and out-of-date quickly. The organization of the room to include the functions important to teens (conversation, interaction, study, and technology) with basic furniture elements (counters, computers, and comfortable chairs) and colors and decorations that excite but are easily adapted may be the best approach. This way, the theme can be easily changed with new generations.

IMAGINATION AND WHIMSY

Imagination in design is the province of all the stakeholders in the design collaboration. The imagination or dreaming stage of a project is an open design exercise and should be fun and engaging. It is critical to imagine the space designed for the age of the audience it is intended to serve. The most successful design results are always the result of a collaboration of client and design professionals. The gifted design professional coalesces many ideas into a synthesis of design to reflect the notions and creativity of the participants—staff, board, and community members (a must for teens)—alike.

The children's room will have several distinct areas arranged to invite children, parents and caregivers to move through the space in accordance with the child's conceptual development. . . . Each of the areas should serve as an imaginal landscape of the developmental period. The space should invoke a sense of creative discovery while also allowing containment for the projection and experience of the child's own imaginal field—a real field of dreams that encourages and supports a variety of imaginative feelings and creative thought. (Lushington 2008, 50)

Adolescent spaces, on the other hand, are most effectively "imagined" with teens. Young adults gravitate toward trendy, popular décor, but it is often difficult for adults to determine just what that décor would look like. Different communities and differ-

> Images should flow naturally from the library's function to stimulate the imagination and to offer children a variety of materials and ways to experience these materials. Explicit themes may be of interest during the first visit, but they become stale and boring on repeated exposure and have little relevance to the imaginative world that library books create. It may be better to create frequently changing, interactive learning experiences with a variety of exhibits mounted on mobile carts or fitting right into the bookshelves.
>
> —Nolan Lushington (2008, 51)

ent groups of teens are the library's best bet for gaining much-needed specific input. Bolan reflects on selecting themes for teens:

> Potential themes for teen spaces are everywhere. Just take a look at what's going on in the world and what's popular. . . . [Be careful] about not choosing themes and related décor that are either too adult or too juvenile. . . . pick something that will be popular with males and females. It is essential that you involve teens in this entire process because you might think you have the best idea in the world for a young adult area but teenagers might have a totally different opinion. (2003, 58)

A synonym of imagination is fantasy. There is a place for fantasy in space design for children. This may be fantastic shapes and inventive fenestration or the manner of introducing natural light into space. Fantasy may be a simulation of the constellations, as in the Enoch Pratt Free Library's central library children's program room. Fantasy may be a larger-than-life mural created by a brilliant illustrator, such as Maurice Sendak's mural "The Wild Things" in the Richland County (S.C.) main library—described for us by library director David Warren:

> It's like a park. It is beautiful. Especially when the sun comes in the morning and it goes through the trees and it catches shadows just like the mural. The mural one sees is of "The Wild Things" swinging from the trees, with actual trees in front of the mural. It's three dimensional. When you walk in you see the live trees and behind it you see the mural with the trees and they all just blend together, so that the "Wild Things" look like they are hanging on real trees rather than just on the mural.

Many youth spaces can be enhanced with themed or decorative whimsical elements. Think of whimsy as something intended to be unusual and amusing—but in fact of little definitive purpose; there is a place for such whimsy in design for young people. Everything in art and design does not need a particular purpose. To delight and amuse is, in and of itself, serving a purpose.

In the Eastwick branch design of the Free Library of Philadelphia, the VITETTA team converted a leaking, obsolete fireplace story pit into a "train place" with an accompanying mural (figure 6.2). This renovation had a limited budget, and the mural included a scene with a cowboy on a horse (symbolizing the west) facing an otherwise specifically local array of themes—airplane, trains, and skyline of Philadelphia. The "train place" included ideas from the branch staff, administrators, and the design team, focusing on a whimsical interpretation of notions, which together successfully transformed the space into a fun, inviting, and accessible place.

THE "WOW!" FACTOR

Though avoiding themed environments in the extreme may be a goal, libraries do have to compete for the general public's attention. We want children and teens to choose the library as a destination, and we also want the library to have a vivid, welcoming environment "right from the start" of the visitor experience. To accomplish this, architects and designers along with youth services staff have reached outside the library's traditional past to other venues for creative ideas and dramatic effects. To some in the field, this has come to be known as the "Wow!" factor.

FIGURE 6.2   Story area before renovation (left) and after (right), Free Library of Philadelphia, Eastwick Branch, Philadelphia, Pa. Architect, VITETTA. Used by permission of the architect.

Photo credits: Joanne Bening/VITETTA

When VITETTA started the Free Library of Philadelphia branch renovations, there were so many mixed messages that we held a special, long meeting and talked about what "Wow" meant. What was the preschool or the children's area supposed to be? Themed? Not themed? Some replied that it shouldn't be themed, some that it should. Should it be a special interest area? Every library should have a special interest area—sometimes for children, sometimes teens, or seniors. Nobody could agree on what these things meant. It was difficult to design something when no one on the library side knew or agreed about what any of these things meant.

We had a myriad of ideas of what "special interest area" and "Wow" meant. At the conclusion of our meeting, we finally agreed on an approach that carried through all eighteen of the VITETTA renovations. And it was what we defined as the "Wow!" factor: that patrons came into the building after it was renovated and stood there and their mouths dropped open and they literally said, "Wow, this is different." Something had happened; they didn't come in and say, "Oh, okay, it looks nicer—maybe?" It was everyone's goal that in each branch, when anyone walked in off the street (even if they had not been in the building before), they would say, "Wow, there is something really special about this place."

STRUCTURES AND OBJECTS

Objects to integrate into youth spaces may include sculptural art, architectural objects/fragments including colored glass, and structures that define space such as kiosks or

FIGURE 6.4 Curve World learning area with the Vortex, Indianapolis–Marion County Public Library, Central Library, Indianapolis, Ind. Used by permission of the library.

FIGURE 6.3 Reading cylinders, young children's area, Santiago Public Library, Santiago, Chile. Architect, Cox and Ugarte; Design Consultant, VITETTA; Industrial Designer, NAVE. Used by permission of the library.

tented areas, curved walls, arbors, or special doorways. Tenting or other structures within a space can create fun zones for special activities in the library. The Amsterdam (Netherlands) Public Library has circular pods for children of different ages that include entertaining places to sit, computers at different heights, and other functional and fun accommodations (see plate 11).

In the Santiago (Chile) Public Library, architects Cox and Ugarte created futuristic cylinders, some suspended from the ceiling of the children's area as though they are levitating above the floor (figure 6.3). These elements bring together space-age fantasy and imagination while providing practical, cozy zones for small children to gather and read or be read to. Children flock to sit in or under these colorful forms. Although these wonderful elements may evoke images from science fiction, they are timeless and not specific to a particular story or theme.

A space itself can encourage participation and enthusiasm for literacy and learning. The Learning Curve at the central facility of the Indianapolis Marion County Public Library is a great example of reinforcing programming with design or vice versa (figure 6.4). The design of the space encourages contact with different areas of learning and growth through the organization of the space itself. The Learning Curve (http://curve.imcpl.org) offers a typical array of programs with titles like "Curve World," "Introduction to Robots," and "Star Search." The space is arrayed with collections, special features, lighting effects, and fun places to sit, read, and experience information. Natural light is abundant by day, and carefully designed interior lighting invites people into and through the space at night.

The Learning Curve creatively combines all of the necessities of a children's library—shelving, seating, and computers—into objects unto themselves. The shelves, for example, are not just rows of stacks but sculptural elements that define the space with special lighting. The computers, including portable computers on stands, are among the many inviting settings in this space and each an object of sorts. The library brought in the interactive entertainment team Funny Garbage to launch Curve World, an interactive literacy learning game, to coincide with the launch of the dynamic space. The Funny Garbage website describes the space:

Let's face it: we all grow up hoping one day to have the chance to hurtle through space piloting a rocket-propelled wheel of cheese. It goes without saying. Well, now lucky students visiting The Learning Curve at Central Library in Indianapolis are able to *live* that dream—while strengthening literacy in information, technology and media along the way—as they blast off into CurveWorld!

Curve World is actually a game-like interactive educational experience that is part of the Learning Curve. Focused on improving students' understanding and use of evolving digital media, CurveWorld provides a hands-on, immersive learning environment that engages the user's creativity and motivates intellectual curiosity.

To begin their exploration of the virtual cosmos, children construct personalized transporters—strapping rocket boosters to lipstick, flying-V guitars and, yes, cheese—to navigate through space. After take-off, students chart their own courses, interacting with each other while also creating and sharing art, audio, video, and other projects. Through these activities, kids gain practical experience with real-life technology in a safe, nurturing environment.

When considering the construction of a major element or structure, it is best to work with a professional firm that has experience in building this type of element and, if possible, experience installing the structure or object in a library or other public facility. There is enormous detail in this type of construction, and it needs to be fully integrated with the overall design of the youth space. Professional companies produce detailed plans that lead to the successful implementation of the idea.

Denelle Wrightson elaborated on this theme as she told us about building the garden area in the children's room at Schaumburg Township District Library. They subcontracted to Chicago Design, people who could take a sketch and turn it into reality.

If you are doing it in a vacuum, fine. But to integrate into our building, we needed to know the exact dimensions and the heights of the tree so we could make sure the lighting was right and change the ceiling and work with the flooring and exactly where one would end and the other would start. Yes, those details were like pulling teeth out of them. One of the lessons I learned, as our firm moved forward and tried to do things in other libraries, was that we took the drawings so far and then, depending on the project and the size of it, brought those drawings to a subconsultant who would detail the drawings and build it under the contractor so that there was coordination.

PERMANENCE AND TIMELESSNESS

Because redesigning or building new space is a major investment by the community, it is important for the design team to include timelessness in the equation when selecting elements, particularly more permanent elements such as furniture, carpeting, and colors. It is best to avoid anything trendy or easily outdated. Whatever is done needs to last a while, be pleasant and flexible, and should not be exaggerated. Remember, walls can be repainted with relative ease and often, but carpets and furnishings are with the library for years. For example, the vibrant colors in the teen space in the Rockwall County Library (see plate 19) could be easily modified to represent a future color trend.

Be wary of allowing materials into the design that have permanent colors that are part of a current color trend, including surfaces that cannot be repainted or inexpensively replaced such as plastic laminate, hard-surface resins for countertops, prepainted light fixtures, and permanent signage. The fashion and mercantile design industry sets color trends *each year*. General trends may last several years, but it behooves retailers for products to become quickly outdated. Although it is customary in the hospitality industry to change color schemes and update interior environments every five to seven years, few if any libraries can justify or afford to do this. Therefore, the interior designer is expected to be sensitive and sensible when it comes to selecting finish materials and colors with timelessness in mind. This does not mean, however, that it is necessary to engage in a *timeless* fanaticism that results in drab and boring environments.

Timelessness can also be in the eye of the beholder. No matter how diligent we are in striving for "timeless" design, color and stylistic trends abound in the products available at any given time. It is worthwhile to look at an existing space without prejudice to a particular fad or trend of the past. For example, many libraries built in the 1970s integrated orange plastic laminates or gold end panels. Often in renovations, staff and community develop a dislike for such "trendy" elements of a past generation. Yet in many instances these very elements are part of a cohesive design language and can be cleverly integrated within a renovated space.

For example, clear anodized aluminum storefronts were extremely popular in the 1960s and '70s. In the 1980s, powder-coated (painted) finishes from the factory became available. Buildings from the 1980s to the present therefore include a broad array of painted metal window and door frames in colors from pink to red to aquamarine. Though the color preference of a prior generation may not be the current preference, it is important to consider incorporating these elements into a renovation rather than replacing (which is costly) or recoating (which is futile in most cases). Clear anodized window frames can be cleaned and will last for another generation. Many also accommodate reglazing (new windowpanes) for thermal efficiency.

FLEXIBILITY

Flexibility is a critical element in designing space for youth. Libraries planned now must be able to accommodate the unknown technology, programming, staff needs, and materials of the future. In our interview, Jeff Scherer commented on the need for flexibility:

What is really interesting about children's areas is that you cannot define the task in advance like you can in all the other departments in the library. So, where people get into trouble, at least from my experience, is when they try too hard to define the task in advance. And what I find are the most successful children's programs or areas are those that understand the structure of how children learn, but don't try to box them in. [The design] allows for the space to evolve and change fairly rapid over time, [particularly] if you have the right financial, service, and staffing understanding of how that change has to happen. Too often the spaces are way too limiting for that kind of spontaneity to occur.

School-age and teen areas need to be particularly flexible. Activities and needs are driving factors in how the space is used at any one time or for any one purpose. Moving furniture to accommodate activities is a favorite pastime, and it is not so unusual for groupings of peers or activities to require different seating and table configurations. The summary of a 2008 LAMA presentation on top building trends noted that new buildings need to focus on function, not form. Open spaces with reconfigurable furniture and materials, furniture and shelving on wheels, easy setup and breakdown of room arrangements, and the flexibility of a space to be used for more than one purpose are the goals for the modern library (Camarata 2008, 2).

Jeff Scherer continued:

Within a given twelve-month period you can have one child move from one kind of sedentary activity to a very active area or vice versa. And then you get up in the upper ten- to twelve-year-olds and you start getting very precocious kids, kids that are moving up into adult collections very fast or who also want to move back. So, what we have been trying to do is focus on or rethink how to program library space for teens. . . . We have been doing what we call "place mapping," and what that is trying to break down activities into a three-dimensional grid. You have some activities along one side and other activities on the other side—and trying to show the community that where these two points intersect is not a fixed thing. It's continually evolving. And it changes the amount of space that's needed for different activities; it's going to change depending on the rhythm of the day or the year. So if it's after 3 o'clock, it's one size bubble. If it's before 3 o'clock, it's a different size bubble. If it's June, it's different than it is a week before finals.

The most important part of the design in regard to flexibility is the structure of the building. To achieve flexibility, it is best for the architect and structural engineer to coordinate the building plans and space design from the concept phase. For instance, in one-story buildings there is no need for repetitive structural bays. It is critical that the design team keep the space as free of structural columns (and bearing walls) as possible. In the Horsham Township Library, the architect/structural team was able to create a space of 10,800 square feet without columns. Columns are considered impediments to flexibility and sight lines. Although they are structurally necessary, their arrangement, spacing, and sizing can all be managed and controlled by the design team. Many libraries suffer severe inefficiencies because columns were integrated by the architect as "decorative or space-defining" elements.

Be sure to know the architectural symbol for columns on floor plans. During the October 2000 Association for Library Service to Children/American Library Trustee

Association's National Institute "Up the Leadership Ladder" seminar in Baltimore, a librarian noted that she had been shocked, after the completion of her building, that what she thought were round tables on the floor plan were in fact large round columns—and there were many in the space. Not only was she shortchanged in table quantity, but the sight lines and flexibility of the space were seriously compromised. Architectural and engineering drawings are complicated and contain many symbols that library professionals are not necessarily trained to read. It is imperative to ask questions of the architects and engineers and not make assumptions. If something on the drawing does not look right, chances are that it may not be right or what you expect.

Walls and columns are not easily movable, but it is important to keep flexibility in mind when selecting furniture, shelving, and carpeting. It may be helpful to standardize some things—meeting room chairs, computer furniture, shelving—throughout the library or an entire branch system to increase the possibility for moving things around easily from room to room or from branch to branch depending on need. Carpet tiles rather than broadloom may be easier to keep clean and fresh and can be replaced more easily.

Other things to keep in mind that provide for a flexible environment include shelving on casters, sled-based chairs, a multitude of electrical receptacles distributed throughout the room, light fixtures designed for task flexibility, modular acoustical partitions and sound-dampening materials, and minimal fixed walls and features. Architect Lou Khan, highly regarded for attention to detail, commented on his plans for the Kimball Museum of Art in Fort Worth: "I don't like to see space nailed down. If you could move it and change it every day, fine" (1978, 47).

ELIMINATION OF CLUTTER

Libraries are the most accessible public buildings on earth and often are architectural masterpieces—landmarks in the community. Conscientious library administrators, diligent in maintaining the integrity of the space, help customers realize the full benefit of the library experience. The Richland County (S.C.) Public

---

The children's and young adults' library design stage [at the Santiago Public Library in Chile] was very intense and had the intervention of multiple agents. Work was focused in three directions—architecture, design, and community.

The building in which the library [was constructed] was formerly a state warehouse. Although a building of such characteristics might be thought to allow plenty of flexibility due to its sizeable halls in open levels, the renovation was limited to the already existing spaces. It was then suggested that the library should be designed in direct relation to the user—the human being—not only taking into account the activities and functions proper to a library, which are constantly changing. In this sense, the means, rooms, and spaces, and the activities and areas of the building should be able to be modified. The library should be constructed bearing in mind possible and future uses, human as well as technological growth and development.

This is particularly important when considering an infant and juvenile library. The shapes, materials, and the relationships people used to have with children and young adults are not the same ones that existed thirty years ago. And thus it is easily predictable these will not be the same in the next thirty years. The protagonist role children and young adults have today in a country's undertaking and political decision making; the level of participation they have in school, family, or city; the incorporation of an important and massive number of technological advances; the transformations in the educational and cultural national planning scheme—all must be considered at the moment of designing and building of such features.

The interior design has to consider potential transformations. Nothing should be static; everything should be potentially malleable. Graphic and industrial designers had to consider suitable furniture, signage, and color. Infant and juvenile libraries must be developed in such a way that children and young adults can find the information arranged according to the topic instead of books organized by numeric and alphabetical codes.

Most of the library users belong to the poorest areas of the city. In their small and generally overpopulated houses, it is unlikely to have adequate spaces for comfortable study or leisure activities. Then, the library must be a comfortable and cozy space, an expansion of home—a place they feel is their own.

—Gonzalo Oyarzun (2009)

Library system is one that has beautifully maintained buildings—free of clutter and providing services second to none—all of these things combining to earn a *Library Journal* "Library of the Year" distinction in 2001.

Yet many libraries struggle to create and maintain the dignity of a clutter-free environment. The situation is exacerbated by well-intended customers who deposit all of their old or unused books and other items right at the front door of the library. Although these gifts may be welcomed for Friends' book sales, they nevertheless take space and add to the clutter, especially of small, storage-strapped buildings. Libraries are often cousins to attics and basements. Old furniture, lamps, and decorations wind their way to the public library from both customers and staff. Susan Kent summed it up: "Public Libraries are the only public spaces—except parks—that are completely accessible to all sectors of the public with no constraints" (2005).

Youth services librarians are particularly prone to creating, saving, and reusing programming materials as well as displaying an inordinate number of fliers and brochures on the low stacks generally available in children's spaces. Similar to teachers, children's librarians collect items that are used in storytime and reading clubs. Props, signage, and decorations are often created by staff and young patrons as part of an activity session. During the design phase of the project, it is important to recognize these activities and provide adequate storage and display areas for the materials.

Though it is wonderful that libraries have an overarching mission to be completely accessible, this is also a liability when it comes to tidiness and clutter. And make no mistake—a clutter-free, attractive environment is as important to the success of the library as it is to any retail store. Keeping clear lines of sight, understandable pathways, and intelligible signage are all part of the success of any retail business; so too for libraries. Keep in mind that the library is not a domicile for staff and frequent customers. It should not be papered with personal photographs and temporary signs. Personal belongings and furnishings should stay at home. Who wants to come to a library that looks like an overflowing attic?

If the governing agency has a policy for excess furniture and equipment, make it a priority to discard the items quickly following procedural guidelines. Everything from old computers and fax machines to broken chairs and old card catalogs clutters libraries everywhere. Storing these items is wasteful, since they are taking up expensive square footage that could be used for other productive purposes, even if in the basement. The easiest way to manage clutter is to establish a policy and enforce it consistently, removing most of the personal anguish from keeping the library beautiful, tidy, and welcoming.

CONCLUSION

The library is an amazing place, and the resources it provides are invaluable for many young people. The goal of most modern libraries is to create an inviting environment—one that conveys that children and teens are welcome. Whether the goal is to "Wow" children and families, to entice teens with trendy decor, or simply to provide a clean, pleasant place to begin lifelong learning, design is instrumental in achieving the vision. Clarifying the vision of how the space will convey welcome and determining how the priorities of the community are to be reflected in the building or space design are goals of the design process.

How children and teens react to and interact with the new space is initiated in the design team's willingness to explore their own imaginative thought processes as well as others', particularly teens. The functioning of the library and the ease of use by patrons are results of the design team's focus on flexible and interactive environments and the selection of materials based on thoughtful consideration for permanence in relationship to the design. Allowing the architect to think out of the box in creating a new library—one that has a balanced consideration for function—ultimately results in a dynamic, well-planned library.

PLATE 3
Mixed use teen area with performance space, Middle Country Public Library—Selden Branch, Selden, NY. Building Architect, Hardy Holzman Pfeiffer Associates; Teen space architect, Swartz Architectural Group; consultant, VITETTA. Used by permission of the consultant.

PLATE 2
Mixed use teen area with juice bar, Middle Country Public Library—Selden Branch, Selden, NY. Building Architect, Hardy Holzman Pfeiffer Associates (Holzman Moss Architects); Teen space architect, Swartz Architectural Group; consultant, VITETTA. Used by permission of the consultant.

PLATE 1
Story room with sliding glass doors, Horsham Township Library, Horsham, PA. Architect, VITETTA. Used by permission of the photographer.

PLATE 4
Children's area, Minneapolis Public Library, Minneapolis, MN. Architect, Pelli Clarke Pelli. Used by permission of the architect and photographer.

Photo credit: © Jeff Goldberg / Esto

PLATE 5
Exterior view of ImaginOn illustrates use of volumes, scale, proportion, and color—mixed use facility for children, Charlotte, NC. Gantt Huberman Architects with Holzman Moss Bottino Architecture. Used by permission of the architect and photographer.

Photo credit: Tom Kessler

PLATE 7
View of red sided "Museum Corner" jutting out of exterior wall—site of planned Nature Explorium. Middle Country Library, Centereach, NY. Used by permission of the photographer, courtesy of the architect. Architect, Hardy Holzman Pfeiffer Associates.

PLATE 6
Children's space with varied activities, The Hjoerring Public Library, Hjoerring, Denmark. Architect, Bosch & Fjord. Interior design, Lammhults Library Design. Used by permission of the photographer.

PLATE 8
Children's area with a balanced and harmonious space, Rancho Mirage, CA. Architect, Meyer Scherer and Rockcastle, Ltd. Used by permission of the architect and photographer.

PLATE 9

View of prominent children's area—colored glass clerestory as beacon denoting importance of Story Tale Place inside—Horsham Township Library, Horsham, PA. Architect, VITETTA. Used by permission of the photographer.

Photo Credit: Andrea Brizzi

PLATE 10

Windows from adult/children's seating area with Story Room, Lexington Public Library—Northside Branch, Lexington, KY. Architect, Omni Architects; consultant, VITETTA. Used by permission of the photographer, courtesy of the architect and consultant.

Photo credit: Frank Döring

PLATE 11

Children's pod, Amsterdam Public Library, Amsterdam, Netherlands. Architect, Jo Coenen & Co. Used by permission of the photographer.

PLATE 12

Ottoman for parents and children, Santiago Public Library, Chile. Architect, Cox and Ugarte; Design consultant, VITETTA; Industrial designer, NAVE. Used by permission of Santiago Public Library.

PLATE 13

Young Adult Room illustrating use of color with paint and carpet patterns, Horsham Township Library, Horsham, PA. Architect, VITETTA. Used by permission of the photographer

PLATE 15
Teen area with seating mix, Lexington Public Library–Northside Branch, Lexington, KY. Architect, Omni Architects; consultant, VITETTA. Used by permission of the photographer, courtesy of the architect and consultant.

Photo credit Frank Döring

PLATE 14
Early Childhood Area with rubber flooring and pads, The Idea Store, London, United Kingdom. Architect, Bisset Adams. Used by permission of The Idea Store.

Photo Credit, The Idea Store

PLATE 17
Fountain with child, Middle Country Public Library, Centereach, NY. Architect, Hardy Holzman Pfeiffer Associates. Used by permission of the photographer.

PLATE 16
Interior of space zoned for teens, Southfield Public Library, Michigan. Architect, PSA-Dewberry. Used by permission of the architect and photographer.

PLATE 18
Exterior viewing prominent childrens area, Middle Country Public Library, Centereach, NY. Architect, Hardy Holzman Pfeiffer Associates. Used by permission of the photographer, courtesy of the architect.

PLATE 20

Early childhood and parent center, Children's Public Library in Muscat, Oman. Architect, VITETTA/COWI. Used by permission of the architect.

Image Credit: VITETTA

PLATE 19

Multi-use teen space, Rockwall County Library, Rockwall, TX. Architect, PSA-Dewberry. Used by permission of the architect and photographer.

Photo credit: Judd Haggard

Chapter 7 | **Mood and Ambiance**

When choosing light, colors, textures, patterns, and other material elements, it is important, right from the start, to decide on the mood of the building or space being created. The staff and design team have to come to some mutual understanding of the tone and feeling they want to present to visitors. How should people feel when they are in the building or upon entering the building? What should be their impression? How does the building relate to the community at large? Carol Brown discusses designing libraries as destinations:

Furnishings, materials, colors, and lighting are just a few of the design elements in a building that make it an inviting place in which to be. In public libraries, one of the catchphrases often used in recent years is "the library as destination." In other words, library staff wants people to come to the library because it is a comfortable, attractive, and pleasant place to spend some time, like a modern shopping mall, park, or a movie theater. (2002, 6)

Having discussions around overall impressions and coming to agreement on the tone, mood, and ambiance desired help the design team make selection decisions on potentially sensitive elements such as color and composition of materials when they come up for selection.

COLOR

Color, perhaps more than any other single design element (other than light), including the color that light casts, affects the mood and mission of space. Joseph Albers in his *Interaction of Color* reflects that "in visual perception a color is almost never seen as it really is—as it physically is. This fact makes color the most relative medium in art" (1963, 1). "A color is affected, for example, by other colors in surrounding areas and by the light that falls on it. Colors viewed under an incandescent light source will appear different from the same colors viewed under a fluorescent light. In selecting colors, therefore, it is important to view them under the same lighting source (artificial or daylight) that will be used in the final building situation" (Brown 2002, 104).

Color and tone are great moderators of physical space. Color can be used to create the illusion of greater or smaller space. Color and pattern can combine to create scale, warmth, and excitement in a space. Architect Rem Koolhaus mixed color metaphor in the new Seattle Public Library with retail and entertainment venues to create a mood unique to any public library. Tones can distinguish volumes and harmonize physical

117

elements in the space. The role of color and the appropriateness of color also have a cultural correlation.

The role of design is to balance many factors and considerations. It is important to anticipate the behavioral effects of color on young people in the design of youth spaces and to consider the integration of color throughout the entire building, not just the children's and teen spaces. Thoughtful use of color to create balance in the environment is essential to successful design.

Selection Process

Color is very subjective. During the design process, choosing colors from the vast array available may prove to be one of the most controversial tasks. Kim Bolan emphasizes that "color reflects personality, mood, and interest, setting the scene for any area . . . [and] can convey a wide range of feelings, ideas, and meanings" (2003, 69). Staff or board members may be "hung up" on colors they personally like or dislike. People often have strong opinions and cannot get beyond their own preferences. As Albers noted, "It should be learned that one and the same color evokes innumerable readings. In order to use color effectively it is necessary to recognize that color deceives continually" (1963, 1).

The recommendations of the interior designer, based on past experiences and expertise, should be taken seriously and often help the group come to a final consensus. Deciding on a color palette is best done at or near the beginning of the project and should be led by the design professionals, with input from the staff. One strategy in the selection of colors is to have an initial meeting to discuss what colors will work or not work with the library and the community. Are there particular cultural sensitivities to be taken into consideration? Are there any local colors from the community at large that the library would like to consider? Will the library be making use of any older furniture that needs to be integrated?

Before VITETTA began working with the Free Library of Philadelphia, there had been major disagreements about color. One of the things VITETTA did in the very beginning was to try to mitigate the controversy in color selection by simply asking the question of all the stakeholders: "What are your thoughts about this particular building? It's not so much what you like—I love the color purple or I hate the color purple—it's what do you think color-wise are the do's and don'ts or the things that will make this building work? Maybe it's a reflection of the community. Maybe it's a reflection of where the building sits; it's in a landscape and thus it should be earth tones. What do you think?"

With this quick design exercise, the design team started out using color suggestions that came from the group of stakeholders, not something the lead architect or interior designer happened to like. We took direction from the people we were working with in a given branch, and we did not impose a particular philosophy. When we went back to present to the group of stakeholders, we stated that the color palate was something that came out of our original conversation.

In fact, lead librarian Hedra Packman told us that "color was one place where the design team was really, really important to the library. The librarians could choose colors, but we were, kind of, guided. It was not an 'I want purple' kind of decision. It was like, 'Well, what do you think? Don't you think a muted purple or a purple accent?' It was very subtly done."

Color Palette

A conversation should take place between the library staff and design team about the relationship of young people and color, which is a relatively subjective issue. Color philosophy has a broad range in terms of an appropriate palette for children and teens. There are different schools of thought, everything from vibrant primary colors to subdued secondary colors or mixes of greens and blues.

An important design factor regarding color is harmony and continuity in the design. Albers reflects that "color systems usually lead to the conclusion that certain constellations within a system provide color harmony. They indicate that this is mainly the aim and the end of color combination, of color juxtaposition" (1963, 39). Libraries should not have areas separated by disparate color schemes; it is one library building, expansion, or renovation and one color palette. In any one building, the color should be consistent, using a common theme or thread. This is not to say you should not vary from area to area, have something special, or even use color to distinguish areas in a harmonized manner. Children's and teen areas may just "punch up" the color palette—a splash—or emphasize one shade over another.

Architect Denelle Wrightson discussed several issues regarding the color palate in the children's area at the Schaumburg Township District Library. As part of the renovation, the children's room was partially designed with a park theme.

Green was a given. But the board really wanted something timeless. They didn't want anything trendy; burgundy (a kind of burgundy used with cherry wood) became another basic color. We used those colors as a backdrop and added contrast or complementary colors with the green theme throughout, and then punched it up with softer colors. We didn't want to necessarily go with the red, blue, and yellow children's kind of thing. We wanted it to fit—tie in—with the other colors in the building, so that the same carpet carried through.

Range of Color

Spaces for young people may be most appropriate when they are muted, quiet, warm, and soothing or cheerful, bright, and lively. When choosing a color scheme, recognize that there are many nuances of each color and they can affect the ambiance of the space. There are primary, secondary, tertiary, and complementary colors; neutral, soft, and quiet colors; bright and lively colors. The range is unending, and how colors are applied, the mix of textures and materials, and the interaction with light all play into how the overall color appears to the user and observer.

Although traditional thought may lead the design team toward the use of primary colors, great spaces for children need not be limited to this palate. Consider the wide range of hues, patterns, and colors that abound in picture books. In recent years, interpretations of the storybook through murals and themed environments have enhanced many otherwise ordinary library environments. The quintessential ingredient in the picture book, or storybook for young children, is the illustration. Illustrations present an array of fun and stimulating to mysterious and enchanting images, ones that burst with colors of every hue.

The careful use of color is no less important in the design of space for children than in the illustrations found in beautiful children's books. This is not to say that vibrant primary colors or even warm secondary colors are essential, but that color is very much a medium of design. Every space has color. And, according to Albers, "any color (shade or tint) always has 2 decisive characteristics: color intensity (brightness) and light intensity (lightness). Therefore, color intervals also have this double-sidedness, this duality" (1963, 34).

Variability

Chemist François Delamare and physicist Bernard Guineau point out that the computer age has actually increased our distance from colors. "The average human observer can readily distinguish some 100,000 colors; what are we to think of new systems and programs that claim to offer us a range of hundreds of millions of colors?" They also observe that in the virtual world information is merely coded, but in the real world we have "an affective relationship with the materials [colors] themselves" (2000, 126). This reality bears itself out in everything that has applied color in environmental design. It is important to be aware that a tiny paint chip or a color on a computer monitor does not create the same perceptive characteristics in a real application.

The variation from chip or screen to the real world may be dramatic. Further, the application of an actual (true) color to different materials results in entirely different affective relationships. Think about painting a drywall partition, then continuing the paint over existing brick, onto board siding, and then onto a concrete wall. How very different the perception of this—the same pigment and color—because of the material beneath it. Then increase the affective variables with variation in light (both natural and artificial light), and the differences become even more dramatic. To achieve a pleasant and harmonious color balance, it is important that a design professional with experience in the translation of color into real space and textures assist in the process of color selection and designation.

Designating where color is to be used, how it is to be used, on what textures and materials, and with what type of lighting are as critical as the selection of color itself. How many young adults have described painting their bedroom as not just an early act of independence but a first foray into space design? And how many have experienced the shock of picking a favorite color—only to realize that four walls and a ceiling of that color are not only *not* what was desired but unpleasant, perhaps even revolting? Of course, in regard to color, not all design professionals are created equal. It is prudent to be sure of their color sensibility and sensitivity to the users before

In a period of flux and expansion, it is not surprising to see the revival, here and there (for example, in the persuasive vocabulary of marketing and advertising), of the antique colors, drawn from the manuscripts and treatises of the past: ocher, oxblood, cinnabar, carmine, auburn, azure, buff, tan, russet, chartreuse, cresson, scarlet. These colors bear history not only in their names, but in their very molecules; they are the heirs of art, craft, and popular tradition. They remind us that pigments and dyes have affective and symbolic attributes, too, which are probably a bit neglected in our day.

—François Delamare and Bernard Guineau (2000, 127)

engaging in this part of the design process. Color, as a matter of taste, is subjective. Therefore it is important to keep an open mind and to think of the design with broad vision—rather than the paint chip that strikes a fancy.

Amount and Use of Color

Color is influenced not only by the choice, combination, and array of colors but also by the amount of color. A skilled design team balances the amount of color and also considers the altering effect of colors in relationship with one another—a phenomenon reviewed comprehensively in Albers' *Interaction of Color*. Think of entering a space only to make a rapid exit because it is oversaturated with color. Often restaurants and cafés suffer from this. Oversaturation results from the amount of color, saturation level, scale and volume of the space, and sources and amount of light.

The surfaces on which color is applied have a great influence on the mood and perception of the space as well. A color appears very differently, not only as it relates to other color (as on a color card, used in Albers' studies) but in vast horizontal and vertical planes/surfaces that meet each other in various ways and places. The floor color appears differently with the graduating height of viewers; thus, the color is perceived as more intense by small children than by adults (not to mention the developmental differences in the retina). It is critical, then, to view flooring samples laid out on the floor, not on a tabletop. The perception of the color and pattern changes dramatically from one horizontal plane to another. Colors painted vertically to match the width of the open bookshelves create a colorful backdrop for the collection and add depth and dimension to the teen room in the Horsham Township Library (see plate 13). As time moves forward this color pattern can be modified without great cost.

The use of color on vertical surfaces—paint on the walls—is one of the most cost-effective ways to add warmth and interest to space. According to Bolan, "It is important not to be afraid of color. . . . instead, think unconventional and 'fresh,' never hesitating to be unique. Choose colors that excite and motivate" (2003, 69). But just as it is important not to be afraid of color in children's space design, it is important not to be afraid of too little color. A muted, mannered color scheme that resulted in a warm and hospitable children's environment was successful at the Richland County Public Library, for one example.

The horizontal plane of the ceiling is another that can have color applied. Other than shades of white, ceiling color should be restrained and coordinated with the lighting designer. Colored ceilings can reduce the light level and alter the mood of the space by casting the glow of the colors used. Green and yellow are particularly problematic for ceilings. Even light blue—a popular solution—should be used sparingly for special feature areas, such as sky simulations. Dark colors on ceilings, even portions, can darken the space and will most likely create a dismal place. Although it may be appropriate for a *special* program room to have a ceiling painted black, in general black ceilings are a poor solution for a library—especially in children's space. Black ceilings are fine in restaurants and night clubs, but they are performing a different task there and are at counterpurpose with the mission of the library, which promotes learning and literacy.

Cultural Sensitivities

Each library must consider its own community and the cultural aspects of the population mix. Ann Curry and Zena Henriquez observe that "library customers vary in age, education, ethnic background, and aesthetic preferences, but despite this kaleidoscope of users, a public library building must somehow address the needs of all community members" (1998, 89). And it is not just cultural and ethnic backgrounds; it could be neighborhoods.

One of the best methods to determine the cultural sensitivities of a community is to conduct focus group meetings. These focus groups, which can cover a range of design considerations including color, should be managed by a design professional or library consultant. They can include children from a very young age to young adults. In preparing the feasibility study for the first children's library in Oman, the library board and VITETTA conducted a focus group with twenty-two boys and girls from the surrounding area. These children represented a cross section of socioeconomic backgrounds and included several from the local orphanage. One teenage boy concluded that "the building should be like Omani traditional forts with paint colors that are easy on the eyes like beige, blue and yellow."

Some colors have strong symbolic messages in certain cultures, and it is important to be aware of these and to balance the color direction with local perceptions. Some colors may need to be avoided to maximize the appeal of the space and create a universally loved and inviting place for children, their caregivers, and teens. The design team must be sensitive to these cultural considerations and remember that it is possible to bring about the best color solution for a particular location—a palette that embraces everyone in the community. A good example of working with cultural sensitivity toward color—at the Franklin Branch of the Hennepin County Library project in Minneapolis—was described in our interview with Jeff Scherer:

We talked about the cultural issues of color. We know from certain communities that we are working in that color is a big deal politically. You can insult someone if you don't do it right. You are tailoring designs to the community on a really micro level. For example, in the Somali culture there are certain patterns that are harmonious and positive and there are certain patterns that are taboo. And in Mexican culture certain bright colors are part of their heritage and some of those same colors are danger signs to the Somalis. [This generated] a really interesting mix. [During the project] we had a community meeting. We displayed all the colors and found colors that worked with both cultures. Just having that conversation was pretty interesting.

In the Richland County Public Library's expansion, the design team agreed that they did not want anything too distracting. The library wanted nothing that was too busy. They chose a minimal use of bright colors, with flooring and carpeting in two shades of gray that were easy to look at. Still, there are patches of color too, colors that sort of pop out at interesting places. These places are "happy places" and make use of

The use of the primary colors and the shades of wood that were selected [for the Middle Country Library expansion projects] and the cinnamon colors that were picked are very appealing to all different kinds of cultures. Both of the buildings have that feeling and tell different cultures this is a welcoming place to be. It's exciting, it's dynamic and you are here. And while there are many computers and we used a lot of metal, there is a great feeling of warmth in the building that has to do with the shades of color that were selected.

—Daria Pizzetta (interview, October 2004)

"happy colors"—Caribbean colors—beautiful blue, a beautiful orange, a hot pink. In South Carolina this is called rainbow row, like a Caribbean row of houses.

In the Free Library of Philadelphia branch renovations, the neighborhood became the focal point. Philadelphia is known as a city of neighborhoods, and each neighborhood has its distinct character, its self-image. It was important that each building be treated as a separate library from that standpoint. Colors changed from building to building, and each branch decided on its children's art theme or subject matter, its brand. Themes were meant to be prominent, not hidden in a corner. The designers did not tell the branch what it had to be, although they made suggestions. The branch had to decide. One selected transportation as the theme because it was near transportation—the airport and trains. Another selected an African plains theme. Each selected what felt appropriate to the branch and the neighborhood. Then it was up to the design professionals to figure out how to incorporate the colors and theme into the design.

Nolan Lushington voices concern about remaining flexible on design features, including color selection:

The library design should be sensitive to opportunities for responding to the cultural aesthetics of the populations served. Banners, colors, patterns, furniture types and decorative touches can be attractive responses. Beware, however, of rapidly changing demographics. . . . Avoid ethnic wall murals or major design elements that are difficult to change. The library's great virtue is that it is a place that celebrates diversity with constantly changing organic materials. (2008, 68)

The physiological reaction of people as subgroups to color is an increasing area of research and should be considered. The advertising and marketing industry is at the forefront of this research, even if limited to focus group study. In the end, the mission of the children's library is to foster lifelong learning. Heeding simple lessons from available color research and the expertise of the design professional bolsters the success of the space designed. Yet again, the simple, subjective reactions of individuals may obviate much research and "expertise." In discussing the color of existing steel trusses in the Selden building of Middle Country Public Library, a teen focus group participant exclaimed, "Purple rocks!"

What is appealing in the Middle Country Library's interior space is that there is a richness of materials. We used a lot of color, texture, pattern, and visual stimulation for the children's side, which also carries over to the adult side. You don't draw a line in the center of the building and say this is one side.

And you look at these buildings and think somebody really cared about this work. It was built as a public building. It's beautiful and it must have been really expensive. But we managed to do this on a budget that was allotted to us. Through our experience and some experimentation with how to apply the materials, it resulted in a very rich composition. It's really warm. We used stained flake board on a lot of the wall surfaces. Some of the boards have a natural stain; some of them have an orange stain. We made patterns out of the boards. It is really interesting visually to look at along with the blue carpet, which was complementary to the orange. And the whole thing just tied together really well.

—Daria Pizzetta (interview, October 2004)

COMPOSITION OF MATERIALS

Materials affect mood and ambiance. Color is affected by other design elements in the building, including colors in a surrounding area and the light that falls on it. Wall textures and floor patterns interact and can help to emphasize certain colors or mute the overall tone of the space. This is where the experience and skill of the design professionals (collating appropriate color palates, knowing various flooring and wall materials, using materials and patterns to direct traffic, making use of everyday items in artistic ways) become an imperative part of the process. Good professionals utilize their knowledge to make all of the elements function in a cohesive framework without seeming frenetic or disjointed.

It can take a variety of features—wall treatments, fabric, carpeting, and elements such as wood, tile, glass, and metal—working effectively together to create an aura of mystique or harmony. A user's perception is affected by texture and pattern and their interaction with color; smooth finishes may appear lighter than heavier textures; objects and spaces may seem larger or smaller depending on the colors selected. Bolan writes that texture "pulls a space together, stimulating the eye, adding depth to an ordinarily flat space," to create "an exciting and interesting overall effect, provide variety and contrast," and "convey atmosphere" (2003, 74). And remember that books and other materials housed in the library provide a lot of color, texture, and pattern. The combination or integration of all of the various elements satisfies the user's perception of the space and is a testament to good interior design.

Pam Sandlian describes the composition of materials used in the children's room of the Denver Public Library.

> The cool sea of aqua carpet with the whimsical squiggly colorful lines, the rich curly maple custom wood shelving built to curl around a perfect children's collection like a comfortable arm chair, computer stations built for three and four children to collaborate, an open craft room available throughout the day, a perfect view of the city from the Adirondack chairs in the fiction area, a helicopter magazine shelf, a programming space that looked like a copper castle or a Jules Verne space vehicle. (1999, 6)

Patterns

Pattern is an integral part of every space. Being aware of the function of patterns in the design of spaces for children and teens serves to enhance the design. And though the use of pattern in the library can augment the opportunities to further the mission, the use of too much or conflicting pattern can confuse or detract from the space. It is critical that the expertise and sensibility of the design professional be respected with regard to design involving patterns.

Each building material has pattern. This is true even of drywall. The pattern may be subtle and formed by the texture of the material, but there is pattern nevertheless. It is common to think of pattern only as textile patterning, but wood has pattern, metal has pattern, the organization of bricks on the wall creates a pattern. In the synthesis of designing space, think of the patterns relative to all the materials to be used. Some patterns are complementary, others conflict. This is true in textile patterning and the creation of clothing or upholstery ensembles as well.

The design professional must be cognizant of the myriad patterns that are evident in the library's collections and equipment, all of which must be taken into account in the design of the space. The books themselves perform too frequently overlooked, but critical, jobs: attenuating sound and generating patterns. Books, colorful and lively in their different thickness, depth, and height, create a panoply of patterns. The organization of the shelving is also a pattern generator. Many libraries suffer from the

FIGURE 7.1 Children's area pathway in carpet, ImaginOn, Charlotte, N.C. Architect, Gantt Huberman Architects with Holzman Moss Architecture. Used by permission of the architect and photographer.

dreariness of endless book stacks uninterrupted. In the design, consider using shelving to create patterns, zones, and areas of interest while reinforcing the circulation of the collections.

Pattern designs in the flooring and wall covering can also enhance the space and reinforce the mission of the library. A floor pattern can direct children from one area to another or create special zones for reading or activity (figure 7.1). It is wise, however, to resist patterns that encourage unwanted activity in the library, such as hopscotch or other floor games. When deciding on fabric patterns, it is important to consider the practical as well as the aesthetic impact of the choices. Some patterned fabrics, for example, hide soiling and normal abrasion/wear. This is of concern especially in the children's space, where frequent cleaning may not be an option.

Since the library is full of varying materials, types of furniture, lighting accessories, and other building elements, sometimes the most successful enhancement is to minimize the use of additional patterns. Carol Brown warns: "Be careful with too much pattern. If a highly patterned carpet is used, the upholstery on sofas should have very little pattern" (2002, 110). Remember that many busy elements will be added regularly by library staff as well, such as hanging objects, colorful displays, posters, and materials advertising programs and services. Displaying on the tops of bookshelves is common and also adds to the visual "clutter" if not planned for.

FIGURE 7.2   Floor to children's area before renovation (left) and after (right). Free Library of Philadelphia, Bustleton Branch, Philadelphia, Pa. Architect, VITETTA. Used by permission of the architect.

Flooring and Carpeting

The horizontal surface of the floor is integral to children's and teen spaces. The floor is the surface that young children are physically closest to and therefore the most noticeable to them, and teens often are most comfortable sitting or lying on the floor or on floor cushions. Connections in the young people's areas to the floor surfaces may begin at the entrance to the library, not necessarily just at the entrance to the youth spaces. In large metropolitan libraries, the entrance may be formal and cues to locate the children's and teen rooms may be subtle, but in neighborhood libraries the floor surfaces and patterns can reinforce the cues and even direct caregivers, children, and teens to their respective areas, as in figure 7.2.

The floor material most commonly used in youth areas in North America is carpet. Usually this is specified

Photo credits: Joanne Bening/VITETTA

as carpet tile, a vinyl-backed rolled product, or broadloom. These products are available from several high-quality carpet manufacturers. The tile products allow the maintenance staff to replace severely soiled tiles or tiles in high-traffic areas easily with surplus tiles (known in the trade as "attic stock"). It is important that the architect include in the specifications a designated amount, in count or percentage, for attic stock.

Many libraries opt to use carpet tiles for all areas, not only for cleaning and upkeep but to accommodate wiring throughout the building. David Warren, director of the Richland County Public Library, gave us one example: "Flexibility is truly a key to functionality of this building. We put in floor tile carpeting, but we have flat wiring. Everything is flat-wired in the building, so we can move anything that requires power to any place we want it just by picking up the carpet tile and putting it back down." Raised flooring systems are another broad approach to provide flexibility in power and data management. The Vancouver (B.C.) Public Library has raised floors throughout. This allows for an exposed concrete ceiling, slightly vaulted in some bays, and provides for future adaptability of the floor/furniture layouts.

Broadloom is another carpet type appropriate for some installations. Being glued directly to the subsurface (usually concrete), however, this installation is more difficult to alter or remove for future updates. Broadloom also lacks the backing that cushions the carpet, decreasing its lifetime compared to rolled goods and carpet tiles. Broadloom may be perfect for a meeting room where wheeled book trucks will not be present and therefore a double-glued pad can be used. It is also common in hospitality environments and generally offers more patterns and colors. This may enhance the meeting room, especially in a historic building.

In Europe, South America, and Asia, hard-surface flooring is more common in libraries, including the children's spaces. The trend to hard-surface flooring in North America may increase in the coming years. Advantages include ease of cleaning, reduction of allergens and germs, consistency of aesthetic appearance, and longevity resulting in amortized cost savings. The disadvantages include the initial cost and acoustics. The acoustic concerns are valid in an enhancement project where only finishes are being updated. The integration of hard-surface flooring in the library requires careful design coordination with the wall and ceiling surfaces to ensure that the appropriate sound attenuation is achieved to maintain a reasonably quiet library. Scandinavian libraries serve as models for achieving this balance; they have aesthetically attractive, practical hard-surface floors—usually seamless wood flooring—with acoustically engineered space that is quiet and pleasing.

In a children's room that integrates hard-surface flooring as part of the design solution, there can be appropriately zoned areas for infants and toddlers with carpet inset or area rugs. Hard-surface floors are generally not recommended for infants and toddlers, although there are successful installations in early childhood spaces in Scandinavia, perhaps a cultural phenomenon that would not work in North America.

[Libraries] get big [groups] of kids at story hour and at program hours. How do you orchestrate those kids to get to their spots and the right spaces and all that kind of thing? In the Las Vegas [Public Library] we actually put little stars on the floor with a number that indicates a place in line. Children get to sit on that number; they find their number and that's where they sit. And the best numbers are up front—first in line. They make a game out of it. We designed the line to go one hundred kids long before going into the program. Sometimes they do activities in line, so the kids have things to do while they are waiting to go into story hour.

—Jeffrey Scherer (interview, June 2005)

Medium-hard surfaces such as rubber flooring may be more practical as a compromise solution for very young children (see plate 14). As sustainable flooring materials continue in their development, new materials that adequately serve this need for in-between flooring will likely become available.

Currently available and appropriate hard-surface floor products include terrazzo, terrazzo tile, hardwood, colored/finished concrete, vinyl composition tile (VCT), Marmoleum, rubber tile, rolled vinyl flooring, and natural stone/brick. Ceramic/quarry tile is not recommended for any area of the library where rolling shelving, book trucks, or hand trucks are constantly being moved through the space. Other materials such as polished granite and marble do not meet the friction coefficient required for public spaces; they are too slippery. It may be beneficial to note this and require that the architect avoid use of such materials in these areas. Ceramic/quarry tile is perfectly appropriate, however, for kitchen and toilet areas. Natural stone or interior brick can also be problematic, although if considered carefully and specified with smooth joints it can provide a sustainable and attractive solution in entry spaces, ramps, and cafés. Granite (flame finished), blue stone, and slate are examples of natural stone that may be suitable. It is critical to include accommodations for the use of natural flooring, such as heavy-duty rubber wheels on rolling delivery equipment.

Materials can be changed to create direction, zone, or path. Retail stores have mastered this mixing of materials to direct people to specific areas and even to captivate and promote a sale or luxury item (think of hardwood aisles leading to a plush carpet with a boutique clothing collection or jewelry). Mixing materials in libraries can accomplish the same goal, such as directing children to the children's area on a terrazzo aisle to arrive at a special hardwood or carpeted floor zone where books and computers can be found. The same can be accomplished with changes of color or material pattern within the same material type. Daria Pizzetta use such techniques at the Middle Country Public Library:

With the carpet we created a path that leads visitors and tells them where to walk. This is how to circulate through the space. It's delineated on the floor where one is going or where cross-paths happen. It also helps to section off spaces where the book stacks occur and where the tables occur. Visitors know where to sit and where to walk, and it's very easy for the children to read how to circulate through the spaces and how to go about finding books.

Paint and Other Wall Treatments

Almost every wall surface and many ceiling surfaces in contemporary buildings receive paint. Distinguishing surfaces with varying paint textures and colors can create interest in the space. Paint is used to define areas, add warmth or life to a space, and create mood. Not only the color but also the texture or sheen of the paint affects the perception of space. Most public spaces are painted with a version of "eggshell" finish paint. Picture the very low sheen of the shell of an egg and you have an idea of how an eggshell paint finish appears. With only a slight hint of shine or gloss, it is good for walls and holds up better with cleaning than a flat finish paint.

High-traffic areas with water and food may be better painted with semigloss or epoxy paint. Epoxy paint is most often specified for toilet rooms and provides a highly water-resistant and washable finish. There are many compositions of paint and different binders (the agent that holds the pigment together) to accomplish specific tasks. The architect generally specifies the paint type for the building, whereas the interior designer or architect designates the colors. The facilities department or maintenance staff may have preferences for paint type. It is a good idea to ask whoever will be performing touch-up painting to determine the preferred type and even a brand that is available locally.

Another consideration is using low-VOC (volatile organic compounds) paint. The quality of appearance is not altered, but the quality of the environment is enhanced. Low-VOC paint also contributes to the sustainability of the library and helps achieve the LEED certification that many public entities now strive for.

Indoor air is three times more polluted than outdoor air, and according to the U.S. Environmental Protection Agency it is one of the top five hazards to human health—due in large part to paints and finishes, which release low-level toxic emissions into the air for years after application. The source of these toxins is VOCs, which until recently were essential to the performance of paint. But now most paint manufacturers produce one or more non-VOC varieties of paint—durable, cost-effective, and less harmful to human and environmental health.

Since most public libraries are constructed or renovated in a public bid environment, it is important to set the criteria and performance requirements, since the manufacturer or brand of paint is not guaranteed in most cases. Though most, if not all, paint manufacturers can computer-match any color chip, it is advisable to select colors from the manufacturer's colors in order to restock and match "touch up" painting in the future. This may require reselecting/adjusting colors slightly if a contractor submits a different manufacturer than the one used in the design phase. The library can work with the design professional to determine the best strategy to deal with these issues.

Paint can be applied to the structure of the building—concrete or steel columns, beams, and trusses—to add interest. Exposed ductwork and other mechanical/plumbing apparatus can be considered for decorative effect. This decision must be considered carefully, though, because painting ducts and pipes can have a positive effect or can highlight appurtenances that should not become features.

Wall treatments need not be limited to painted drywall, although this is usually the most economical solution. There are many other possibilities including perforated wood or metal panels (with sound-attenuating batting behind), fabric-wrapped acoustic panels, and upholstered walls. Creative use of exterior building materials may add interest and excitement to the interior, such as the hardie board (a cementitious painted siding) used at the Museum Corner in the Middle Country Public Library (see figure 5.2, plate 7). Extending exterior building materials into the interior can also add warmth and character to the space, especially if the exterior material is a natural stone, brick, or wood. High-impact-resistant washable panels may be appropriate in select situations; these might be made of plastic laminate or other polymer/resinous materials.

Fabrics

The use of fabric extends from upholstered seating to upholstered (or fabric-wrapped) wall treatments, window coverings, room dividers, and special features. Any fabric specified for a public library must be manufactured for use in public or commercial spaces. There are thousands of fabrics manufactured for residential applications, but they will not stand the wear and use in a public environment and do not generally have appropriate flame-retardant treatment.

Commercial fabrics are tested for wear and abrasion, and it is important to know the performance characteristics of the fabric as much as the aesthetic character. The most common testing methods are known as the Wyzenbeek and Martindale tests. Both methods test the surface wear of a fabric caused by contact with another fabric. The capacity of the fabric to resist the abrasion of clothing fabric with normal use of seating, for example, is critical to determining if it has a suitable life expectancy. The standard many design firms have used in recent years is that fabric should withstand 30,000 double rubs (Wyzenbeek method) to be suitable for public or commercial (heavy-duty) use. Because of vast strides in the textile industry, it is now possible to obtain fabrics that withstand 200,000 double rubs or more. The interior designer can help library staff determine the balance of performance and aesthetics to make appropriate selections.

With new technologies and treatments, there are an increasing number of fabric treatment methods for durability. Some chemical products impregnate the fabric to create moisture resistance. Patterned fabrics generally help hide soiling, but patterns are not always desirable as part of the aesthetic composition. Solid color vinyl or leather fabrics may also be appropriate. Beware of any fabric that will be in direct sunlight, especially west- or south-facing exposures. Fabrics fade and vinyl (sometimes called leatherette) dries out and cracks. If the ability to wash or wipe down a chair is critical, the trade-off of reupholstering the vinyl every five to ten years may be well worth it.

Although it is important to consider patterns of the fabric as they relate to other patterning in the library, solid color fabrics are rarely a good solution for a public environment. When a solid color is desired, it may be preferable to select a slightly varied woven material in order to at least minimize the appearance of normal wear on the fabric.

Most task seating manufacturers offer a "standard" or "graded in" fabric that will withstand many years of normal use without showing wear. It is best to use the darker colors, particularly charcoals and grays, for these seats. The lighter, brighter colors show wear sooner and also become dated, most likely before the library can afford to replace them. The black, navy, burgundy, and brown task seating fabrics show lint, dust, crumbs, and other small particles. The "standard" or "graded in" materials are a preapproved array of fabrics that have been tested with the specific seat components.

The library may, however, choose COM—"customer's own materials." COM does not mean that the customer actually provides the fabric; rather, the customer (designer) selects a fabric from any commercial manufacturer of textiles and specifies this for the upholstery. Normally the fabric is priced by the seating manufacturer and becomes part of the order. The manufacturer of the seating must coordinate the schedule with the textile manufacturer to ensure the timing of production and delivery. COMs provide the greatest latitude in selecting fabrics. It is important to know, however, that some fabrics do not work with certain seating products. This may be caused by a pattern or weight of the fabric or the attachment mechanism of the seating. COMs are often problematic in regard to task seating and conference-type seating and should generally be avoided for these applications. They are most beneficial for lounge seating.

Fabric is sometimes used for curtains or for special tenting or other treatments in interior space. Curtains present two challenges for a children's space. First, they are most likely within reach and therefore can be clung to or hung on, especially by small children. Second, curtains attract dust and mites. It is important to consider these factors before using curtains. One example of an appropriate use of curtains is the integration of a theater grade curtain in a program space for story hour, puppet theater, or young adult performance space. These fabrics are available with integral flame-retardant characteristics, with heavy-duty hardware available to provide a secure attachment. Be sure the hardware is attached to structural steel or masonry with adequate anchoring.

Any fabric that is hung vertically or horizontally needs to be cleaned regularly. These fabrics create a dust haven—a serious health consequence for many users, especially those with allergies and asthma. Tenting can be very clever and create vignettes of space that are cozy and inviting—just be sure to consider how these constructions will be cleaned and maintained, and develop a protocol for their maintenance before incorporating them into the finished space. Upholstered or fabric-covered walls are the least problematic of fabric surfaces, for they are a true 90 degrees from the floor and do not attract much dust. Many of these surfaces can also be vacuumed or wiped down with relative ease, unlike curtains, tents, and awnings.

Make sure that all design team members understand the selected fabric. Fabric samples come in generally small sizes—often one to three inches square—which is much too small to evaluate even by a skilled interior designer. Do not hesitate to require large samples of fabrics and other materials so that the library can reasonably envision the final finished appearance. Most manufacturers provide a "memo" sample upon request—usually about one or two feet square. If this is not large enough, ask for a yard or two of the fabric. Offer to pay for the yardage if the manufacturer will not provide this large sample size free of charge. It is much better to truly understand the effect of a fabric and spend a little extra money than to order a quantity of furniture only to be dissatisfied with the result. The dissatisfaction can be both intense and fiscally irreversible.

ART AND GRAPHICS

Some of the most stunning interior spaces in the world have, as an element, great art. "Thousands of examples of Roman-era mural paintings, decorating rooms like wall-paper, have been found across the Roman world. Most are composed of large panels with elaborate ornamental motifs: bands and stripes, leaves, architectural elements, or branched candlesticks. Figurative scenes and landscapes, called emblema, are often inset within these panels" (Delamare and Guineau 2000, 26–27).

Likewise, art and graphics can play an integral role in creating a timeless and enduring space for children. The integration of art, graphics, and interior mural painting can be found throughout the centuries. The incorporation of graphic (wall and ceiling) treatments can be accomplished to provide a timeless element that augments the experience of the space.

Often in children's rooms, library staff prefer to display picture book characters as part of their new space. Although these images are attractive to children and bring timeliness to the design, the rights to their use are often hard to acquire. Book characters are protected by copyright, and it is necessary to obtain permission, and in some cases to pay a fee, to use any copyrighted character. Keep in mind that the publisher and illustrator control the exact color shades, figure designs, and environments and sometimes want to control the actual mural. At the Richland County Public Library, the director worked in tandem with Maurice Sendak to place a design of his "Wild Things" in the children's room (figure 7.3). Another consideration is that, by limiting the selection to only one or two characters, a great many more popular and enticing characters are "left out."

The practical application of graphics in contemporary library spaces for children and teens is usually best accomplished with the advice and consent of the architect/design professional. The lead design professional can help determine the most appropriate setting for such vignettes as well as the most practical and cost-effective means. In part, because space assignments in public libraries are subject to change over a period of years, it may be advisable to create wall murals, paintings, or other graphics on removable surfaces, as seen in figure 7.4. This also helps facilitate repairs and cleaning to both the building surfaces and the artwork itself.

In some cases, the most practical solution may be applying the illustration onto wall and ceiling surfaces. This can be done by either painting directly onto the surface or applying a print version of the art/graphic-like wallpaper. These graphics do not have to be elaborate murals, as stunning as they may be. In the Lexington Library Northside branch, the VITETTA design team selected a series of graphic images simulating circuits/electronics, available for purchase on the Internet, and designed their coloration and placement as the backdrop for the computers in the teen area. In the Horsham Township Library, the VITETTA design team sketched a color pattern for vertical paint stripes to serve as the backdrop behind the shelving in the young adult room (see plate 15). The colors of the stripes were based on the building palette, and the design reinforced the character of this warm and inviting space (see plate 13)—yet it was accomplished with minimal cost.

Libraries that are part of a city or county system may have available the "1 or 2 percent for art" program of the governing entity. These can be wonderful programs that enhance our environments with art. On the other hand, many of these programs are run through a form of commission in which the selection of artist is outside the library management's or architect's control. Often in this scenario the artist is selected, then commissioned for a series of works for a building or perhaps the entire library. Sometimes the artist is given virtually free reign on subject and media. This can prove detrimental to the success and appropriateness of artwork in spaces for children in the

FIGURE 7.3 Entrance to children's area with Sendak artwork, Richland County Public Library, Columbia, S.C. Architect, Eugene Aubrey with Stevens and Wilkinson. Used by permission of the library.

Photo credit: Richland County Public Library

library. It is critical in this type of scenario that the library management and, if possible, the architect meet and work with the commission to ensure that the art created for the children's space both reinforces the design of the space and is complementary and appropriate.

When there is no imposed authority to handle the art, the library administration may rely upon the architect/design professional or directly commission an artist or graphic designer. To achieve cohesive, harmonious space, it is advisable to either work through the architect or forge a team of architect and artist. It is important to remember that, if the library is commissioning the work, then the library has the right to dictate the subject matter. The interpretation will be that of the artist. If an artist balks at being provided the subject matter for a children's space, it is best to find another artist.

It is equally important for the library to consider the placement of art and its integration with the architecture. This point reinforces the need to include the architect in the placement and coordination of art in the library, particularly in the children's area. The architect may be able to accommodate specific art if the architect and artist work together early in the design process; that is, the art may be part of the comprehensive plan, not just a feature added later. Even in the case of panel art or framed art, it is beneficial to contemplate placement and purpose in the design development of the building or space.

Architect Jeffrey Scherer described a good example from a Fayetteville, Ark., project:

We organized the whole design around the four elements: earth, fire, water, and air. There are four big zones in the children's library, and each of those—their colors, the fabrics, and patterns—are centered on those four elements. An artist was commissioned for each of those four areas to do a mural that surrounded the window. The window box, which is sort of a little sitting area, is almost a realistic kind of fantasy about the animals and creation myths that represent the four elements. So, with the earth, there are plants and air; there are birds and water; there are fish. And in fire, there is this sort of upheaval of the earth and the volcanic thing.

We took this mythology of creation, the science, and the color as the theme for the children's area instead of saying red, yellow, blue, and green. The artist did a little explanation. The kids read it. The colors all relate to that. And we hope it is high enough quality art that it is going to last a while. . . . let the art itself be the thing that elevates the space and communicates with children.

FIGURE 7.4 Children's computers with local motif: timeless, yet inexpensive, easily changeable applied graphics, Lexington Public Library, Northside Branch, Lexington, Ky. Architect, Omni Architects; consultant, VITETTA. Used by permission of the photographer.

Photo credit: Frank Döring

COLOR SELECTION AND FINISH BOARDS

During the design process, the design team presents samples of various suggested materials and colors intended to create the composition of space. These are often called "loose sample" presentations. It may be useful for this stage of collaborative work to be conducted in the design professional's office. This is generally more efficient, for the office has its own collection of samples and catalogs. This ready access saves time in reviewing and adjusting the schemes. Even if the design professional's office is a distance from the library, it helps the key library decision makers to remove themselves from the existing library environment for the exercise—to "think out of the box" literally.

An inexperienced designer may look for a cute coordination of little squares in each textile, wall pattern, and floor pattern being assembled for a particular space. Sometimes this is effective, but often these types of coordinates are trite. It is important to understand the vocabulary of your design professional as you begin working together. Many design solutions require visioning that is beyond the reach of the layperson. A two-story space wallpapered with little squares may be a smashing success and a brilliant solution, or it may be as vastly disappointing as it is vast in area. Design professionals, especially interior designers, often excel in this part of the visioning. A designer who can truly visualize is a person with a gift and, just as with a virtuoso violinist, the gift (or talent) plus years of training and practice render the virtuosity. The client needs confidence in the capability of the professional to guide and direct these decisions.

At the end of this process, when all of the colors and finishes have been selected, the design professional prepares a final color and finish board. These collages of paint and finish chips, carpet squares, wall textiles, photos or pictures of the furniture, upholstery samples, and other materials make up the total character of the room or building. They provide the design team with a visual guide to how the library or youth space may feel or be perceived by users and staff. Sometimes the professional may prepare a mockup or model of particular areas of construction to help the design team "imagine" the space. In addition, the interior designer prepares a color schedule that lists colors and where they will be used in each space. This may be in the form of a spreadsheet or, preferably, a floor plan with such notations.

CONCLUSION

Many elements of design contribute to the mood and ambiance of space. Creating the appropriate setting to reinforce the mission of the library is a collaborative effort among design and library professionals and other stakeholders including library board members and staff. The selections and designations of everything from paint type and color to seating fabric and carpet style all forge the design language of the space. Understanding and communicating the design intent are essential to creating a place for the community—a welcoming yet dynamic library. Every detail, from the fabric patterning to the brick coursing, will work in synergy to create a special place for children and teens.

Chapter 8

Financial, Political, and Administrative Considerations

A successful design process often acts as a positive agent of change and can influence the future administration and development of the library and the role of youth services within the library setting as well as in the greater community. The budget needs to cover not only the cost of construction but ongoing maintenance costs and staffing issues that may arise out of the design or size of the space. A new building or additional space may require more custodial care. Using sustainable building materials or design, though generally more costly to build, may lead to energy savings in the future. The placement of public service desks may increase or decrease the number of employees required to staff the area, and integrating self-check may decrease the number of circulation staff or free them for other beneficial tasks. Increased usage, in most cases, is a result of creating new space, whether for the entire library or just youth areas. Each of these factors has a defining effect on operational costs.

Creating new space often leads to an examination of the library's organizational structure and services, provides a platform for changing those structures and services, and exponentially expands the knowledge of professionals who operate in different yet complementary fields. As the library design/project team work together, each member develops better communication and relationship-building skills that can often be transferred to future collaborative projects and programs. Renovated and expanded youth spaces also provide opportunities for fund-raising and marketing, greatly enhancing and solidifying the library's role as a family-centered community institution.

ASSESSING FINANCIAL RESOURCES

After the initial planning stages and completion of the Program of Requirements, the design team needs to start assessing project cost data. In addition to the cost per square foot (which is generally determined locally), the other cost factors include whether property needs to be acquired (for new or expanded buildings), the level of quality of furniture or special aesthetic elements, the types of finishes and materials to be used, how much millwork is to be built, and whether old furniture or shelving is to be incorporated in the final design.

Cost Estimates

In the case of planning a new building or a major expansion, the consultant team generally prepares a budget for the project on the basis of relevant cost data on a square-foot basis. The cost estimator or architect usually gathers relevant local or regional data for similar recent (one to three years) projects, factors in the current escalation (annual percentage increase experienced in the local construction economy), and arrives at a relevant budgetary figure. It is always better to keep these estimates on the conservative (high) side in the early planning stages and be realistic about escalation to the year the library will (not hopes to) actually see the project funded—two, five, ten years out. It is also critical that local cost data be used for these early estimates as well as for subsequent detailed estimates.

A new library construction project in Florida is no more relevant to a library construction project in Illinois or Massachusetts than a similar library project in Ecuador. A building boom can dramatically affect construction costs. It is beneficial to know the trend of development and construction in the region. Sometimes accelerating a project's start or bid date renders better bids because of the local economy. Deferring the project usually causes the cost to increase, since escalation and inflation mitigate any possible benefit of a future but not guaranteed slowdown in area construction.

For renovations, cost can rarely be computed on a per-square-foot basis. There is much selectivity in a renovation, and so a comparable cost per square foot for new construction will not necessarily have any bearing on the project cost for a local renovation. Likewise, the cost of renovating one building may vary greatly from another because of the condition of the buildings and the extent of work necessary to accomplish the new design. In the Free Library of Philadelphia renovations, the VITETTA team, working with a project manager and cost estimator, saw a dramatic cost variance per square foot from building to building—even in the same vicinity of the same city.

A library consultant, project manager, architect, or cost estimator can provide a cost estimate based on all the varying elements and factors. The library consultant can normally provide relative costs from related projects for budgeting purposes in the early planning stages. An architect or project manager can usually provide an "order-of-magnitude" cost estimate during concept/schematic design, and some architects offer more detailed construction cost estimates. Order-of-magnitude estimates are generally a mix of comparable systems' costs per square foot or unit (such as surface square foot of stone veneer) and specific design items for which specific cost is assigned. It is generally preferable to work with an independent professional cost estimator for very detailed construction cost estimates during the preparation of design development drawings and construction documents. A cost estimator is best suited for the project if the firm has experience estimating for other library projects, particular familiarity with the local construction environment, or both.

As the project progresses through schematic design and design development, the project team oversees the plan as outlined in the Program of Requirements and keeps a watchful eye on the anticipated project cost. Since public libraries (in most cases) are constructed within the realm of public bidding statutes, be mindful that the only *real* cost estimate is the actual bid. Therefore, it is important to maintain budget/estimate contingencies and create possible alternates for the bid. Alternates are areas of work or specific items that are listed in the bid with enumeration and can either be added to the sum of or deducted from the bid. Deduct alternates are usually not as advantageous to the library. Unit costs are rarely used in public sector bids, but where they are used they can be implemented as equal add/deduct unit costs, therefore keeping the unit costs realistic. Unit costs could be advantageous for cleaning and restoration of exterior masonry, for example.

An Initial Estimate

In larger projects, a thorough space study estimates the needs of the new or expanded library accurately. In smaller projects, the library director or board may have a figure in mind for how much can be spent to renovate or redesign the interior of the space. This can also happen when buildings are donated and the library is expected to "fit" within the space. In any case, the planning process is always the preferable way to go, and an architect or library consultant can help staff determine the space required and delineate the requirements in writing. A team of architect and library consultant offers the most comprehensive solution, with the operational, service considerations accounted for and projected by the library consultant and the parameters of design and construction evaluated and accounted for by the architect.

As part of the space study, an initial assessment of financial resources—current and future—is required. Though the space study should be based on sound judgment and analysis, those involved in the planning process often need some understanding of the range of resources available and what the administration and board intend to raise. As with most plans, it is best not to raise hopes that are inconsistent with what can realistically be done to accomplish the goals. At the same time, it is important not to constrain the planning process with a fixed amount with no room for "dreaming."

In the early stages of planning, rough estimates or budgets are used to begin thinking about the capacity of the space that can be envisioned. Throughout the design process, the development of various plans (bubble diagrams, schematic designs, and construction documents) brings the estimates closer to reality. During the space study, financial issues must be discussed. The project team may have to modify the overall goals and objectives of the project. The architect requires budgetary guidance before beginning the actual design phase. This is one of several parts in the planning process where a library consultant can be particularly helpful.

Once the architect begins the conceptual design, the irreversible cost to the library has begun in earnest. Although it is good to allow for visioning and "dreaming," it is equally beneficial to the library to work with the library consultant (or architect) and the potential funding sources (including the local government) to determine a realistic target for funding *before* extensive design work. If building a 25,000-square-foot addition is not feasible, then it is better to design a 10,000-square-foot addition that will actually come to fruition. There is a delicate balance here of not planning too small and not planning too big. Right-sizing the project to accomplish the service mission and to realize the project is the goal. In some cases, the need may justify much more construction than the local tax base or private benefactors will support.

Libraries in many states must pass a local referendum for new library construction. Generally these libraries develop a Program of Requirements with a library consultant, hire an architect to prepare a conceptual design (often quick and relatively inexpensive), and then promote the project in the public sphere to garner support and votes. A similar approach may be beneficial in areas where the political and funding process are different—where perhaps a county or township council determines whether a project will be funded. Rather than design an entire facility (only to find that it will not be funded), it may be wise to garner the needed support and votes prior to the large investment of time, energy, and money.

During the entire design and building process, the cost of construction is an ongoing issue. From the beginning, it is important to recognize and account for not only cost efficiencies but the costs of services to be provided in the space in the future. At all stages of design, cost assessment must include input from library staff who will be the ones to use and manage the space and be responsible for ongoing operational budgets.

Publication of the Budget

Public libraries must follow the statutes of local and state governance. It is important to not only understand the options for bidding or procuring construction services and furniture but also to understand the requirements for when and how estimates must be made available to the public. It is in the best interest of the community served that detailed construction estimates *not* be available to potential bidders. Although many reporting services request an overall estimate of the value of a project in order to generate bidder interest, publication of specific details can actually increase the cost of the project. This is especially true in a local economy where there is much construction and the bid environment is not expected to be competitive to begin with.

It is also important to understand that in some jurisdictions contractors who provide cost estimates to a public entity may be prohibited by law from bidding on the project. Better to hire a professional cost estimator than to eliminate a good potential bidder from the running by getting a free or discounted cost estimate from said contractor. It is advisable to review these matters together with the architect *and* the library attorney before commencing the project. This will facilitate and ensure the most competitive and cost-beneficial approach available to the library.

Budget Priorities

During projects that involve multiple buildings or those with limited funds, it is particularly important to keep focused on the mission of the library and the goals established by the library staff and design team. During the Middle Country Public Library expansion of two buildings, it was decided—early on—to use the same materials in both buildings. Middle Country staff felt (and still feels) strongly that the library is "one" library and that using the same building materials would underscore that concept. Another goal of the design team was to use most of the money that was raised on the building footprint and overall space. It was important to gain as much meeting and public service space as possible. This priority left limited funds for furniture and millwork. Many of the library's

The space planning consultation process must always, in my view, start with the people who use the space. While strategic managers ask for space efficiency at an acceptable cost to them, the people who manage the services (and therefore the space) need to be involved from the beginning of the development of the design brief, through the schematic design, design development, cost planning, construction and handover. Requirements can only be met at an acceptable cost to the client and, due to this, some requirements might be reduced—especially through the cost planning stage. The library managers, at least, and best of all—if it can be achieved—the library staff also need to know what is reduced or varied through all stages so that they can know and be prepared to manage the result. It is bad enough to have space reduced for some functions because of cost. It sometimes ensures that the functionality is reduced because of cost planning. This affects space planning.

—Graeme Murphy (2002, 1)

stacks and furniture had to be reused, which then necessitated a particular color scheme that integrated the new and old furniture and shelving.

In the Free Library of Philadelphia project, a budget was set for each branch. The overall budget was, however, a moving target, because various sources of revenue were coming into the branch projects. All the same, the project had a strong commitment to certain priorities that helped settle matters. It may have been nice to have a new light fixture somewhere, but that was cost prohibitive and unnecessary; the money had to go into floor patterns for the children's area. Whenever the project team thought they were going to go over budget, it came back to the priorities. Whatever the wished-for shopping lists, they would not eliminate the special carpet patterns, the graphic design panels, the mural.

Sometimes budgets go up and down. It is important to keep a shopping list ready and to understand that it can be a problem not only to overdesign but to underdesign. What if the design is for a low budget and then, all of the sudden, an extra $150,000 of funding becomes available designated for capital improvements? It can be difficult to use these funds effectively when the design is complete.

Project Management

Managing the budget is an ongoing task that is often a primary job of the project manager, someone on staff, a project consultant, or a representative of the architectural firm. It involves the management of funding resources with the coordination of the schedule and scope of the project.

After the budget is set, the architect needs to move forward without the staff micromanaging the budget. It is the job of the architect to reflect the design team's goals and to offer a variety of materials and suggestions for building the building or renovating the space within the parameters of the budget. In the Free Library of Philadelphia renovation project, the architect was provided a formula for spending—60 percent for youth and 40 percent for adult. It was up to the architect to stay within those broad ranges. Nor micromanaging the project can sometimes be hard from a librarian's point of view, since most of the time library staff must keep a strict eye on how their programming and book budgets are spent.

Multiple Projects

Budgeting and managing the budget for multiple projects can present some issues, whether working with a main library, a branch, or several branches or if the overall budget is split among many buildings. When you are managing a multiple-branch budget, there is also the issue of how to take care of the main library relative to the branches. The whole idea of having or not having resources in all the communities that are fairly equal is an ongoing problem.

With the Free Library of Philadelphia projects, for example, it was the intent of the library administration that every branch be treated fairly, equally. If you went into one of the renovated branches in the absolute poorest neighborhood, and in one of the branches in the wealthiest neighborhood, you were to see the same quality. There might be different colors, different fabrics, but the quality was to be consistent.

Real Estate

The real estate in a village, town, or county encompasses public, commercial, and private spaces. Every community seeks to set aside commons, or public spaces, and one of the most popular uses is for building a public library. Acquisition of land to build or expand a library can present a multitude of challenges. Sometimes libraries must request land for a new building, expansion, or parking lot from another municipality such as the county, town, or local school district. These parcels of land are often controlled by councils, legislatures, or boards, and the transference of property rights can become quite contentious or combative.

Sometimes land or an older building is donated that may or may not be in the best location or requires the costly removal of asbestos. When an older building is acquired for adaptive reuse as a library, it is likely to be a former retail store or office building. In Denton, Texas, the public library acquired the former grocery store. The architect was tasked with creating not only a viable interior plan for the branch library but also a new facade that would provide a dignified appearance as a library while inviting children and families into the space through its welcoming transparency (figure 8.1).

When real estate issues ensue, it may be best to work with a consultant, particularly one with experience working with the municipality or owner or one knowledgeable about land issues. In most cases, these types of issues need to be resolved before the building is designed.

Questions to Ask about Project Costs

What is the current local estimate of building costs per square foot for a new library facility? Expanded space? Renovation of existing space?

What are some of the extraordinary costs associated with the project that need to be understood, such as the addition of an elevator or parking garage or the purchase of land? Major artwork or themed area?

Will the library need to purchase property?

What is the estimate or range established for carpeting, chairs, tables, computers, and other furniture or equipment?

Will the library be able to use existing resources such as shelving, furniture, computers? What can be salvaged? What must be new?

Will the library need to rent space during the construction process? Has rental space been identified and what is the cost?

Is there a shopping list of special items that the staff would like to purchase if "extra" funds can be found?

How is the project being funded? Existing capital budget? Floating a bond issue or mortgage? Raising private funds?

Does partial funding already exist? Can the project begin, particularly the design process?

Does the state or municipality have access to other capital funds for library projects? What is the process for accessing these funds? Is it a competitive process? What is the timetable?

FIGURE 8.1 Exterior before renovation (top) and after (bottom), Denton Public Library, North Branch, Denton, Tex. Architect, Meyer Scherer and Rockcastle. Used by permission of the architect and photographer.

What is the estimated time frame for designing the building/space? For the construction or renovation?

How does the planning and design phase interact with other important timetables? Is there an upcoming operating budget vote? Does the municipality need an estimate as part of a large bond issue?

Must the library prepare for a bond issue vote? When will this take place and what materials need to be prepared for the vote?

Will there be a fund-raising campaign? When will this begin? What is the targeted goal for the campaign?

RAISING FUNDS

Raising money for the construction or redesign of existing space can seem daunting. In most cases, it takes various funding sources to complete a project, and it is the interconnection of all the sources that makes for a slippery slope or an exciting ride—however the library views it—to create the new library or space successfully. Some libraries use only bond money and an existing capital fund that has been built over years. Other libraries are awarded grants or a major donation that underwrites some or most of the costs. It is not just prudent but essential that the project team, particularly the library director, understand all the facets of funding needed to complete the project and have a plan of action for how the library will go about achieving the funding goal.

It is particularly important for the library director to work in tandem with the architects and a public relations firm when embarking on any form of raising money. Whether the library needs a public bond vote, bond money or capital funds from a town council or county board, or private funding, the project team members must be on the same page repeating the same message. Before a public vote takes place or funders are approached, it is a good idea to get support from the key members of the community. If there are any dissenters, it is always best to know who they are and what they are objecting to. Bringing them over to the library's side, or at least getting them to tone down the rhetoric, can make or break the passing of a bond vote or special legislation.

Bond Vote

Many libraries that aim to build a new library building or undergo an extensive renovation or expansion project need to ask their residents, through a public process such as a bond vote, for approval. Sometimes the municipality's governance structure (town council, county legislature) conducts a vote at a public meeting. After formal approval has been granted, the governing body floats a bond or takes out a mortgage to cover the major cost of construction. These funds are then paid off over the duration or life of the bond or mortgage.

This process can often be politically charged. If the library functions as an arm of a municipality, it is often competing for funds with the fire or police departments, parks, and other public venues. If the library has the authority to conduct its own bond referendum or vote, there may be competition with the school or fire district, which may need to raise money from the same tax base.

It is imperative to investigate and understand the entire process and who the major players are before conducting the vote. Each community is different and each political situation can present different obstacles. Identifying those individuals and groups the library needs to work with and understanding the capacity in which they need to be worked with are of utmost importance.

When the Middle Country Public Library began its foray into the building process, it hired the services of Hardy Holzman Pfeiffer Associates to conduct a space study and design an expansion and renovation of both the Centereach and Selden facilities. To be successful, the library needed two things from the school board: a parcel of land for a parking lot and an agreement on a date to conduct a bond vote. It was decided that it would be beneficial to work with a public relations firm—particularly one that was sensitive to public library/school district issues—to accomplish these goals.

After considering the matter for some time, the school board finally agreed to give the library some land for the parking lot. The bond vote proved to be another story, since the school district was also conducting a bond vote for repairs. The library decided to wait for nine months after the school bond vote before asking taxpayers to vote on the library's bond. During this period, the library began the onerous work necessary to get the bond vote passed—reaching out to groups and individuals in the community to elicit their support.

The important thing to keep in mind is that what seems simple and upfront may turn into a political situation that can negatively affect the outcome of the bond vote. Networking with city officials, school board members, the town council, the planning commission, and others can mitigate negativity. If handled properly, this type of networking and communication can also initiate the first steps toward gaining public support for the project. Many of these stakeholders not only vote, they influence their constituents, who also vote—and so in effect their vote counts in more ways than one.

Passing the bond vote is usually the most critical step to getting a new building or major renovation. Working with a public relations consultant may prove to be one of the best first steps a library can take to achieve this goal. This consultant can not only approach the municipality but design the public relations and media campaign necessary to pass the bond vote.

Capital Funds

The capital fund is a special fund set aside for major capital projects and may provide a portion of the budget for a new building, expansion, or renovated space. Money from this fund can be used to fund professional fees, including the architect's fee. Alternately, the library may consider this fund for special enhancements such as artwork, a videoconferencing center, or a discovery center that the board feels is too politically sensitive for a bond vote. In some instances, the library may choose to use capital funds to underwrite the entire renovation of an area. This is often not recommended if an expansion is part of the process, however, since most libraries need public approval for adding square footage, which in many cases results in an increase in annual operating expenses.

When we were doing our bond referendum [for the Richland County Public Library], we got approval to have [the vote] and then we discussed the dates. I looked six months out, and that was February and the second Tuesday of that month was the 14th—Valentine's Day. What a perfect day to have a specially called referendum for a public library! We had a campaign, a very professionally run campaign, built around "If you love your library, get out and vote." And, of course, we used the heart and the idea of the heart of the community. And we built the library in the very heart of downtown. Those are all points and things that went into our marketing, our selling the concept, getting voter approval, getting funding, and creating something that people love and consider to be so important to this community.

—David Warren (interview, March 2005)

Exterior of library, Richland County Public Library, Columbia, S.C. Architect, Eugene Aubrey with Stevens and Wilkinson. Used by permission of the photographer.

Photo credit: jaybrownephotography.com

Grant Writing, Individual Solicitation, and Corporate Support

During the Middle Country Public Library project, it was decided that in addition to the $12 million bond issue, which would pay for construction of the buildings, the MCL Foundation and Friends of MCPL could help secure an additional $1 million for special spaces and activities within those spaces. Our strategy was to identify past donors and reach out to them through personal solicitation and grant writing. Varying levels of recognition for donors became the cornerstone of the campaign. It took several years to raise the money, and the campaign was conducted throughout the building process. Major individual donors were solicited first, and they became leaders in the fund-raising effort.

Various levels of giving were attached to naming opportunities throughout both buildings. Foundation and library board members, the Friends, staff members, and corporate supporters matched their ability to pay with the level of recognition they desired. Donor recognition signage was designed to blend with the building materials and continues to be used for those who want this type of opportunity.

For corporate support, the library had a two-pronged approach. One involved soliciting funds through a form of sponsorship, focusing on recognition within a certain space or for a specific collection. The other was through grant writing. The library had been successful in raising money for Family Place and several other projects. But many corporate foundations do not contribute to capital campaigns as a matter of policy. The thought was that the MCL Foundation could raise money for the building project if the emphasis was on services that would be provided using the additional space and materials (not just the facility itself). It was decided that these gifts could fund computers, special furniture, and collections as part of the activities or programs to be provided in the new space. This strategy proved successful.

Sometimes a building project can be used to attract private donors or special donations, but most libraries that attract outside gifts have built these relationships before the building project occurs. The Richland County Public Library had (and still has) a long-standing relationship with authors, illustrators, and publishers. It regularly taps these relationships to garner support for children's programs. When the library was designing its central facility, one of these relationships was serendipitous. The well-known children's book illustrator—and good friend of the library—Maurice Sendak agreed to allow the library to create a larger-than-life mural from his *Where the Wild Things Are*, along with two large entryway "Wild Things" figures (see figure 7.3). This wonderful art is both the focal point of the space and a dynamic portal into the children's room.

Private funding comes in many different ways, sometimes with restrictions and sometimes without. Once in a while, a person leaves money in a will to support the library, and this allows the library to do whatever is needed to move forward with services. This unrestricted gift can often be used to partially or wholly fund a capital project.

Hedra Packman described how one major funder stepped forward to support the renovation of the Free Library of Philadelphia's branches:

The William Penn Foundation marked its fiftieth anniversary with a major gift to the children of Philadelphia through the Free Library. This gift—the "Model Urban Library Services for Children" (MULSC) Grant—provided $18 million over three years to renovate and put technology into the children's areas of thirty-three branches; a "Learning for Life" print and electronic basic skills collection in every library; and a "Bits and Bytes" program that would hire adults and teens to assist and train the public in the [use of] new technologies. MULSC also provided training for all seven hundred library public service staff—librarians, library assistants, guards, and custodians—in new technologies and customer service to children, teens, and families; seed money to revitalize the central children's department; and a beginning endowment to ensure maintenance and replacement technology for children and teens into the future.

This multifaceted grant from the William Penn Foundation is a good example of how funders perceive libraries, their changing culture, and the types of activities needed when space is renovated to support children and teens. Educating the "old guard" of library service staff and reflecting new priorities go hand-in-hand with designing and building dynamic spaces for youth.

It is important to remember that the various funding streams must be coordinated. In an unusual move, after the Free Library of Philadelphia received its major grant, the City of Philadelphia worked with the Free Library Foundation to coordinate capital funds for infrastructure improvements with the grant funds designated for children's services enhancements and new computers. At the Middle Country Public Library, the library director and the head of community relations had to coordinate the funding from the Foundation, the bond issue, and the capital fund.

STAFFING AND MANAGEMENT CONSIDERATIONS

During the design and construction of the building or space, management and the design team need to be cognizant of how the new space could affect staff, patrons, and service delivery. As stressed in chapter 1, good communication is the key to management of the construction process itself as well as to staff issues that are bound to arise and patron feelings about the new space.

Managing Staff during the Construction Process

It is important that design team members have ongoing contact with the staff during construction. Most teams find that identifying a point person—often the head librarian or library director—for communication purposes helps alleviate anxiety, provides a conduit for questions and concerns, and educates the staff on many issues that arise during construction and renovation. Remember that the public services staff have regular contact with the public. If they understand what is happening, they can educate the patrons. Without this type of two-way communication, the staff and public are often left "clueless" and become annoyed and discouraged.

Some libraries use an internal newsletter or communiqué to update the staff regularly about what is happening in any one day, week, or month. These updatable fact sheets can be designed for staff and public alike. In addition to expecting regular updates, the public and staff will have ongoing questions and concerns. It is important that a process be established to address these concerns rather than ignore or downplay them. During construction of the Middle Country Public Library's facilities, it was decided that a staff manager would be designated on a daily basis as the point person for problems from the public service floor. This manager checked in with staff on a daily or hourly basis—during the worst of the construction process—and passed along to administration questions or problems. This procedure was particularly helpful in empowering the staff to handle issues as they arose at the public services desk or in helping patrons who were upset with the construction.

Providing tours during the construction process can help educate and inform the staff (and maybe even patrons or officials) on the progress of the project and serve as an introduction to the new design. Architect Sam Miller discusses how important the concept of including and educating staff can be to the successful acceptance of a building: "Some of the staff had a hard time visualizing what the library would look like. So, when the building was under construction, [the director] took library workers on tours through the building, so they could see what was coming" (quoted in Wallace 2005, 51).

Acknowledging and recognizing the strengths of the staff can lead to a successful integration after the construction process is completed. Their acceptance and embrace of the new space and the changes that occur as a result will ensure that customer service retains its past quality and efficiency while new services can be rendered; the more staff are involved and included, the more empowered and better prepared they will be.

> After years of planning, we realized the issues of creating a fabulous library. Some of the most important issues in libraries are those of service and philosophy. We found those elements essential to our success. The aesthetics of our space enhanced our services, but we could have had a wonderful library without the beautiful new building. The richness of the space created an experience that was nearly perfect, but the design alone did not create our success. The most important element in creating our library was our staff.
>
> —Pam Sandlian (1999, 12)

Staff Reorganization

As a result of a building or renovation project, staff often need to readjust to the design. Sometimes this involves accepting the use of security badges or buzzers at public service desks. It may be that a guard must be added during parts of the day. Sometimes, however, the change is more drastic and affects the organization and management of the library. When designing spaces, these changes may provide a once-in-a-lifetime opportunity for changing the way the library works.

After a building renovation or expansion program, floor space is often increased and staff experience increased use and a change in how the work flows throughout the library. Sometimes the office space is relocated and demands a new way of doing work. Public floor space may become larger and more spread out, which may require additional staff. In other situations, the children's department may be separated from teen services, requiring different staffing and a reorganization of the management structure.

Self-service, often introduced during a building or expansion project, is popular with children and teens. This type of service reduces the number of checkout staff needed, which may result in a reduced number of employees or a redeployment to other departments in the library. Viewed from an organizational and managerial position, such changes are more efficient, but they can create some unhappiness with the staff members involved. Mike Madden, director of Schaumburg Township District Library, offered us these comments regarding his building project's impact on staff:

> Through the building process, the library was forced to restructure the existing staff organization. The design of the building provided an opportunity to think outside the box, and a new organizational structure was created that helped the library better manage the new space and services. It wasn't easy and in some ways painful for some employees. Having them involved in the planning process helped most of them accept the new structure.

Ownership and Turf Issues

Increasing the size and role of youth services in the library may create ownership or turf issues. One issue revolves around responsibility for the parents' collection and the provision of information services to parents in their role as a child's first teacher. In some libraries, the parents' collection resides in the adult room, and staff may not be comfortable relinquishing this audience. In this case, a special display area with revolving collections placed in the children's area may address the problem satisfactorily. In some libraries, materials are duplicated and placed in both areas. For others, the design may allow for the collection to be housed in an area that straddles the adult and children's rooms. When the design includes seating, collections, and services for parents of young children, the library must decide how to resolve this placement issue.

The proportion of space devoted to children and teens, and the excitement that can easily be created in support of youth services, may engender another difficult issue among the various departments. In discussing the political and fund-raising opportunities for the establishment of the library as a cornerstone of the community, youth services often take center stage. Because of this popularity, children's and teen spaces have been growing disproportionately during the past decade. This can generate feelings of jealousy among staff members. It is wise to be aware of this and find points of inclusion and overlap where they exist. Reinforcing the importance of popular adult services (e.g., support for seniors, business and health information services) can help.

During the Middle Country Public Library's building project, the administration knew that there could be an issue in the development of the main library. Although Family Place and teen services were driving forces for the expansion, the adult department was out of seating and shelving room and, in fact, needed more space proportionately. To alleviate this condition, the library made a special effort to gain support from the business and workforce communities for a design that combined several critical adult services—finance and law collections, career information and counseling, and adult literacy—into one overarching service named the Miller Business Resource Center. The building design, space allocation, and layout ultimately supported these different audiences and their reflective programs.

Although adding space allows children's and teen services to expand, a renovation that provides more space to these audiences generally means less space for adults. In the Free Library of Philadelphia branch renovation project, this was a clear objective. Reflecting usage and the wishes of the funder and library management, the branch was to be redesigned with children and teens in the forefront. In many cases, this may not be a problem, since nonfiction materials (in general) are circulating less because of the Internet and increased use of online resources. It can, however, still create a touchy issue, and the design team needs to be aware of it. Preparing adult services librarians and circulation staff for an increase in children's and teen services is paramount.

In the Free Library of Philadelphia grant-funded project, a substantial part of the grant was intended to hire teens to assist and train the public in the new technologies and to train all seven hundred library public service staff in new technologies and customer service to children, teens, and families. Although the library had often provided staff training opportunities, the emphasis on working with children and teens and also hiring teens was new. This broadened the staff's consciousness about the importance of library services for youth and fostered appreciation of the teens among the adult public.

Targeted Age Ranges

Whether to split youth services into the various age groups (e.g., early childhood, school-age, teens) or keep the entire youth services intact and managed under the auspices of one department is another issue that affects the direction of the building design. If the building is small, dividing them may not be in the best interests of overall management. It may be more advantageous to have one department head and one desk to staff, with librarians trained to work with the range of ages. In this scenario, those who enjoy the preschool and parent population may be more often scheduled to work in the mornings. As the day proceeds, librarians who enjoy school-age children and teens may staff the youth services desks.

In many libraries, a division between younger and older youth may be the preferred option. This often requires separate service desks and spaces with specially trained staff and programmers, which in turn may increase the overall operating budget. It is important to understand from the start how the design and enlarged (and separated) spaces can permanently alter library service.

Knowledge Transfer and Maintenance

When new products are integrated within the library, it is critical that staff responsible for properly using or maintaining the equipment be educated on its proper use by the vendor. Library staff must end up with the knowledge, skills, and internal expertise to maintain all the new service and material products.

> When working with partners, remember that they will leave and you and your staff need to have the skills to keep the library running. Thus, knowledge transfer is key. Knowledge transfer is integrally linked to some perpetually favorite topics: maintenance, training, and the ongoing issues of technology and change projects. These issues must be considered during the project, institutionally, and in all decision making. . . . The realities of future function can't be afterthoughts; they must be part of the design process. (Peterman 2001, 6)

After the construction process is complete, some of the biggest hurdles to overcome often involve maintenance and upkeep. Children's use of materials such as paint, glue, and glitter requires ongoing cleaning and, in addition to the typical labor required for maintenance, can leave a residue, affect the color of carpeting, and stain or mar furniture. The sculpture built in the reading garden at the Middle Country Public Library uses sensors that produce moving books and spouting water (see plate 17). These sensors, extremely sensitive to movement and temperature, require ongoing upkeep by the sculptor. Had the design team thought about this problem beforehand, they might have decided to use fewer sensors, place them differently, or find alternative ways to control the public's interaction with the fountain.

Library director Mike Madden told us about another unforeseen problem, at the Schaumburg Township District Library:

> The hardest part of maintenance, regarding the themed area, revolves around two issues. . . . When you have the rubber foam kind of thing, it doesn't last and we need

to keep replacing it. We are trying to think of a better solution—better product—for that. . . . The other thing is the cleaning of leaves and the trees. The main issue concerns blowing from air ducts, which creates a big mess in the whole department. You are stirring up dust, and to control that dust is a tricky thing. We have to clean up leaves regularly because they accumulate dust.

The architect and project manager should remain involved for at least the first several months after the project is completed. During this time, the architect must prepare a list of supplemental deficiencies (any work, usually minor, that remains to be completed or corrected) and follow that work up with a final walk-through review to ensure satisfactory completion. All of the control and maintenance manuals must be collected (usually submitted by the contractor to the architect for review) and provided to the appropriate staff responsible for upkeep and ongoing operations. Final copies of the construction documents with approved modifications made during construction (called "as-builts") need to be delivered to the library before the construction company leaves the project (also usually, but not always, submitted to the architect for review). It is also beneficial to the library to obtain an electronic file containing the complete construction documents for the project from the architect. The architect/engineer may require a special fee or a release for the electronic files. It is best that the library maintain a copy of these electronic documents for future reference and facility management.

Workspace

New workspaces and the design of staff workstations on the public floor may create strong reactions on the part of the staff. Those who are accustomed to formal, imposing desks may be uncomfortable with more flexible, less formidable workstations. Ideally the staff are involved in the design of the workspace but, even with this involvement, some staff members may be unhappy with the changes. Do not minimize their discomfort; this is a time for discussion and communication around the role of the library in the community.

After staff are moved in and functioning within the space, they may ask to rearrange furniture or collections to suit their old styles—"It's the way we've always done it." It may be best to tell staff that they need to leave everything "as is" for a period of one year or eighteen months, before moving things around or changing the environment. This will give them and patrons a chance to adjust and get used to working in the new space.

Office space can also be an issue. During the Middle Country Library expansion, the professional offices were reconfigured from three separate department office spaces into one open office area organized with low partition walls. At first, the adult and children's services librarians were not that happy, since they had lost their department offices and, they initially thought, their identity. Within a short time after moving in, however, they began and continue to express their satisfaction with this office design. Communication and team building among the librarians serving all of the various audiences have added to the library's ongoing creativity and out-of-the-box thinking.

IMPACT ON SERVICES

For both the staff and the public, living through a building project is a transforming experience. New, renovated, and expanded libraries attract new users, bring back those who (for some reason or other) had gone elsewhere for services, and create a buzz about the future of public libraries. In general, communities are very proud of their library; a new building or redesigned youth space energizes those feelings of pride and excitement. There may also be criticism of the new space and activities that take place within it.

Libraries often experience a surge of use in a new space, including an increase in circulation statistics and program attendance. Sometimes the staff is overwhelmed with this increase. It is important to acknowledge the growth that comes with the additional space by providing emotional support to those who are engaged with the public on a daily basis. Hedra Packman told us about such increases at the Free Library of Philadelphia:

Use jumped amazingly in each branch. Circulation went up; use went up; new people came to the library. We had issues with how to deal with these new people; they were coming for computers (and they still are)—not for books—which offends many librarians. We did have a jump in use by teens who [consequently] attracted more teens to the library. One of the branch managers was an adult librarian and she was very concerned, in the initial month or two after reopening, that the children's circulation exceeded what had been the total circulation or usage for the whole branch before the renovation—it was double the adult. But after a period of a year, it leveled out. The increase in clients has remained at that level. [Regarding] the adult circulation, it took longer for word to apparently get out in the adult community. Eventually, adult use increased so that it was the same proportionately.

Things changed dramatically at the Denver Public Library too:

Everyday in the Children's Library was much better than a day at a Disney park, but in many ways needed to be orchestrated on a smaller but similar scale. Our workload doubled, and of course our staff increased only slightly. Our success was tied to a staff who had willingness and a dedication to look at our work in new ways and to develop a team environment with a mixture of structure and looseness. Each member needed to have the flexibility to complete their responsibilities using their own work style and meet the staffing needs of the group. We developed a sort of intuitive ecosystem of managing ourselves and this style seemed to work best for a group of hard working people in a rapidly moving, fairly stressful work situation. We had moved from a boutique library setting to a fast paced McDonald's environment where our challenge was to provide a very consistent product on a massive scale. We were successful, but to sustain this workload on a long-term basis required a staff of tremendous commitment, beyond any regular 9–5 job. (Sandlian 1999, 13)

Renovations and expansions of youth areas are generally embraced positively and often have a great impact on library services overall. Librarians often describe experiencing a kind of real-world change in the library that exceeds the philosophical mission. The *reality* of implementing the priorities of services to children and teens was a "real eye-opener and systemically changed the institution of the Free Library of Philadelphia" (Peterman 2001, 3).

Ongoing Communication with the Public

Once the library is built or the children's or teen area is completed, it is important for staff to hear what the public has to say about the new space and, if necessary, make improvements or respond to criticisms. Speak to community groups about the project and arrange tours as requested both during and after the construction. Invite people in, including neighboring library colleagues. Listen to their comments and suggestions.

It is important to keep track of some of the changes and reactions to the new space, which just naturally will attract more users and elicit many comments. Staff should keep notes throughout the building process and keep them up after the project is completed: "Note things that work well and things that don't. Ask your focus group participants back to see how they think the new space is working and if it is what they wanted. Survey the other library users and see if they think the new design is working. Document their comments and keep your notes safe; you never know when you will need these pearls of wisdom and hindsight again" (Boon 2003, 158). Use every means available to communicate—a comments page on the library website, an in-library comments book, a drop box for suggestions.

At the Middle Country Public Library in Centereach, the lobby has a welcome desk staffed by a member of the community relations department (figure 8.2). The welcomer's job is to assist people in understanding where to go to resolve a problem, access a service, or find a meeting. They let staff know when a visitor has arrived, answer the main phone console, and serve as dispatchers, directing callers to the proper place. A running log is kept that records comments and suggestions from visitors.

As soon as the building was completed, the library realized that the welcomer was located in one of the most strategic spots in the building and that this position could help managers and administrators hear complaints firsthand, respond efficiently, and solve problems. It was also a good place to gather impromptu comments (good and bad) about the new building. What were people thinking when they first walked in? What do they say when they leave? The welcomer records all of the comments and activity on the computer in a daily log. These comments have been recorded and categorized since opening day: positive/negative, building related/service related, coffee machine and copier help, and so forth. In subsequent public relations materials, these comments provide invaluable quotes about the library and the building. For maintenance purposes, the library can track complaints and come up with better solutions. For service purposes, notary and fax services were instituted immediately because of the number of requests for them.

FIGURE 8.2 Welcome desk, Middle Country Public Library, Centereach, N.Y. Architect, Hardy Holzman Pfeiffer Associates. Used by permission of photographer, courtesy of the architect.

Photo credit: Tom Kessler

Handling Criticism

The converse of the adage "Those who do nothing are never criticized" is extremely apt for anyone who goes through a design and building project: "Those who do something are almost always criticized." Be prepared for the critics, for rarely is a project conceived and executed that is not criticized for something, whether the expenditure, the architectural style, or the color of the carpet. This is normal—to be expected and not taken personally. Develop a strategy to channel the critics and point out the universal benefits of the project—and win over the critics.

Questions to Ask after Construction

How does the new youth space stand up next to some of the characteristics that the design team identified for innovative, futuristic libraries?

Does the design focus on materials or people? Observe how the people inhabit the space rather than how the materials inhabit the space. What are some of the patron comments about the new youth space?

What were some of the objectives outlined by librarians, administrators, and marketing professionals for the youth areas? Evaluate the new space or building relative to those objectives.

What is the library celebrating? What do you see first when you enter? How are people welcomed into the new library or space? Do the children's or teen areas stand out?

Does the new space feel like a learning lab in which children and teens are experiencing new ideas? Is it interactive and dynamic? Are there multisensory areas that encourage patrons to look, touch, listen, read, and talk? Is there a buzz?

Are there recognizable spaces for age groups and activities? Through observation, is it easy to recognize who should be using the space? Are there personal and group spaces? How many new patrons are using the library or space?

Are computers and other media stations found throughout the building or space? How many children and teens are using this technology?

Does the new space acknowledge the community in its design? Is the color palate comfortable? Is the environment pleasant to be in? Does the new space have elements of a hotel or bookstore? How is the display area functioning?

Are furniture, shelving, and equipment flexible and adaptive? Can furniture and shelving be moved easily? Are books displayed in a marketable way?

Is the area light and spacious with easy patron flow? Is it intuitive to the user? How about the signage? Is it readable? Is there too much or too little?

Are staff easily seen and available? What is the level of staff acceptance of the new space? What are staff members' perceptions of the new youth space?

What are the maintenance issues? Can they be corrected easily?

DESIGN LAUNCHES, GROUNDBREAKING EVENTS, AND CELEBRATIONS

Three types of acknowledging events often accompany a major building or space renovation project: launch events to unveil the design to the public, groundbreaking events at the beginning of a project, and celebrations at its completion. Their importance lies not only in recognizing momentous occasions in the life of a library but in signifying the initiation of something important and the final stage in an often strenuous period. Most important, these events can be used to propel the library forward into the future, providing an opportunity for greater communication and accompanying support from staff, patrons, funders, and key stakeholders.

A design launch is an opportunity for the architect and library to present the design and the new vision for services to interested community members. This may be a simple affair—part of a township commissioners meeting or an on-site library event. It may also be part of a design competition, where the finalist designs and winning entry are displayed publicly. In other cases the design launch may be integrated with fund-raising efforts.

In Muscat, the design launch was a formal event held in a hotel ballroom, the goal of which was to provide a look at the design of the Children's Public Library in Oman and attract donors to help fund the building. Carefully organized by board chair Dr. Samira Moosa and the board of directors, this event was used to introduce the fundamentals about what a public children's library is, why it is important to children of all ages, and, most important, how the library would foster the culture of Oman in this global age. During the event to launch the library, H. H. Dr. Mona Fahad al-Said, honorary board chair, offered the following vision:

Our children are the foundation of our development, and in order to have a strong foundation, we need to equip them with the skills they will need to acquire and use knowledge. Having said that—I would like to emphasize that our own culture should be the starting point for such an endeavor.

Culture is a way of life and society plays a great role in fostering—in children—its culture in order to maintain their identity in this global age. Therefore, the Children's Public Library is more than just a library where children will read books. Its main objective—besides spreading and supporting a reading culture among children in Oman—will be to seed good values in the growing child and stimulate and support the child's thirst for knowledge. It is hoped that this library will be a lighthouse for knowledge in Oman.

This library will serve as a knowledge resource for both children of different age groups and their families, in addition to being well equipped for the use of children with special needs. It will offer a variety of books, journals, reading corners, movies and educational resources through the use of recent educational technology to serve its users' needs. This educational and learning ambiance will take place in a family-friendly atmosphere. (al-Said 2008)

Acknowledging and celebrating the completion of any project is important, particularly when it has taken months or years and a great deal of individual effort to bring to fruition. These celebrations can range from quite simple to elaborate affairs, but in all cases it is important to invite everyone who was involved in the project as well as those who are potentially affected by the services to be offered in the newly designed space. Remember, though the celebration recognizes the completion of a project, the real significance is that the new space is a stepping-off point into the future of the library's services. This is a time to say thank you and look forward.

A groundbreaking ceremony or opening celebration can be small or large, depending on the needs and resources of the library. The Middle Country Public Library decided to use the "official groundbreaking" of the Centereach building expansion to formally announce the MCL Foundation's $1 million enhancement campaign. Dovetailing the two provided an opportunity for the library to bring together the general community with elected officials, donors, corporate supporters, and staff—allowing all stakeholders to join their efforts in creating the "new" library for a "new" century.

A Grand Opening

David Warren, director of the Richland Public Library, described how they celebrated the opening of their library:

In Richland, we found opportunities to do some exciting things the whole week when we opened the library, and we also raised local funds. We had $50,000 given by two firms to sponsor our opening week activities, which started with the benefactors and a black-tie dinner. It was held in the children's room under the trees; a beautiful dinner by this famous caterer with all this antique china, and so forth, and an orchestra playing the music from Maurice's "Wild Things Opera." We also had nights just for staff—both current and former staff members in the community, and the Friends of the Library. Almost 2,000 people were here for the Friends' night.

For our grand opening, we had a parade from the old to the new library led by the Fort Jackson Military Band. We had children's groups performing, including a children's community choir that wrote an original song (which we have used in many different ways since the grand opening). We had all the officials, and our oldest employee—who was something like 84 at the time—carried the last book from the old library to the new one. For the parade, we invited all the schools to come and march in the parade with signs that children created. These signs were all original and said things like, "We are going to where The Wild Things are." Hundreds of children participated from different schools, marching the three-block distance. When you have that many children involved, you get their parents and the grandparents. The press reported 10,000 people attended. Having involved children was key.

A Modest Affair

The Middle Country Public Library had ribbon-cutting events for both buildings. They were intentionally designed to be a culmination of the project; a recognition for all of the funders, supporters, elected officials, the design team, and staff who were involved in or lived through the expansion; and a starting point for future projects that may be initiated because of the library's new spaces. Each of the events was held approximately two months after the actual opening of the building and timed for optimum public relations opportunities. The library wanted to mark a historic occasion while taking advantage of a public relations opportunity that could propel the library into the future.

Small but Significant

The Wixom (Mich.) Public Library serves a population of 14,000, and the children's room of 3,372 square feet underwent a complete renovation in 2008. Jane Kahan, the children's librarian, sent us some information on the ribbon-cutting event they held to celebrate the grand reopening. The theme for the library's project—animals and the alphabet—was chosen by the department to match a commissioned mural from a memorial donation. The invitation reflected the new theme and was sent to board members, Friends, city employees, donors, other libraries in the library cooperative system, former employees, local teachers and principals, and the design team. The general public was invited via a front-page article in the library's quarterly newsletter.

The celebration began with formal remarks by the library director, recognizing the donors and many others who contributed to the success of the project. Big scissors were borrowed from the chamber of commerce. Children were entertained with custom balloon animals, and everyone enjoyed a specially designed sheet cake that looked just like the animal alphabet blocks on the new portal. Punch and animal crackers, lovely floral arrangements, and party favors enhanced the event. Approximately 200 people attended the celebration—despite a severe winter storm. Everyone had a good time.

Tips for Events

The event (large or small) needs to be thoroughly planned. Who is to be invited? What is the program of the day? How will it be orchestrated? Who will speak? Who will cut the ribbon? What refreshments will be served?

Don't miss this opportunity to thank all of those involved in the design, construction, funding, and management of the project.

Use this event to propel the library and its services forward. Think big (even for a small project). Remember, "children are our future." This phrase should resonate throughout the entire event. Elected officials, funders, parents, children, and staff will relate to this message.

Involve children, teens, and their families in the event itself. Integrate hands-on activities. Are there any special clubs or groups that are already sponsored by the library? Engage them in the program of the day.

When scheduling the event, it is *not* necessary to hold the ribbon cutting or grand opening on the day the library or space is first opened. It may be best to wait until initial adjustments to the physical plant are made, staff members are comfortable with patrons' reactions to the space—both positive and negative—and the staff in charge of community relations and public programming are prepared.

CONCLUSION

Creating the vision for a new library space for children and teens is a wonderful and rewarding experience. It is like planting a seed that will grow into a beautiful tree, and then more trees will be seeded from it—trees of learning and knowledge. The journey from the vision to reality has many steps, some more arduous than others. Balancing the vision with the financial, political, and administrative realities is instrumental in the successful realization of the project.

A variety of issues during the process and after the project is completed are to be anticipated and are best managed if the design team is aware of them and addresses them throughout the design phase. Staff comfort and knowledge help alleviate the likelihood of the worst-case scenario and make the adjustments more palatable and, in some cases, challenging and exciting. Celebrating with all of the stakeholders—staff, board, funders, elected officials, patrons, design team members—is the culminating step in the process. Enjoy!

References

Albers, Joseph. 1963. *Interaction of Color*. New Haven, Conn.: Yale University Press.

Blum, Andrew. 2005. "Project: Play." *Metropolis*, April, 82–86.

Bohrer, Clara N. 2005. "Libraries as Early Literacy Centers." *Public Libraries* 44, no. 3 (May/June): 127, 132.

Bolan Taney, Kimberly. 2003. *Teen Spaces: The Step-by-Step Library Makeover*. Chicago: American Library Association.

Boon, Lesley A. 2003. "Designing Library Space for Children and Adolescents." In *Planning the Modern Library Building*, edited by G. B. McCabe and J. R. Kennedy, 151–159. Westport, Conn.: Libraries Unlimited.

Brown, Carol. R. 2002. *Interior Design for Libraries*. Chicago: American Library Association.

Camarata, Corinne. 2008. "Top Building Trends." Panel presentation for LAMA, American Library Association Mid-Winter Conference.

Chekon, Terry, and Margaret Miles. 1993. "The Kids' Place." *School Library Journal* 39, no. 2 (February): 20–24.

Cooper, Ginnie. 2005. "Laptops, Coffee and Carpeting: The City's Libraries Today." Symposium sponsored by the New York City Department of Design and Construction and AIA New York Chapter, New York City, July 14.

Cranz, Galen, and Eunah Cha. 2006. "Body-Conscious Design in a Teen Space." *Public Libraries* 45, no. 6 (November/December): 48–56.

Curry, Ann, and Zena Henriquez. 1998. "Planning Public Libraries: The Views of Architects and Librarians." *Library Administration and Management* 12, no. 2 (Spring): 80–89.

Dahlgren, Anders C. 1998. *Public Library Space Needs*. Wisconsin Department of Public Instruction. http://dpi.wi.gov/pld/pdf/plspace.pdf.

Delamare, François, and Bernard Guineau. 2000. *Colors: The Story of Dyes and Pigments*. New York: H. N. Abrams.

Demas, Sam, and Jeffrey A. Scherer. 2002. "Esprit de Place: Maintaining and Designing Library Buildings to Provide Transcendent Spaces." *American Libraries* 33, no. 4 (April): 65–68.

Esmay, Michael. 2006. "Library Administrators, Leadership, and the Building Expansion Process." *Library Administration and Management* 20, no. 3 (Summer): 121–127.

Feinberg, Sandra, et al. 2007. *The Family-Centered Library Handbook*. New York: Neal-Schuman.

Harvey, Todd. 2005. "Selecting an Architect." *NYLA Bulletin*, Fall, 5.

Holt, Glen E. 2008. "ImaginOn: The First Twenty-First Century Public Library Building in the U.S." *Public Library Quarterly* 27 (2).

Huntington, Barbara. 2005. "Early Learning Initiative for Wisconsin Public Libraries." Bulletin No. 0510. Madison: Division for Libraries, Technology, and Community Learning, Wisconsin Department of Public Instruction. http://dpi.wi.gov/pld/earlylearning.html.

Imhoff, Kathleen R. T. 2005. "Marketing to Diverse Populations." Presentation manuscript, Management and Marketing Section. IFLA conference, Bergen, Norway, August 10.

Jones, Theodore. 1997. *Carnegie Libraries across America: A Public Legacy*. New York: John Wiley and Sons.

Kahn, Louis. 1978. *Light Is the Theme*. Ft. Worth, Tex.: Kimball Art Foundation.

Kent, Susan. 2005. "Laptops, Coffee and Carpeting: The City's Libraries Today." Symposium sponsored by the New York City Department of Design and Construction and the American Institute of Architects, New York, July 14.

Lushington, Nolan. 2002. *Libraries Designed for Users*. New York: Neal-Schuman.

——. 2008. *Libraries Designed for Kids*. New York: Neal-Schuman.

Marano, Hara Estroff. 2004. "Biorhythms: Get in Step." *Psychology Today*, April 28, www.psychologytoday.com/articles/200404/biorhythms-get-in-step.

Molz, R. K., and P. Dain. 1999. *Civic Space/Cyberspace: The American Public Library in the Information Age*. Cambridge, Mass.: MIT Press.

Moss, Peter, and Pat Petrie. 2002. *From Children's Services to Children's Spaces: Public Policy, Children and Childhood*. New York: Routledge Falmer.

Murphy, Graeme. 2002. "Space Planning for Libraries." Presented at The Inside Story: A Library Interiors Forum. Library Network Unit of the State Library of Victoria, February 4–5.

NADF. 2007. *Learning with Nature Idea Book*. Lincoln, Neb.: National Arbor Day Foundation and Dimensions Educational Research Foundation.

Oyarzun, Gonzalo. 2009. Draft of presentation for the IFLA Library Buildings Section and Libraries for Children Section: If I Were the Director. Milan, Italy, August 26.

Peterman [Packman], Hedra. 2001. "The Free Library of Philadelphia: The Library of the Past to the Library of the Future." *Journal of Youth Services in Libraries* 14, no. 2 (Winter): 3–8.

Prince-Ramus, Joshua. 2005. "Laptops, Coffee and Carpeting: The City's Libraries Today." Symposium sponsored by the New York City Department of Design and Construction and AIA New York Chapter. New York City, July 14.

Ramos, Theresa. 2001. "From the Outside In: Library Renovations from the Perspectives of a Project Manager, an Architect/Designer, and a Technology Consultant." *Journal of Youth Services in Libraries* 14, no. 2 (Winter): 9–13.

Richie-Sharp, Shelly Ann. 2003. "Influence of Friedrich Froebel: The History of Kindergarten." www.froebelweb.org/web2003.html.

al-Said, Mona Fahad. 2008. Children's Public Library in Muscat, Oman. Transcript of event to launch the library; introductory remarks. Muscat, Oman, November 1.

Sandlian, Pam. 1999. "Information Playgrounds: Creating Children's Libraries." *Public Library Quarterly* 17, no. 2: 5–13.

Sannwald, William. 2008. *Checklist of Library Building Design Considerations*, 5th ed. Chicago: American Library Association.

Science Daily. 2006. "Daylight Savings: Building with Natural Light." *Science Daily* (Massachusetts Institute of Technology), November 15. www.sciencedaily.com/releases/2006/11/061114194440.htm.

Sloan, Robert. 2002. "The Inside Story: Developing a Signage Strategy." www.libraries.vic.gov.au/downloads/Library_Network_Unit/robert_sloan.doc.

Wallace, M. C. 2005. "Do I Need an Architect or Not? Some Things You Should Know." *Searcher* 13, no. 9 (October): 48–54.

Index

You may also be interested in

Teen Spaces, Second Edition: This fully revised edition includes step-by-step instructions and easy-to-use templates, the latest information on teen spaces policies, new ways to involve teens in the space-renovation process, updated tools, worksheets, instructions, and vendor information, inspiring illustrations and discussions of what other libraries have achieved, and best practices for developing teen spaces.

Countdown to a New Library, Second Edition: Packed with helpful checklists and worksheets, this revised edition includes updated references, standards, materials, and resources; tips on efficient HVAC systems and evolving rules for LEED certification; and information about new technological issues.

Building Science 101: Designed for libraries where construction of a whole new building is not feasible, this book offers step-by-step instructions for improving the energy use of existing structures, with methods for being environmentally and fiscally responsible.

Moving Your Library: Author and experienced mover Steven Carl Fortriede has everything you need to get the job done quickly and efficiently with step-by-step directions, diagrams, spreadsheets, and photos.

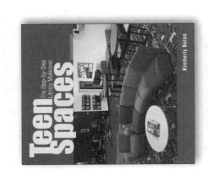

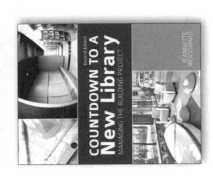